TO Jack

You have
Been an Inspiration...
Welcome Aboard. -

With love,

Sam

Aug. 17, 1984

The
WARM-UP

☆   ☆   ☆

SAMMY ☆ SHORE

William Morrow and Company, Inc.
New York 1984

In Memory

*I dedicate this book to my mom, Lena, who
when I was twelve wanted to take me to Hollywood—
because I could move my stomach like a
belly-dancer . . .*

*. . . and to my father, Hyman, who was pissed
because he had to give me two dollars a
week for trumpet lessons.*

*And a special thanks to William Van Doren,
who believed in this book from its inception
and who put things where they belonged; to
Rudy DeLuca, who helped me create The
Comedy Store; and to three special ladies
in my life—Beverlee Dean, Pat Golbitz,
and Mother Seton.*

Library of Congress Catalog Card Number: 84-60212

ISBN: 0-688-03315-6

Printed in the United States of America

First Edition

1 2 3 4 5 6 7 8 9 10

BOOK DESIGN BY PATRICE FODERO

FOREWORD

Being in show business for over seventy years, I've watched all the great comedians of this century walk out on the stage and make people laugh. There were funny ones, unfunny ones, and a great many in between. Sammy Shore belongs in the funny category, a comedian who has his finger on the pulse of fresh humor. He's more than just an opening act, a warm-up for the star who follows him. He's a hilarious Little Giant who is capable of filling the room with laughter as the "*only*" act on the bill. I know because I've seen him in action, and he belongs with the best.

Now, as an author, he branches out into a new area, to prove that he possesses more than a mere funnybone. He has a heart. Sammy's story is the story of every man struggling to achieve happiness within himself. Just as I thrill to see him on the stage, I was thrilled by the feelings and emotions he so poignantly revealed between the covers of this, his first, book.

You'll love it. I did.

—MILTON BERLE
February 7, 1984

AUTHOR! AUTHOR!

Someone once said to me, "That stuff you do about your father in your act, it's hysterical! You ought to write a book about him."

"My father?" I said. "Who would want to read about my father?"

I thought about what he had said, but not being a writer, how was I going to write? My friend, who happens to be an author, had said, "Just write about what you remember. It doesn't have to have a beginning, middle, or end—just do it!"

I came home that evening, and on a legal pad I started writing down things I remembered about my dad, Hyman. And for the next three years I did not stop writing.

I called friends, read them passages about him. "That's cute," some would say. "Not so cute," others said.

The more I wrote about Hyman, the more I could appreciate who he was, although he was no longer around. And through my writing I was finally able to love my hostile, wrathful pop.

No, *The Warm-up* is not about Adidas and Puma, but about a continuous search to be comfortable with oneself. It's about the number-two guy in life—not the star!—the underdog who's always trying to please the boss, the wife, the parents, who has an undying thirst to be liked. As a "warm-up" for the stars, well, let's say my journey was just a little rough.

But through my experiences I was able to stop my addicting vices and stay alive to tell about it.

I'd like to dedicate this book simply to people, with the message that there's hope in any endeavor or situation.

CONTENTS

PROLOGUE

JULY 31, 1969—LAS VEGAS—THE INTERNATIONAL HOTEL. In thirty minutes, Elvis Aron Presley of Tupelo, Mississippi, will walk out onto an immense stage for his "comeback," his first personal appearance in more than twelve years. Between two and three thousand specially invited persons—European royalty, bankable motion-picture stars, solid-gold recording artists, household faces of TV, powerful press—are milling about, sitting down, visiting, squirming, laughing, and looking around at each other in the audience. They are all waiting for the King, the ultimate royalty, the only one of them whose first name alone brings universal recognition and excitement. It is the show of the decade.

Shaking in the wings is a slight, curly brown-haired Jewish man who is completely unknown to most of those who sit and wait. Partly for that reason, it is he who will first face the bright lights and even brighter luminaries. He is the "warmup comic" hand-picked by Elvis's guiding force Colonel Tom Parker, Bill Miller, entertainment head of the International, and Elvis himself. In the eyes of the elite crowd, this professional funnyman will have one big liability from the start: he ain't Elvis Presley.

The picador is the man who goes out before the matador, when the bull is in his strongest and meanest disposition. He teases and antagonizes the bull so that later the matador can come out and make his fancy passes and play with the bull and do with it what he pleases until, finally, he kills the bull.

This is the picador's Super Bowl—a break no other comedian has ever had—a chance to walk out there and warm up Elvis Presley's audience. He's worked twenty years in various dives and third-class resorts just for this moment. All of his dues, all the nights of sweat and struggle, have brought him this one-night trial subscription to fate.

What was I thinking?

I was not thinking, I was dying. In a few moments I'd be stepping out onto a stage that has never been tested by a comedian. Every comic has been vying for the privilege. Every major talent agency has been courting the Colonel to get him to pick its comic as the one who would be right for Elvis. Sammy Shore was picked.

In anything of importance in my life I was always in panic. I could never handle confrontation or pressure of any kind—and now this!

I stood backstage alone. My mouth was completely dry. Perspiration was dripping down the sides of my body. The prevailing feeling was doom. My brain was sending frantic signals throughout my body, tensing my muscles and preparing adrenaline for the oncoming shock. The war is just a few seconds away.

But, as it turns out, this was just the beginning.

1

MIRACLE MICROPHONE

"Drive carefully," she said.

"I will."

I got into the XKE. It was brand new. So was everything else—the shoes, the shirts, the tuxedo, my material. Everything looked great, but it didn't help. I turned the key and the motor came on like a jet on the apron of a runway. I waved to Mitzi as the car began to move. She waved back. It was 7:45 P.M.

I headed north on the San Diego Freeway. Darkness was settling in, a few rays of light still hanging on in the sky.

Vegas was 285 miles away. I could make it in four and a half hours if I kept up the pace—seventy-five, eighty miles an hour. Not too many cops on the freeway at night. The farther behind I left LA, the more isolated I felt. If I did get stopped by a state trooper, at least I'd have someone to talk to.

I began to see signs. ELVIS IS COMING! OPENING THE INTERNA-TIONAL HOTEL. JULY 31ST. I began to get that icy feeling again.

Just three weeks earlier, I'm sitting in my dressing room at the Flamingo Hotel, Las Vegas, drying myself with a towel. I'm still coming down from the high of my warm-up for Tom Jones, feeling good about myself. The show's over; I hear the musicians coming down to their dressing rooms. A knock at the door. Maybe it's a fan coming back to tell me how good I was. I don't yell "Come in!" I jump up and open the door. There stands Bill Miller, the Flamingo's entertainment director, Colonel Tom Parker, and Elvis Presley. I think I'll shit.

"Brother Sam!" Bill says.

"Hi, Bill," I manage to say.

"Elvis and the Colonel would like to say hello. They just caught your show."

"Sure, come—come right in-n-n." I'm stuttering.

The Colonel puts out a hand and I'm shaking it. "You're quite a funny boy," he says in his southern drawl. "I like that black preacher you do, reminds me of back home. Shake hands with Elvis."

I'm shaking hands with Elvis Presley, wondering when I'm going to wake up.

"Really liked your show, Sammy," he says.

"Thank you, Elvis. It's an honor for me to meet you."

Bill speaks up. "How would you like to do the warm-up for Elvis at the New International Hotel in three weeks? Elvis and the Colonel would love to have you in the show."

I look around like I think they're talking to someone else. "You want me in your show?"

Bill nods, smiling. "We all agreed you'd work very well with Elvis. What do you say?"

I have to swallow first. "I'd be honored and thrilled to share the same stage with—"

"Great!" Bill doesn't wait for the rest of my fancy speech. "I'll call your agents tomorrow and work out the details."

LAS VEGAS 100. I was coming to Barstow. Almost everyone on the way to Vegas turns off the freeway here for gas and coffee. I pulled up to a Denny's restaurant and headed for the counter.

There were groups of tourists, laughing, giggling. Truck drivers traded wisecracks at the counter. They all seemed so happy. I couldn't believe they had much anxiety about the work they did. Why couldn't I be like them? It's just a job, being funny. I told myself: Just do it!

Back in the car, as I approached Vegas, I started to become obsessed with the possibility that I might walk out onstage and completely forget my act. That had never happened to me, but there was always a first time. I started going over my material like I was cramming for final exams.

It's really nice to be here at the International. . . . They really treat you fantastic here. . . . They just sent a Rolls Royce over to the airport today to pick me up, which is kind of silly . . . because I came in at the Greyhound Bus Depot . . .

Wasn't that surefire stuff? I went over it twice, wondering if it was really funny.

And the room they gave me is unbelievable. I don't have a Gideon Bible . . . they got Charlton Heston on a chain.

And can you believe the size of this show room? Do you know some of the acts they're planning to bring in here? In January the pope is going to work the balcony . . . four shows a night. . . . Then the entire Arab-Israeli war is coming . . . but only for a week.

And did you know, folks, they have a youth hotel? . . . Only hotel with a sandbox and a pit boss.

How do you like the bright lights in the casino? It's like an operating room . . . they remove everything.

I just finished working with Tom Jones. . . . I remember one night he had a bad throat . . . his fly went out and did two shows.

I should really have them by now. Then go into a couple lines about Elvis and the Colonel.

People ask me, "What's it like working with Elvis?" All the girls trying to sneak down to his dressing room past the guards. I said, "Elvis, what's with all the guards? Why don't you go where the girls won't bother you?"

He says, "Where?"

"In my dressing room . . ."

But Elvis is the greatest. . . . This afternoon his manager, Colonel Tom Parker, walked over to me and said, "Boy, you're good. I like your brand of humor."

I said, "Gee thanks, Colonel, and I like your chicken."

He said, "Well then, lick my fingers, boy."

I got to Vegas a little after midnight. After miles of black desert sky, the city was a piece of hyper-bright daylight in the dark. The people everyplace seemed to be jumping. I pulled up in front of the International, so big and expansive it scared me.

One of the car hops came over like he knew me and opened the door.

13

The Warm-up

"Hi, Sammy, just getting in? Remember me from the Flamingo? Richie—I used to be a bellboy over there."

Now I remembered, and I asked how things were at the new place.

"Fantastic, Sammy. Hey, that's great about you opening with Elvis. Good luck—it's really gonna be something. People're calling from all over the world trying to get a room just so they can see Elvis. There's no rooms till after he closes, not even for the king of England."

I felt a cold shiver that stopped at the base of my spine, only because there wasn't a tail to keep it going. I didn't even think to ask Richie who the king of England was.

I walked into the casino, the world's largest. It had tremendous chandeliers, like an imitation of the Winter Palace. The pit bosses all wore tuxedos, men and women dealers alike in baby-blue ruffle-fronted shirts. I never thought I'd see pit bosses in tuxedos. People crowded around the tables like money was being handed out free. A new hotel in Las Vegas—like a new girl in town, except this one was a princess—an empress! Barbra Streisand had just opened the hotel, and Elvis was to follow. With me, of course, but there were moments when I felt I was just there to see Elvis like everyone else.

I must have given off that kind of feeling, because when I got to the front desk, the beautiful young woman behind the counter hardly gave me a glance.

"Can I help you, sir?"

It hurt that she didn't know me. I was nuts—here I wanted so badly to hide, but I also wanted recognition from the entire population of the world.

"I'm Sammy Shore. I'm opening with Elvis this week here. There must be a reservation for me . . . around somewhere," I faltered.

"Oh I'm sorry, Mr. Shore, I didn't recognize you. I'm new here." She looked through her reservation spindle. "Yes, I do have your reservation. You have a suite on the top floor, right down from Elvis. Mr. Shoofey made it for you personally."

Alex Shoofey had been general manager of the Flamingo when I played there and had just become president of the International. He had put me in a suite next to Elvis? Oh my God! I never had a suite. I didn't *want* a suite. I just wanted a plain room. I couldn't handle that much attention. I was getting nauseous. Should I call Alex and tell him I don't want the suite?

14

MIRACLE MICROPHONE

I nodded to the girl. "That's very nice. Thank you."

I was saying to myself, Sammy, you're entitled. You paid your dues, Sammy. You *should* be getting the best. My nausea got worse.

I got my key and headed for the elevators. I passed a dress shop, a fur shop with minks and sables in the window, jewelry stores, beauty parlors, a drugstore—a shopping center built into the middle of the hotel. There was a bank of elevators for floors 16 through 30. My key read 3016–18. I stepped into an elevator and pressed 30.

When I stepped out on the top floor, I saw beautiful carpeting in greens, reds, and blues, with red linen material on the walls. The paintings were all originals. It was, to me, almost like a palace. I found my room. Two enormous doors in an antique style, with brass handles. I felt like I had come here straight from my dad's miserable rooming house in Chicago, where Mom slaved in the kitchen and we were cramped in little rooms. If only they could see me now, their little Sammy standing in front of his own private suite. Somehow it all made me feel wretched.

I opened the door and just stood there gazing. The Italian furniture, the finest decor available, more original oils, watercolors, and prints. I opened the door to the bedroom and couldn't believe it. Not only was there a circular bed with a mirrored ceiling, but lacy white drapes surrounding the whole thing. The bath was decorated in red and green and offered a sunken marble tub, separate male-female bathrooms, including a bidet—I didn't even know what that was.

I opened the wide glass doors separating the suite from the balcony and walked out. Behind me, just above me on top of the hotel, the giant letters I-N-T-E-R-N-A-T-I-O-N-A-L flashed on and off. I looked down. A half-joking thought entered my mind: Go ahead, Sammy— jump off. You'd be the star. They'd forget about Elvis.

I could see just about every major hotel. There was the Stardust, with its huge, million-dollar sign flashing: LIDO DE PARIS WITH A CAST OF 100's. Kitty-corner from the Stardust was the Riviera, announcing: DEAN MARTIN. The people; the traffic, dominated by yellow cabs; everything and everybody rushing from hotel to hotel despite the lateness of the hour; a flow of walking, running, riding dots looking to get lucky, to find the friendly slot machine, the personally destined table, the mythical hot hooker, whatever you wanted. Maybe you couldn't have it, but there was equality of opportunity to make yourself crazy trying.

15

The Warm-up

***

What a far cry this was from the "international hotel" where I grew up—my father's rooming house at 936 North Wells Street on the near north side of Chicago, the Watts of that era. There were twenty-four rooms, and he made sure they were always rented. As I said so often in my act, he had three-dollar rooms, four-dollar rooms, and five-dollar rooms. They were all the same rooms, it just depended on whether you had three dollars, four dollars, or five dollars. I'll never forget the day he bought the rooming house for eight thousand dollars and was trying to think of a name for it. He came up with quite a few candidates, including the Wells Apartments and the Off Lake Shore Drive Singles, but when he found out what the lettering was going to cost, he put up a board that said ROOMS.

Even where we lived, upstairs in our own apartment, he rented one of the bedrooms to Charlie, a Japanese short-order cook, and one to Burt, a Filipino musician. Nothing would be vacant. My mother and father slept in the dining room because my dad wanted to have another room available for rent. I had one room and my brother Bernard, his wife, and baby son had another. My brother Phil, a policeman, lived on his own but was always around. My oldest brother, Morris, was twenty years older, married and gone. I honestly was apprehensive about staying out too late at night, worrying in the back of my mind that my dad might rent out my room!

God forbid if one of his roomers was a day late with the rent. He would not wait till the next day. That evening he wouldn't even eat his dinner, he'd be so aggravated; he'd tighten up his belly, roll up his sleeves, and head for the showdown. He had so much intensity heading down those stairs, he could have been subbing for Gary Cooper in the final scene of *High Noon*. He would pound on the door with a vengeance. He'd never send his wife or anyone else to collect, he enjoyed being pissed and letting them know they couldn't get away from Hyman Shore, landlord.

The door would open and reveal "the roomer," as Pa would call him. Or he would call them by their room number, saying to Ma, "You know, number seventeen is late with the rent." And my ma would know that the poor fellow was in trouble.

Most of the roomers were on relief, as they called it in those days. And many times their checks would be late getting to them. But that was no excuse for Hyman.

16

"Good afternoon, Mr. Johnson," he'd say. "Are you comfortable? You have enough heat in the room?

"You got the lights on, I see. You know all of that costs money. When I rented you the room, that was all included in the rent. I'm a nice person, and I just wouldn't even think of asking you to pay for the utilities. Everything is included—free! Except the rent, which as of now is two days late. Maybe you have a couple of loose dollars you could give me till you get the rest of it, hopefully by tomorrow.

"To show you what a nice person I am, I'm going to leave the lights and the heat on—till tomorrow, when you bring me the rent. If the eagle don't fly tomorrow, you're not going to be able to see in this room or feel any heat. Because by five o'clock tomorrow, if I don't see you, your room will have a large-size padlock on it! And don't try to skip out! You know my son's a cop!"

I was scared to death of my father. That's where I got so good at being scared. Whoever created the image of the last angry man must have spent some time with Hyman. He used to sit all day in the used furniture store he called Hyman & Sons, on the ground floor of the rooming house. Why he put "Sons" on the sign I'll never know, because he never gave a damn about any of us, at least as far as I could see most of the time. For the most part he resented us because he had to clothe and feed us, diverting his attention from himself and his obsession with money. To people who didn't have to live with him, he was a "character." He was five feet tall, 138 pounds, wore thick glasses, and had a Russian-Yiddish accent.

I remember all too well how he used to sit in his store screaming at the top of his lungs, "Goddamn sonsabitches!" "Bastards!" "Fuckin'!" Only there was never anyone around! he just enjoyed his screaming. He was a professional yeller—a Rolaids junkie, that's what he was.

There were days when he would just sit in that store and gaze out at the street waiting for someone to come in, someone to attack. If nobody showed up, he'd let my mother have it.

On hot August afternoons he'd sit in his favorite chair and wilt, just staring at the motionless fan in front of him, miserable, wanting to turn it on but loathing the cost of electricity. When I was in my teens and starting to use the phone, he became so upset about my calls that he actually had a pay phone installed.

"You want to use the phone—pay for it," he'd say. "What do

you think I'm running here, a free phone service? It's not enough that I feed you and you got your own room?''

Every day, after cleaning up in the store, my mother would walk up three flights of stairs to our apartment, make him lunch, bring it down, and pray that he would like it. "It's almost three o'clock, Hymie, I thought you might be getting hungry," she'd say, "so I brought you down a sandwich."

Often he'd respond by sneering and lifting up the top slice of bread. "Sandwich," he'd growl. "You'd call this a—I wouldn't feed this to a cat! It's goddamn tuna, you know I don't like tuna. Go upstairs and get me a piece of chicken." As she turned away he'd throw in another jab. "And I don't want your goddamn milk, either. Bring me a beer!''

Bernard, ten years older than me, was really my father's best helper. He didn't know any better. Whatever Pa wanted, Bernard was there. He was scared of his own shadow. Ma once told me about Pa having had a nervous breakdown long before I was born. I always figured Bernard must have been conceived then. He never said anything, just stared. I never got to know him. He was always in the store, and I never heard my dad say anything to him except to call him stupid when he did something wrong.

The store was a sight: stoves, dressers, linoleum, dishes, chairs— you name it in the world of utilitarian junk, Hyman had it. The only trouble was getting to it. God forbid you wanted to see a sofa buried somewhere in the back in a pile of other furniture. Hyman was the kind of salesman who would talk you out of the one you wanted and sell you the one he could get to. You did not walk out of that store empty-handed if he could help it.

Like the time a lady came in looking for a sofa. She wanted a green one that was way in the back, at the bottom of a pile. My father talked her out of that one and sold her a cream-colored sofa in front. "You'll be able to see your kids better," he said. He thought that was very funny because the lady was black.

One evening during a blizzard with howling winds and below-zero temperature, my dad was really mad because he'd just had to go down to the basement to shovel coal into the furnace. The roomers were pounding on the pipes, clamoring for more heat. It seemed like the roomers were all prisoners and they were getting ready to break out. Coal cost Pa twenty-six dollars a load, and that winter, 1935, was

18

one of the worst in Chicago's history. So every few days he'd have to send for another load. Sometimes, to save on coal, he'd feed the furnace a few tables and chairs he couldn't sell. On this particular evening he started up from the basement dirty with cinders and tired and angry because the cold weather would just not let up.

It was around nine-thirty and I was helping him get ready to lock up the store. He had ways of locking doors, involving several two-by-fours, so if a Sherman tank had tried to get in, its best chance would have been the wall rather than the door. You would have thought this coliseum of junk was Fort Knox.

As Pa headed for the front door to carry out his locking ritual, there appeared a very large black man, about six feet two, who looked like he could crush cinder blocks with his skull—that's how big he was. He wore a cap pulled down low over his eyes and walked straight into the middle of the store, not pausing to handle merchandise like the usual customer. Pa, more than a foot shorter, looked up at the man and fairly shouted, "We're closed, mister. Go take a walk, I'm sold out for tonight. Everything in the store is sold! Come back to-morrow—we got a sale!"

The man took a gun from his pocket, put it to my dad's bald head, and said, "I ain't kiddin', man, this is a stickup. Give me all your money or I'll blow your brains out."

Pa glanced at me where I was standing, next to a pile of kitchen chairs. Ever since I had seen James Cagney in *The G Men*, I had dreamed of a bunch of gangsters invading the furniture store. Some-how I would snatch a gun from one of them and the banner headline in the *Tribune* would read 10-YEAR-OLD BOY CAPTURES HOLDUP GANG SINGLE-HANDED! and there would be my picture with my proud father behind me. But now, with a real holdup man holding a real gun on my father—I have never been so frightened in my life. All I was thinking was why did it have to be my turn to help Pa in the store tonight, why couldn't it be Bernard's?

My dad laughed. "Brains out? Who's got brains . . . you want money? Money you want, that's a joke! You see any customers around here? You want to hold up somebody, go hold up Marshall Field's, they got all the money! Now get the hell out of here before I call my son. He's upstairs and he's a cop!" And with that Hyman imperi-ously knocked the gun to the floor and yelled, "Now get out!"

The guy started to back out slowly, but the thing that really scared me was what my Pa said next. "Listen, mister," he said. "Before you go, would you be interested in a nine-by-twelve linoleum?"

From the balcony, I tried to convince myself that I was really a part of Las Vegas. I had worked here before, of course, but I knew that finally this town could be mine if I wanted it. The thought failed to produce any magic.

I wandered back into my room and headed for the wet bar. I opened the cabinet and there at my disposal were the finest whiskeys and wines. I reached for some ice and a bottle of J&B and poured myself a hefty drink. I toasted myself—"Sammy, welcome to Las Vegas"—and took a swig. There on the dining room table was a beautiful arrangement of fresh flowers in a bowl. I bent down to smell them and found a little white card: "Welcome to the International Hotel, Sammy, and to a successful and exciting opening. Regards, Alex Shoofey, President, International Hotel."

I've just finished my week at the Lake Club in Springfield, Illinois. I'm twenty-two. Hugo, the club owner, calls me into his office. "You think you were funny?" he says. He hands me my check. He opens his desk drawer and pulls out a gun. "Tear up that check," he says. I drive back home to Chicago all hunched down because my stomach's hurting so much.

I put down Alex's card and took the rest of my drink in one blind gulp. The doorbell chimed. "It's the bellboy, Mr. Shore, with your clothes." He brought them into my bedroom and I gave him a ten-dollar tip. Ten dollars to bring up my clothes! My father was doing sit-ups in his grave.

It was after 3 A.M. Rehearsal was at noon. The opening was 8 P.M.; I went on at 8:20. I'd better get some sleep. I lay in the huge platter of a bed looking up at myself in the huge mirror, trying to fall asleep.

It's my opening night at the Copacabana, New York. It's 1956. If you do well at the Copa you're definitely on your way. I bomb, then slowly die. Kaye Stevens is headlining, and she becomes a star due to that engagement. She's the talk of New York, while I'm treading water.

It doesn't help matters on opening-day rehearsal when I show up

20

at the Copa with Mitzi, my wife, and she gets hold of a letter that's waiting for me there. It's from some woman in Detroit, telling me how much she enjoyed my visit and the dinner we had together. Mitzi confronts me in the middle of the rehearsal. I look at the letter; I can't believe it myself. I don't even remember that woman, much less the events described. But it must be true or why would she write it? God knows I spend enough time totally bombed and unconscious. Mitzi's furious, leaves for the hotel. The next day, opening night, the break I've been waiting for, she leaves for home. I'm a mess.

Opening night I go out there and really bomb. I feel awful. I got three weeks to go. Right after my act, Jules Podell, the Copa's owner, takes me into the kitchen and tells me I've got to cut out my southern governor routine. Some important guests from Dixie find it offensive and they're already complaining.

"Great," I say. "My best bit! I kill 'em with that in Miami Beach."

Like any good businessman, Jules knows how to answer my objection. "Yeah, well, that's who complained about it—some customers from Florida!"

I've got to take it out. That kills me at the Copa.

It was 4 A.M. I just *had* to go to sleep. I felt like I was lying on top of a thirty-story funeral pyre. They just hadn't found the matches. I was keeping watch on the bedside clock. In eighteen hours, I thought, I've got to go out there and warm up the audience for the greatest entertainer in the world. I couldn't think of a single comic who wouldn't be drooling over that spot. They weren't afraid of it, I thought. They wanted to be seen by everybody—the world! But lying in that overwhelming bed, in that fabulous room, in that luxurious hotel in the show-business capital of the planet, I was aching to be back in Miami or Detroit, working the little neighborhood clubs for twenty-five or thirty bucks a night.

The Chase Hotel in St. Louis, the Zodiac Room, isn't exactly a household name, but it's the best place for comedy in that particular burg in the year 1952. The owner, Harold Kopler, is out of town when I open, but Jean, the maître d', likes me and keeps me on week after week. In the middle of the sixth week, Jean comes to me before the first show. "Harold Kopler is coming in tonight with a party of people to see you," he says. "I told him you're doing good, so he wants to see. Maybe he'll keep you a few more weeks.''

When I go out to start my act, I can see Mr. Kopler with his party at a front table. My act usually runs thirty minutes. Tonight I finish it in twenty. I'm pressing, my insides are screaming "Please like me!" I've panicked.

I see Mr. Kopler talk to Jean and then leave.

Jean calls me over. "Sammy," he says, "Mr. Kopler would like you to finish out the week and close.''

One of my biggest breaks early in my career is opening at the Eden Roc in Miami Beach with Billy Eckstine. It's another horrendous experience. Partly to blame is the fact that I have to cut out my trumpet, since Billy also plays trumpet and doesn't want another one in the show. Aside from that, I just bomb. I look in the paper the next day, and the reviewer says, "Opening the show was Sammy Shore," followed by a column of blank space. I don't understand. Mitzi and I go out and buy three or four more copies of the paper, but they've all got the same mistake—blank space under my name. Then I realize it's not a mistake. It's the review.

I finally dozed off sometime after four-thirty. When I woke up the clock said nine forty-five. I computed the remaining time: ten hours and thirty-five minutes and I would be walking out onstage.

I took a shower, grabbed my music case, and took the elevator for the show room. The casino was even more packed than last night. I decided to go out in front and see if they had put my name on the marquee.

When I emerged from the glass doors into the furnace heat and blinding light, I couldn't believe my eyes. The letters *E L V I S* were so gigantic they reached from the top of the marquee almost to the bottom. In the tiny space left was *S a m m y   S h o r e /Sweet Inspirations, Bobby Morris Orchestra*. I really hadn't known what to expect. I thought maybe big billing would give me some of the confidence I needed. But after a moment, I decided to be happy to see my name at all.

As I approached the door to the show room, back inside, the security guard stopped me.

"I'm sorry, sir," he said. "No one is allowed in here now."

"But I'm Sammy Shore. I'm in the show."

MIRACLE MICROPHONE

"Who?"

I repeated my name. I even had to warm up the security guards! I felt like running away.

"I'll have to check," he said. "Stay here and I'll be right back." A few moments later he came out. "I'm sorry, Mr. Shore, I didn't recognize you. Go right in. I'm really sorry."

"Hey, that's okay," I said. "I mean, how long have I had my face on all those Wheaties boxes?"

I walked into the show room. It was monstrous. The ceilings were a mile high—very bad for comedy. The side walls had statuary of angels looking amazingly real, along with larger-than-life-size figures of gentlemen and ladies in full dress of some previous century bowing to each other. This was a hall for comedy?

From where I stood, the stage looked like the runway for a B-52. The orchestra was playing "Love Me Tender," and at center stage Elvis Presley was getting ready to sing. He had on a black, beaded jumpsuit and dark sunglasses. The man was incredibly handsome. He was surrounded by a handful of guys and girls doing his background vocals.

I headed down the side of the show room toward the stage. My steps were cautious. My heart was pounding and the skin under my arms started popping with sweat. Elvis was singing; I felt like I was in fantasyland. I got to the end of the stage and grabbed a chair so I could jump up and go backstage to find out when I was rehearsing. Elvis was just finishing the song when he saw me heading back.

"Sammy!" he called, and then, in imitation of my act, "Hey, Brother Sam, give me an amen!"

I turned. I was really surprised he noticed me. I walked over and he threw his arms around me, welcoming me to Vegas and the show. He introduced me to his people—the Sweet Inspirations, who opened his shows, the Imperials, who sang in back of him, guitarist and friend Charlie Hodge, and road manager Joe Esposito.

Backstage a minute later I met the stage manager, who told me I was rehearsing at four-thirty, after Elvis, and showed me to my dressing room, right next to Elvis's. Backstage was like an airplane hangar, and you took an elevator to get down to the dressing rooms.

The stage manager left me at the door. I walked in and quietly shut it behind me. The room was unusually nice, decorated mostly with Florentine-style furniture. It also had a touch of England and France, and the bathroom, with its marble tub and Italian tile, was a smaller version of the one in my suite except that the colors were green and gold.

The bar was loaded with every conceivable premium hard booze and liquor. I wanted a drink so badly, but I had learned the hard way—take it easy before the first show. I wanted it so bad to kill the pain in my gut.

I opened my case and sorted out the music for the band. *Band* was the word I was used to, but this was really an orchestra—thirty-two musicians, might as well call them the Las Vegas Philharmonic. I had my arrangements ready.

I headed up to backstage as Elvis was doing his closing song. I waited for him to leave—I just didn't want to see him again.

After trading pleasantries with orchestra leader Bobby Morris, I looked the room over from the stage. It was devastating. This hall was simply not built for comedians.

From out of the middle of the empty room I heard a voice that sounded like a carnival barker's. "Hey boy!" it shouted. "Come down here. I want to talk to you!"

I could make out the dim outline of a man with cowboy hat and cane. As I came to the edge of the stage, I saw it was Colonel Tom Parker.

"Hi, Colonel," I said. "Nice to see you again."

"Listen, boy," he said. "I just want you to do twenty-two minutes tonight, ya hear? Now you go out there and do a good job tonight. A lot of very important people gonna be there. See you later!"

"Yes, sir," I said. I just stood there looking out at all the empty seats and red velour booths.

I'm working the Bon Soir in Greenwich Village with Barbra Streisand, November 1963. It's my first New York engagement after bombing at the Copa. Barbra is just beginning to create tremendous excitement and interest, and the club is packed with people coming in to see the kooky young lady with the unbelievable, unique voice. Everybody knows she's going to be a big star; there's no doubt in anyone's mind.

The Bon Soir is a dark, dreary-looking basement club that only seats around 150, but it's becoming a very important club to be seen in. The era of the big brassy clubs is still in force, but now the TV and record people are starting to look for new talent in the more intimate spots. The hot new acts of the early sixties, from the Smothers Brothers to Bob Dylan, are being seen in the smaller, more hip places.

Streisand has yet to appear on TV. One cold night in late November, Marty Erlichman, her manager, comes in to tell me that things may be about to change.

"Ed Sullivan's coming in tonight to catch Barbra," he says, "so could you cut out a few minutes and keep your act tight?"

I say sure and start working on the Scotch more heavily than usual.

When I do my act and walk over to the bar for my usual refreshment, the bartender tells me I was funny.

"Maybe Ed Sullivan'll give you a shot on his show," he says.

"Was I really that funny?"

"Yeah, no shit, Sam. In fact the boss says to me while you were working, you're really rolling tonight."

I sit at the bar and watch Barbra. She's just magnificent. The room is so still, everyone is hanging on every note, and when she closes with "Happy Days Are Here Again," I've got goosebumps all over. Everyone stands up and cheers. I'm happy for her, yet envious. I know Sullivan has to love her; she's the new Judy Garland.

As the Sullivan party is leaving with Marty Erlichman, they pass the bar. Ed Sullivan comes over, puts his arm on my shoulder, and says, "You're a funny kid, Sammy. Have your agent call me. I'd like to use you on my show."

The next month I'm about to make my first national television appearance on *The Ed Sullivan Show*, the same night as Barbra. I'm waiting in the dressing room watching the monitor, and of course I'm very nervous. I watch Barbra and she's unbelievable—so calm, like she's been on television for years. I'm pacing like someone in a cage. When the knock comes on my door, I'm sure my time has come. It's one of the assistants on the show.

"Mr. Shore, it won't be long now," she says. "Mr. Sullivan is going to run some film clips on Charles Laughton—you know, he just died today, and Mr. Sullivan wants to pay tribute to him. It's a last-minute change, so I don't know exactly when you're scheduled to go on. Just stay here. I'll come and get you when it's time."

"Okay. Maybe you can throw in a piece of raw meat while I'm waiting."

Just my luck—Charles Laughton had to die today; he couldn't wait till tomorrow. Maybe I can join him when I finish the show; that's about how I'm feeling.

A few minutes later she's back. "Mr. Shore, you're on right after he shows the film clip from *The Hunchback of Notre Dame.*"

I hear Sullivan's voice as I'm walking backstage.

"And how can we ever forget his greatest triumph and by far his most highly acclaimed and difficult role, that of the tormented Quasimodo in *The Hunchback of Notre Dame.*"

Audience is applauding.

"We'll miss him," Sullivan says, and then, while the audience is still clapping, he throws in, "And now, ladies and gentlemen, to wrap up our show this evening, a very funny young man, Mr. Sandy Shore." I was so nervous it didn't even faze me that he had said my name wrong.

I start in on my monologue, but right away the stage manager gives me the signal to cut because the show's going to run too long. I panic and try to cut out some of my jokes; my mouth gets dry, and I'm sweating. It's so weird knowing that millions of people are watching me and they don't know I've had to cut my monologue to pieces.

I finish my last joke, and say good night, and walk off. I've done exactly one minute and forty-five seconds.

The stage manager apologizes for cutting my time. "I'm sure next time you do the show," he says, "you'll get more time." I'm hoping he'll also say, "That was funny, even though you had so little time." If they're happy with what you do, they're the first to tell you. This time they don't.

Downstairs in my dressing room again, with the time drawing closer, the pressure was just too intense. My gut alternately tightened like a clamp and opened like outer space. I wasn't into pills or drugs to kill that pressure. Alcohol was the only thing that worked for me, and I was getting desperate for that fix.

No alcohol before you go on, Sammy, not one drop—my old psychiatrist, Dr. Wiggins, had hammered that into me. But my relationship with the black doctor had become strained, and so the man who had literally seen me through my other nightmare openings in Vegas was not here. Just when I needed him.

Mitzi was back in LA with our four kids. Sure, I was the one who told her not to come to my Vegas openings because she made me nervous, but sitting there in my dressing room I wanted to have it both ways. I was just a kid wanting his mommy, except that childhood was supposed to be a few decades behind me.

I poured half a glass of Scotch, added a little water. I sat on the couch, raised my glass and, like desperate people everywhere, talked to myself. "Good luck, Sammy," I said out loud. "Go out there and kill 'em." The liquid descending into me gave me a warm, wonderful feeling. The churning started to let up. Everything's going to be okay, I thought to myself.

There was a knock at the door—a dozen long-stemmed roses sent by Alex Shoofey. I heard the people talking and laughing in Elvis's dressing room. The whole family was there; wife Priscilla, his dad Vernon, the entire entourage of friends and cronies who were always with him. I was alone with my buddies J&B. Once again I was crazed with fear, and I wanted to drink the whole goddamn bottle.

In twenty minutes I'd be on my way up that elevator and down the long walk to the big stage. I got down on my knees. I prayed to God to give me strength and send me hope, to help me through this night.

I had done that on each of my two previous Vegas openings, but then Dr. Wiggins had been with me both times. The first time, I was opening for Trini Lopez. A half hour before I was to go on, I said to the good doctor, "Tim, I just want to be alone for a few minutes," and while he waited outside, I prayed.

Then I opened the door. "Let's go, Tim!" As we headed slowly toward backstage at the Riviera, Tim started doing his thing, singing gospel songs, clapping his hands, spinning around and dancing, and getting me to do the same. "Brother Sam," he said, and sang too, "you are going to be great!" I was like a prizefighter sparring around with a partner just before he steps into the ring for his big fight.

I guess Dr. Wiggins really had a spell on me; he knew how to say the right thing. He was like a witch doctor for me. I went out there in front of Trini, got three standing ovations, and was on my way.

But the more successful I got, the more Dr. Wiggins seemed to need *me*. The relationship became very strange at times. He started calling me, and he became available for me totally, protecting me from everyone. He felt I was on my way—and he wanted to be part of it. Having struggled for a long time, working in psychiatric hospitals and helping patients who couldn't pay him, he seemed to see, through

27

me, a way up and out. He had a wife and two kids. He was bright, handsome, a great tennis player—he had all the attributes for impending success, and now he wanted the rewards.

Many times before an opening night we would stay in the same room, and the closeness of the situation eventually became stifling for me. Althought I truly cared for Tim, I had to tell him that I wanted to begin trying to get through these horrendous openings on my own.

He felt shattered and left out, and after an especially intense pre-opening night, when he said some incredibly painful and embarrassing things about wanting to be a white man, we drifted apart.

But now I shut my eyes and tried to make believe that Dr. Wiggins was there. "Brother Sam, you're going to be great!" I kept trying to see it, to remember and hear it in detail. It was coming, but it was all forced. It wouldn't wash.

Then suddenly something came to my mind that the ghost of Dr. Wiggins couldn't even begin to fight. I got up off my knees and started to dress. My hands were shaking.

I'm back on North Wells Street and Phil, my older brother, is complaining to Pa about my having trumpet lessons. Phil is the next to oldest, and whatever he says carries clout as far as I'm concerned.

In fact I idolize him. He's bald like my dad and he's a cop—and in those days a policeman meant something, especially if you had one in your family. He's fifteen years older than me, and whatever brother love is, I have it for him. He always brings me toys and gives my mother money. He's got the heart of a lion. When I get beat up at school, he comes around in his uniform looking for the guilty party. So when he puts down the idea of me getting lessons, I'm devastated. I never forget what he says.

"Why is Sammy getting lessons?" he says, as if the whole thing is ridiculous. "He's got no talent! Nobody in this family's got talent."

My dad gives me two dollars every week for the trumpet lessons. Ma talked him into it; she says I'm going to be "another Harry James." And every single week I've got to ask Dad for that money; it's agony.

"P-Pa, today's the lesson. Can, can I have the two dollars?"

"Goddamnit!" he shouts. "Again with the trumpet! I just gave you two dollars!"

"Pa, that was for last week's lesson."

MIRACLE MICROPHONE

As I watch him reach into those dirty brown-tweed baggy pants that never fit him but that he wears practically every day, and he digs slowly around in the pocket, I sense how painful it is for him to give me the money. Because he never gets anything in return. He always says, "If you invest, you got to see some returns." All he does is give me the two dollars and I'm free until the next showdown.

I've been taking lessons about two months and I tell my mom that when I come home the next day I'll play the first song I've learned. I feel very secure with Ma; I know that even if I play badly it's good to her. I come home from my lesson in the late afternoon, and the store is closed. I know something's wrong. I'm worried; maybe somebody's sick.

I head up the side stairs to our apartment, trumpet case in hand, I open the door—and it looks like the Second Coming of Jesus. "Sammy's here!" my mother shouts. "Everyone sit down, Sammy's going to play a song!" I think I'll shit! There's my father, my brothers, including Phil, some of the roomers, and practically the entire neighborhood! Some of the people are sitting, most are standing there looking at me, waiting for the sounds that will bring customers into my father's store, or so he hopes. Why not? He's already invested twenty dollars in lessons plus twenty-five for rental of the trumpet, and he's sitting there, arms folded, eyeing me, thinking, And for this I had to close the store! Closing the store, of course, is unforgivable.

I'm trembling as I open the case and put my mouthpiece in the trumpet. I get out my music. I start to play "A Tisket, A Tasket, I Lost My Yellow Basket," currently a big hit. I feel like I'm blowing through one of Pa's rusted water pipes. The thought flashes through my mind of all the roomers getting up and leaving and checking out and my dad coming over to shout at me, "It's all your fault!"

As I finish the last couple of notes, they all start to applaud. My mother's standing, clapping the loudest. "He's wonderful—another Harry James!" She throws her arms around me.

A couple of moments later, my dad picks himself up from his chair, walks over to me wearing something like a grimace but it might be a smile, puts an arm around me, and says, "Sammy, you . . . you shtink!"

In the middle of my obsessive thoughts, as I was getting the last bit of my tuxedo in place, there was a loud knock at the dressing room door.

The Warm-up

"Fifteen minutes, Mr. Shore—and there's someone out here says he knows you."

I opened the door.

Says he knows me? Who could know me better?

There was only one person about whom I could use the phrase "we grew up together." We went through grade school together, through high school and into the navy. We were inseparable. His father was black, his mother was white, and so he was in-between and rejected on all sides. He had always been wiry, with light skin and kinky hair, and he was my size—short. He was as tough as I was scared; he was the definition of *street smart*. Since I was known as a mama's boy, the kids didn't like me, either. And as the only Jew in a neighborhood of blacks, Poles, and Italians, I was like an honorary mulatto as far as my friend was concerned.

I'd heard he was now a shipping magnate in Greece, and I hadn't seen him for many, many years. And there he was, standing in the hallway outside my door, looking fantastic in a tux, with a large cigar in his hand, just minutes before the trial of my life.

"Jesus Christ—Rudy!" I grabbed him and hugged and kissed him. "I don't believe it's you! I heard you were living in Greece. . . . I can't tell you . . . Rudy . . . I'm in shock!"

"Hey, I wouldn't miss this opening for the world," he said, rubbing my head. "I was back in LA for some business, heard you were opening with Elvis, hopped a plane—and here I am."

He took a step back and looked me over. "I'm really proud of you, Sammy. I've been hearing bits and pieces about how you've been doing the past few years—Tom Jones, Trini Lopez—and now you're hot shit with Elvis . . . hot damn, Brother Sam!"

I felt waves of shame and fear along with the incredible relief of having a friend. It was better to have a friend, but Rudy's being there made all the other feelings break loose.

"I'm scared shitless, Rudy," I said, immediately giving back the "hot shit" award. "I really don't want to go out there."

Just then Terry, the stage manager, popped his head in. "Sammy, ya got ten . . ."

"Holy fuck," I said. "Rudy, I just can't do it. You know who's out there? Stars, the world press, the networks—and to see Elvis, not me. They don't know who the hell I am . . ."

Rudy gave me a level look, sizing me up, bringing his image of me up to date from the last time he'd seen me. "Okay, Sammy, I hear ya. But you said something to me that day we were playing Waller High in the semifinals, those unbeatable bastards. You said, 'I really don't wanna play; how we gonna beat those guys; what am I doin' on a goddamn basketball court?' And we got on our knees and prayed and went out there and kicked some ass! You held their high scorer to three points.

"I didn't come here, halfway across the world, to listen to this shit. Those people out there? They're all from Waller High School."

"Five minutes!" Terry shouted.

"Kick ass, white boy!" Rudy said.

I was laughing. I was a guy who always needed a touch of soul to loosen up. Rudy looked around the room while I tied my shoes and poured him a Jack Daniel's and water and me my J&B.

"Let's go get 'em!" Rudy kept hollering, and he kept it up as we headed for the elevator, patting each other on the back and hugging and punching and jiving just like the old days.

Off the elevator and backstage we could hear the music—the Sweet Inspirations were still on. I peeked through the side of the curtain and the room was jam-packed; it seemed like I'd never seen so many people. The audience wasn't reacting too well to the Sweet Inspirations; most of them were talking and looking around the immense room as if nobody were onstage. They were just not interested in three black girls singing gospel music when all they wanted was ELVIS. And I would have to go out there and tame them. For once in my life I felt like a Christian, except I was being thrown to the lions.

The Inspirations finished their last song and were taking their bows. The applause was light and scattered. The feeling was like, Okay already, enough with the Coming of the Lord.

The house lights dimmed and an awesome silence came over the audience, the feeling that *he* was coming closer, that the King was soon to appear, and all that preceded him were just appetizers.

The drum roll started, and over the enormous speakers that were placed all around the stage came the announcement: "And now, ladies and gentlemen, the International Hotel proudly presents the comedy star of our show, Sammy *Shore*!"

Once again the scattering of perfunctory applause, and a few groaning "oh's" as in aw shit. My intro music started and Rudy slapped me on the ass and called me by my Chicago nickname. "Go get 'em, Satch!'' I ran out there and the applause subsided.

Somewhere around twenty-five hundred people glared at me, waiting for me to say something, daring me to fall flat on my face. About all I could see through the lights were little heads and faces and great shrouds of cigarette smoke rising toward the ceiling. I heard the clattering of dishes all around and knew I'd be talking to people who were pissed because their food was late.

And what people. I knew I was facing Cary Grant directly in front of me, in the dead-center booth. Around the room would be Sophia Loren, Elizabeth Taylor, Richard Burton, Raquel Welch, Ann-Margret, Tom Jones . . . . Sammy Davis was to my left with a bunch of his friends; Johnny Carson, Ed McMahon, and their wives were out there; Kirk Kerkorian, who owned MGM, for whom Elvis had made his movies and who owned the hotel; the heads of Twentieth Century-Fox, Paramount, and Warner Brothers—all came to feast on the phenomenon of the decade. But holding up the moment they were all waiting for was me.

For what seemed to me like an entire minute I just stood there, my mouth impossibly dry, the sweat pouring down my face into my eyes. My eyes were burning; I hadn't opened my mouth, and fear seemed to engulf all of me.

I took the microphone off the stand and started to speak—there was no sound coming through! I tried again: "Good evening, ladies and gentlemen.''

Nothing! No sound. The audience started to grow restless.

I hit the mike. Still no sound.

Then I shouted at the top of my lungs: "THEY SPEND FIFTY-THREE MILLION BUCKS TO BUILD THIS HOTEL—AND FOURTEEN DOLLARS FOR A MICROPHONE!''

The audience started to break up.

I twirled the microphone cord and handed it to someone at ringside. "You want some licorice?" Again, the audience laughed. I started to relax. My years of experience were paying off.

I hit the mike with my hand, still no sound. I handed it to a ringsider and said, "Here's a present for you, take it home." I started to recite from Shakespeare: " 'What light through yonder window glows, it is the east and Juliet is the west.' " I started to double-talk Shakespeare, and they began to applaud. They just knew this was not part of my act and that I was ad-libbing.

A stagehand shoved another mike out from behind the curtain. I grabbed it and was certain this one would work, but I had a roll going and I didn't want to stop it. So I pretended to be talking into the mike and that it wouldn't work, either. I was mouthing words. Now I had them all on my side. They were beginning to forget who they came to see.

I started to talk into the mike and it was on and I said, "Now I don't know what to say. I forgot my act, folks!" A roar from the audience.

"What a hotel. Have you noticed the eternal flame in front of the hotel? That's the Tomb of the Unknown Gambler." Applause, laughter. I began to weave in and out of my act. I got into my preacher bit and had them all hollering "Amen! Hallelujah!"

I looked up to the balcony, where more than six hundred people were sitting. "You people up there in the balcony, you wanna be saved?"

They hollered, "Yeah!"

"Jump, you mothers!"

Now they were screaming. I jumped off the stage and started to walk through the audience with my tambourine in hand, hitting some people on the head with it.

"So come with me!

"Walk with me . . .

"Reach out for me . . .

"Touch me . . ." I pointed to a ringsider. "Not *you*, boy." I started back to the stage, hollering, "Are you ready to be saved?"

"Yeah!" they shouted.

"Are you ready to be healed?"

"Yeah!"

"Will you give me your money?"

"NO!"

"THEN GO TO HELL!"

I walked off to my music, "Bringing in the Sheaves."

The audience was wild with enthusiasm. I was a hit. I came back and took a couple of bows and knew that I had conquered, that I'd done the impossible.

I was supposed to exit stage left, because Elvis would be coming from stage right, but in my excitement I didn't know left from right and I went the wrong way. I walked into the wings and there was Elvis in his beaded black jumpsuit, surrounded by his guys—Red, Joe,

The Warm-up

Sonny—and by mirrors, towels, and makeup people. I walked right over and reached out with my hand. He extended his, and we shook. His hand was surprisingly cold and clammy.

"They're all set for you, Elvis," I said. "They're a terrific audience."

He didn't say anything, just nodded. I saw in his face the look of terror—grim and tight.

The fear that I always had, Elvis Presley had too.

2

COLONELS, CLOWNS, AND KINGS

As the months of our first engagement and tour passed, I saw no evidence of any physical deterioration in Elvis. It broke my heart seven years later whenever I saw photos of the man. How could they destroy this wonderful-looking animal? But I should have sensed something from the very beginning of my work with him, when the doctor came by every day with his black leather bag.

"Hi, Sammy," the doctor would say in a drawl, from beneath a dome of white hair. "How's the show?" I was so naïve, I was sure he was only there to give Elvis B_{12} shots.

Perhaps the Colonel was as naïve as I was when it came to drugs and what was really happening backstage. Many nights the Colonel and his assistant, Tom Diskin, would be sitting in Elvis's dressing room when the doctor arrived. I knew that the Colonel, for all his crassness and calculation, had a certain undeniable love and human fondness for Elvis. Why then, didn't he intervene when his boy was being loaded down with pills? During the end, when Elvis started to gain so much weight and it was plain that he was in deep trouble, why didn't Parker hire an honest-to-God psychiatrist to help, if need be to travel with Elvis and spend the whole day with him? Instead of help, all Elvis had around him were leeches sucking on his sickness, suffocating him with, "yes, yes, yes."

The Warm-up

As I reflect on it, it seems to me that the Colonel was more deeply concerned with nourishing his own tremendous ego, the kind of inflated obsession that carried him every night to the roulette wheel, where he would not allow any other players. He would surround and devour almost all the numbers. His gambling sickness cost him tens of thousands of dollars a month.

The Colonel was fat—about five feet nine and 225 pounds—bald, semiliterate, shrewd, and vulgar. His everyday accessories consisted of a color-striped, open sport shirt, baggy pants, cigar, straw hat and cane. He was a southern con man strictly out of a second-rate carnival.

He very seldom watched Elvis work. That was because he was too busy doing a peculiar show of his own, which made me think of what my father's greed would have been like had my dad ever made it big. No matter where we were touring, the Colonel would have Tom Diskin take out a special black briefcase, get the promoter for that arena, and, while Elvis was onstage, help the Colonel count the take and put it in the case. He usually had it timed so that when Elvis was on his last number—his medley of "Dixie" and "Battle Hymn of the Republic"—he had ten minutes to move out fast, like he was holding up a bank. The two black limousines would pull up in back of the arena as close to backstage as possible, Elvis would finish his last song, walk offstage without even taking a bow, and pop right into a limo, where his cronies would wipe him off and tell him how wonderful he was.

I would have the door open for the other limo, into which would jump the Colonel, Tom Diskin, and then me. The people in the hall would still be screaming for Elvis to come out and take a bow, but we were already on the way back to the hotel, following our police escort, the Colonel with as much as a quarter of a million dollars in cash in the black bag on his lap.

Each night of that first gig with Elvis was like opening night all over again. Everybody—every star, celebrity, writer, and reporter—wanted to see Elvis, and I was sitting on top of the world.

When I came off the stage and shook Elvis's hand that first night, I was shocked. I just couldn't understand why such a big star would be so fearful, and seeing him there stiff and afraid was a revelation. No one could fix it for him, either. Once you're out there alone, it's just you, and nothing else—not money, girls, reputation, or power—can do the job.

COLONELS, CLOWNS, AND KINGS

That opening night, drums rolled, music started blasting through the enormous speakers that were hanging all over the place, Elvis's opening song started to vamp, and he waited just a moment. I stood there and watched entertainment history being made. There was no announcement, Elvis just strode out like a black stallion. It was as though Jesus had come to save the world. The entire audience stood up, screamed, hollered: the King had arrived. He was the picture of beauty and power—trim and healthy.

He grabbed the mike and started his opening song, mumbling his lyrics. He really was petrified, although in a few moments the crowd's electricity would touch him and he would be transformed and then transform the crowd in turn.

I had to go down to my dressing room; I really needed a drink to calm down. As I came all the way around backstage toward the elevator, Rudy met me, jumping for joy as if we had just won the championship.

Later, in my dressing room, Rudy and I could hear the shouting and screaming of the audience piped over the speakers. It was happening for Elvis as my friend and I drank to our success. Well-wishers came by and marveled at the outcome of the dead mike, asking me with a little suspicion if it had been part of the act. (No, that's why it worked.) Abe Lastfogel, chairman of the William Morris Agency, came back to make a speech about my "electrifying opening" (a funny choice of words I thought) and to promise me the world on a string, or with no strings.

Every night of the engagement, Alex Shoofey and his cronies would have dinner at one of the International's restaurants: Italian, German, Japanese, French. Alex would sit like a king holding court. He was short—about five feet three—weighed about 150, with a long nose and hair dyed to an Elvis black, and he was a tyrant. His ego preceded him and exceeded him. He looked like a more modern version of my dad, with the same set of balls—lead. He was a "self-made" man, having worked for twenty years at the Sahara from the casino up through the ranks, to general manager of the Flamingo, and then vice-president of the hotel that claimed the title of the world's largest. When Alex walked through the casino, you could see that most of the employees were terrified.

But I was his boy. It seemed that I was the only one who could make him laugh, and when he wanted to laugh I was summoned to court, whether that was the executive suite or one of the restaurants.

The Warm-up

Every one of Alex's associates was like a jester trying to please him, but I was chief fool.

I would finish my first show at ten, change, and head for one of the restaurants. Every night I'd ask one of the maître d's, "Where's Mr. Shoofey?"

"Italian tonight, Sammy."

I'd walk in, perhaps with tambourine in hand, and begin to take over the Italian restaurant.

"Amen, hallelujah!" Alex would shout.

And we would all sit and laugh and drink and try to maintain the proper level of hysteria. I was looking to please, always on, trying to be funny.

Within a couple of years, the International was sold to Hilton. There were several conflicting stories about what happened next. The most popular tale has it that Alex was sitting at dinner with Baron Hilton, Charlie Rich—who was performing in the showroom at the time—and some friends when he made an insulting comment about Charlie. That was unfortunate, so the story goes, but Alex went on to make a much bigger mistake.

"I want you to apologize for the remark you just made, Mr. Shoofey," Baron Hilton supposedly said.

Alex snapped back at his new boss, one of the world's most powerful businessmen: "I don't apologize to no one."

That sounds interesting, but that's not the way Alex Shoofey got canned. The fact of the matter was that Baron and Alex were talking before the show one night—it was to be a show by Charlie Rich—about who was booked for the coming weeks. Baron Hilton mentioned the City of Hope convention he had booked.

"Nobody told me about no City of Hope convention," Alex said.

"I forgot to tell you," Baron said.

Alex snapped, "Who the hell is running this hotel anyway?"

He found out. The next month he was fired. That was February 24, 1972. As of this writing, despite the fact that he has continued to live in that town, Alex Shoofey has never again been employed by any hotel in Las Vegas.

***

"Boy, we like you, boy," the Colonel said. It was the night before we closed our first Vegas engagement, and I'd been called into Elvis's dressing room.

"You did a good job for us. We want you to come on our tour, ten cities in two weeks. How would you like that, boy?"

"I'd love it, Colonel."

"And one of the dates will be the Forum in LA. Think you can handle that big room, twenty thousand people?"

My immediate thought was: never. Twenty thousand people? Was this a USO tour with Bob Hope? I thought the Forum was strictly for basketball and conventions.

"I'm sure I can handle it, Colonel. Maybe I'll go out there and shoot some baskets."

The first stop on the tour was Tampa, Florida. We had two private jets, one for Elvis and his guys, one for the Colonel, his people, and me. I couldn't believe it was happening, me flying in a private jet with Colonel Parker. The only thing that seemed familiar and real was my role as the flunky, gofer, and clown. The Colonel had me take my trumpet everywhere, so I could be the Designated Idiot.

The plane would land, the door would open, one of the Colonel's men would go roll out a red carpet at the base of the stairs, and then, at the Colonel's request, I would come to the door and blow the charge. ("Let 'em know we're here, boy.") We'd arrive at the hotel, and I'd march into the lobby and blow the charge again. "Elvis and the Colonel have arrived!" The Colonel would wind up his Sammy Shore doll and I'd be running all over the place.

In the mornings, at around seven or eight, the Colonel would be pounding on my door. "Let's move it, boy, get the show on the road!" I'd jump out of bed, grab the trumpet, and parade up and down the hotel hall blowing reveille. It was like being in the service, right down to the guys shouting, "Shove that bugle up your ass!"

I was a professional entertainer at the peak of my career, making ten thousand dollars a week, yet I was acting like the warm-up shoeshine boy. The Colonel even had me wheedling food out of hotel managers and schlepping it back to him. "The Colonel asked me to tell you," he'd have me say, "how much he and Elvis have enjoyed staying here at your hotel. Thank you so much for your hospitality. . . . And the Colonel wanted to know if you could pack some lunches for Elvis and the boys. He'd really appreciate it."

The Warm-up

The Colonel's instructions had been clear: "Take everything you can handle, Jew boy." Of course, I knew he was really kidding about that name—wasn't he?

So there I am ferrying lunches, my trumpet hanging on a guitar strap around my neck while I balance boxes, bags, packs of rolls, and whole pies on my way to the limousine.

"What ya get today, boy?" the Colonel would say, and he'd start rummaging through the boxes as we made our getaway.

The Colonel wanted it all, and in every city it was the same. I wondered why I took so much shit from him. Here I was on Elvis's payroll for ten G's a week and he had me carrying bags. If I had refused, if I had reminded him that I was being paid only to perform and not to be a gofer or a porter, would he have fired me? I doubt it. I was doing too well at every concert, and he knew it. Then why did I keep my mouth shut? Because the Colonel's treatment of me confirmed the way I felt about myself. So I did what was expected of me and smiled a lot, knowing I couldn't possibly deserve ten G's a week. I swallowed Colonel Parker's bitter mockery with the aid of my magic soothing elixir, J&B. Through it all, I knew the Colonel had a fond respect for me.

The night of the Forum concert in LA was a big one, like another opening night for both Elvis and me. All of show business would be there among the twenty thousand, including many powerful people who hadn't made it to the Las Vegas shows. Elvis had a new outfit made, all white with beads coming out of the back like a cape; he looked like a snow-covered Batman. He was very nervous and I was more so, since nerves were my specialty.

I remembered what I had told the Colonel, so I came out dribbling a basketball while the band played "Sweet Georgia Brown." I dribbled up the stage to the mike: "Hey, what time the Knicks show-ng up?"

I knew I had them, and I wouldn't let them go. It was an exciting night. I can't describe the feeling of standing in the middle of the Forum with a packed house laughing and applauding and forgetting who they came to see. It was quite an exciting night for the little boy from Wells Street. I came off and shook Elvis's hand, which had become the customary thing for us to do. Once again I saw that he was extremely nervous. He got his beads tangled up in the microphone cord when he went out there, and he really had a struggle getting himself together, but when he did, he completely demolished the audience.

Whenever Colonel Parker came to Vegas for another Elvis opening in the years I worked with him there, it seemed that everyone in the hotel walked in fear. He had the sole power to have almost anyone fired. You would have thought that he, and not Elvis, was the star and that Elvis worked for *him*. He had an entire floor for his offices. He could pick up the phone and within two minutes have the management working on recarpeting his floor because he didn't like the colors.

When he walked into the immense show room of the International, the fixtures seemed to part. Everyone was a puppet, and he didn't bother holding the strings, he grabbed us by the arms.

I felt sorry for the Colonel's semi-invalid wife, who came to Vegas now and then to spend some time with her husband. She could hardly walk, having been stricken with crippling arthritis. Her cane hardly helped her get around, but she was a very proud woman and got to where she was going on her own.

She loved Elvis, and the few days that she would be there, she always came in and struggled her way into the Colonel's booth to watch the show—sometimes by herself, since the Colonel was out gambling. I always felt flattered when she told me how much she enjoyed watching me.

Many nights she would just sit out in the casino at the roulette wheel watching the Colonel cover the entire board. Never a word was spoken between the two while he was gambling. She just sat there watching.

She was a very aware woman. I think she may have seen the coming demise of Elvis before anyone else. She always asked me, "How's Elvis doing?" And in my stupor I'd always say, "Just fine!"

But I don't think she ever voiced an opinion on anything that had to do with the Colonel's business. That would have been sacrilege. Even Elvis had a difficult time talking to the Colonel about those things.

The Colonel was married a long time to Mrs. Parker, as he called her, and when he spoke of her you could at least detect a change, a softening. She was a mere shadow behind his overpowering need, but in his way I think he truly cared.

***

41

The Warm-up

The Colonel's tyranny was the same kind of power that my father had wielded over my mother—until the day my dad had to pay the price for his obsessive greed.

It's the summer of 1958 and autumn is getting close. The previous few winters I've been pleading with my father to buy a little home in Miami, so both Ma and Pa can get out of the cold, especially since Pa's been developing a terrible bronchial condition. He's got enough money—somewhere—and my mother's been pleading too.

"Please, Pa," she says. "You can't stand another winter. Your cough is getting worse."

"I'll take a cough drop; it's a lot cheaper," he says. "And they got hurricanes down there—you could drown!"

I throw in my bit, reminding him about the doctor's advice that he move.

"What the hell does he know, the fat slob. He should talk, all he does is smoke and cough and he weighs three hundred pounds. Let *him* go to Florida, he could afford it for what he charges me."

"Ma needs a rest too, Pa. She's tired of scrubbing and cleaning. It'd do her good."

"Let her go with the doctor. Between them they weigh *five hundred* pounds! They could lay in the water and people will think they are whales!"

His remarks hit her like a javelin spear, but she's silent as always. Just once I wish she would turn to him and say, "Hyman, you cheap bastard, take your money and your store and shove them up your ass. I'm leaving. *You* clean the rooms!" But not Lena; she's always worshiped Hyman, in fear and submission.

After months of our pleading and his worsening cough, Pa starts to understand that we want the new home at least partly for his sake. The three of us get in his Jeep station wagon and head for Miami. The trip is horrendous. "You're going too fast, slow down!" "Not that motel, it's too expensive, tonight we can sleep in the car!" "Let's go back." "Go get a loaf of bread and bologna, we don't need to eat in a restaurant, the food's shitty anyway!"

Finally, after seven grueling days of driving through rain and cold, we see the signs WELCOME TO FLORIDA—MIAMI 257 MILES.

"Pa, look, we're in Florida! We should be in Miami late tonight." He just sits there with his arms crossed. I just know what he's thinking. He's pissed that we talked him into it, that we'll actually have to stay in a *motel* and it looks like he's doomed to buy a house.

We find a beautiful little house—2121 N.W. 25th Street, eight thousand dollars cash, with furniture and everything.

Hyman hates every day of it. "It's too hot here. . . . Phillip is stealing the money from the store." (Phillip, my cop brother, is not only working his beat, but is watching the store and collecting the rent from the roomers.) "I'll come back this summer and be bankrupt!"

Then the day comes when he explodes. It's late March. He's been in the house nearly three months and he can't stand the quiet, the inactivity and, most of all, the constant vision of all the money he must be losing.

"That's it, I've had it with this fucking home and your lousy cooking and this lousy Miami! Tomorrow we're going back to Chicago!"

"But, Pa," I say, "you can't go back now—it's the worst part of the winter, it's five below zero in Chicago. Wait till winter's over."

His mind's made up. The next day I take them both to the train station, call Phil and tell him to meet them when the train arrives in four days. Phil knows as well as I do that Pa's driving thought is that Phil is stealing the money and he's got to go back to save his business.

They arrived at Grand Central Station, Chicago, the evening of March 26, 1959. The winds were howling. Chicago had taken delivery on another one of its blizzards, with the mercury at least seven degrees below zero. The big train eased to a stop, putting an end to four days and nights of my mother and father sitting up in the coach car, weary and exhausted, even though they could easily have afforded a comfortable berth. People were greeting each other all over the platform—hugging, kissing, families reuniting. And standing and waiting for his parents to appear was my brother Phil, in his best dark blue uniform and cap and badge and shiny black shoes.

Slowly exiting the train were his mom, with a little plaid suitcase and brown shopping bag filled with presents, and behind her, Hyman Shore, all tan and wearing the same tweed pants as always, with his suspenders and his little cap.

"Pa!" Phil shouted. "I'm over here." He headed for them.

"Ma, you look wonderful." He embraced her.

"And look at you, Pa, you're so tan," as he hugged him. "How

43

was the trip?'' But no answer came as Phil felt Pa's head droop on his chest, felt Pa give way on buckling legs and fall to the platform.

"Pa, what's the matter? Say something, Pa!" Phil was shouting. "You're home! I made a lot of money for you. Please Pa, say something!"

Hyman Shore died in his son's arms at nine forty-seven that evening. In Phil's pockets was all the money he wanted to give his dad—to show that he was a proud cop who would not steal his father's money.

Meanwhile, I'm working in Miami:

As soon as we drop our kids off at summer camp, my wife feels lost without 'em.
She says, "What'll we do while they're away?"
I say, "Let's move!"

Kids today take it for granted that they're going to go to camp. They don't have to struggle for it. When I was a kid, I had to sell magazines and newspapers all year so I could get money to go. Now it's the parents who have to sell things—the car, the stocks, the house . . .
The beatnik bit:
I have a slight sinus condition, man, so I'm gonna sniff a little decongestant. You cats will excuse me, of course . . . (sniff sniff) . . . Ah-h-h-h. . . . This is the new formula for sinus. . . . Comes in powder form . . . from Indochina . . .
We will now pause for five seconds to let happiness set in . . .
My next poem was inspired by the head-on crash of two tractor trailers. . . . I was in one of 'em. . . . Very messy scene, man . . . bodies all over . . . blood . . . glass . . . and worst of all—my hypodermic was bent . . .
Or the southern governor:
People of this state, I want y'all to know that I-am-interested-in-each-and-every-one-of-you. If any one of y'all have a problem, no matter how small, I want you to come on up here now to the guvnah's mansion, go right on through the front door, walk into my office, and say, "Guvnah, I want to bribe you!"

***

COLONELS, CLOWNS, AND KINGS

I walk into the Weinstein & Sons funeral parlor on the west side of Chicago, unable to believe that my dad is dead. There are just a few people wandering around looking for the right room for their particular loved one. It seems that in every other room someone is lying there like a jack-in-the-box. I'm shaking. I don't know what to expect. Just a few days ago I put my father on the train. I've never known what it's like to experience a death so close in my family.

I know that Pa trusted me and understood that I'm trying to become somebody, not just a cab driver or a cop or his helper, like my brothers. I was something special to him, I think, but he really couldn't show me that.

The only real emotion he showed me was the time I drove all night from St. Louis to get home after one of my early jobs in show business. I arrived in front of my dad's store at about two-thirty in the morning. It was toward the end of the summer, on one of those unbearably muggy nights when the whole city was sleeping with the windows open.

I was completely exhausted and depressed because the owner of the club where I was working hadn't liked me well enough to keep me on. I had all my clothes and possessions heaped in the back of my 1953 Kaiser, which I'd bought that year for twenty-three hundred dollars, a thousand of which had been a loan from Pa, which was a miracle in itself. No one could believe that loan, not even my mom.

I left my stuff in the car, locked it, and started up the side stairs to our apartment. As I approached the door I realized I didn't have keys to get in, and I didn't dare wake up my dad. He'd have me shot at dawn—maybe before dawn—and in any event I really didn't want to disturb their sleep. So I made a pillow out of my shoes and tried to sleep on the floor of the landing.

The daylight coming up in the little hallway window, the cats starting to fight outside, and the sounds of some of the roomers slamming doors as they started off to work meant that my wretched nap was over. I glanced at my prized Bulova: six-thirty. My parents would be getting up soon, and I decided I might as well start to bring up some of my things. I headed down the dismal hallway, past the rooming house on the second floor, Dad's store on the first, and then through another door and out into the street.

I just stood there for a moment. The Wells Street trolley was clanging by, people hanging on for dear life—or at least for the chance to make it to work, as if they couldn't have waited for the next car. I remember thinking that there must be something special about that car, since half the city seemed to be crowded onto it. It was nice, in a way, to be back in the old neighborhood—Tonelli's Candy Store, Pookie's Pool Room, Bonafedi's Barber Shop, Harry's Drug, and down the street, the James A. Sexton grammar school, which I had attended.

I turned toward my car and saw the front window was broken. At first I just didn't understand it—why was the window broken? There was glass all over the seat and glass on the curb. I looked in. All my stuff was gone. I opened the back door and looked all around for my trumpet. Gone—everything gone except one sneaker and a pair of socks on the floor in the back.

I couldn't believe someone would take *everything*. My music, my clothes, and my trumpet were nowhere to be found. I ran down the street. What was I going to do? How was I going to work? I panicked. I didn't know which way to go. I'll tell Pa, I thought. He'll call Phil and Phil will get together with some other cops and catch the thieves.

I ran back up the stairs two at a time. A roomer, a black lady, was heading down the stairs toward me.

"Ain't seen you around, Sammy. You still playing that trumpet?"

"No, ma'am!" I shouted. I careened past her. "They just stole my trumpet, those fucking bastards!"

I came to a stop at our door and gasped for air. I pounded on the door. "Pa, open the door. It's Sammy, someone's broke into my car! . . . Open up, Pa!"

A moment later I heard the shuffling of slippers against linoleum and then the unlatching of the two bolts my father had put on the door. When it opened, there was Ma.

"Semelah is home, Hyman, wake up! He's home!" It was like the coming of the Messiah. She took me into her enormous bosom, kissing me, running her hands through my hair, which was soaked with sweat. "Semelah!"

"Ma, they broke into my car and took all my things. . . ."

"They what?"

I ran into the dining room/master bedroom, where Pa was just sitting up in his bed.

"Pa!" I shouted. "They broke into my car and took all my things! Call Phil!"

He didn't understand, he was still half asleep.

He mumbled, "They broke into your car?"

"Yes, Pa. Come downstairs and look . . ."

Now it took. He jumped out of bed like someone was breaking into his store, grabbed his pants, pulled them on while he was stepping into his shoes and going for his cap, and headed for the stairs.

"They took your what? Car broke into? I don't understand. What's going on here, when did you come home?" He was thumping down the stairs.

"Early this morning, Pa. I was too tired to carry all my things up, and I didn't want to wake you and Ma . . ."

He bolted out the front like the human cannonball I used to see at the Barnum and Bailey Circus, went straight for the car, opened the door, looked under the seats, lifted up the hood, looked at the motor, searched underneath the car, and started to scream at the top of his lungs.

I had heard him yell and shout many, many times, but those were just echoes compared to the way he was bellowing, "You fuckin' bastards, where are you! Bring back my Sammy's trumpet and his music, you fuckin' bastards!" as he ran down the street clutching the baggy pants and pulling on his suspenders. "Come back, you FUCKS!"

When he realized it was all futile, he started walking slowly back toward me. I was leaning against my Kaiser. Pa looked as though someone had taken all the furniture out of his store. His head was bowed, and for the first time in my life I saw his tears. It was then I knew he really loved me.

He started to cry. "Your trumpet, your music, Sammy. How you gonna work?" He was almost sobbing. "Don't worry," he said. "I'll buy you a new trumpet, that one was getting old and had a lot of dents."

"Don't worry about it, Pa. I can do my act without the trumpet."

He heard the words *without the trumpet* and straightened up. "What!" he bellowed. "You're not going to play the trumpet? All the money I spent on lessons?"

He's lying there so still, his tiny bald head on the braided pillow, silver-rimmed eyeglasses magnifying his clenched eyes, arms folded in his lap. He's tan from Florida, so I guess they didn't need makeup.

The Warm-up

I want to touch him, so I reach over and meet the coldness of his hands and I start trembling. The pain in my gut deepens into an empty sensation I've never felt before and tears start to engulf me.

I hear a voice behind me. "Sammy, look at Pa, he's gone!" It's my mother shouting as she comes up to embrace me. "Why did he want to come back—to die, that's why!"

My brothers and Ma's friends are all standing there, seemingly unable to feel anything. But then, Pa never gave any of my brothers anything.

It takes us a week to find all the money Pa had hidden away in the store—in stoves, mattresses, tool boxes, under stairways—the money he had hoarded for a rainy day. We find one hundred twenty-five thousand dollars in singles, fives, tens, twenties, and some new two-dollar bills, all rolled in brown paper bags with rubber bands around them. The money has never been touched, but then Hyman Shore never understood that someday he was going to die.

After we count the money we have Phil take it home, because he's a cop and he can protect it. The next day when my brothers Morris, Bernard, Phillip, and I go to the bank and the teller counts the money again, five hundred dollars is missing.

It took me a little while to figure out. I knew my brother Phillip, the hotshot cop. He always had a wad of dough from some scam he was in or that he had just busted. He loved to buy everybody drinks, and he loved the fact that everyone loved him for being such an easy touch.

He had a beautiful Italian wife who liked nice things, and Phillip loved to get them for her. They had a son who was always beautifully dressed, and they always had the newest car on the block.

Perhaps it shouldn't have bothered me as much as it did—after all, many times Phil had bestowed his extra cash on Ma—but Pa was right. Phillip did take his money.

How do you get through to those kinds of fathers—the ones who don't show anything, unless it's anger. You try so hard to make them love you, to have them tell you you're a good boy, "I'm proud of you."

But who ever told *them* that? Their fathers? Their fathers just taught them to survive. Having never heard, "*I love you, son!*" how can he ever manage to say it?

He might walk down the street with his arm on your shoulder and mutter a word or two, like, "Button up your coat. You'll catch cold." Actually, in my generation, it was the moms who said that, not those kinds of fathers. They were pissed because they had to buy you the *coat*.

The worst part of my pa's death for me was that I knew he really loved me and he just couldn't say it. "I'll buy you another trumpet"—that was the extent of it. I sure wish I had him now. I'd grab his frail body and hug him and tell him, "Pa, you're the greatest. I *love* you, and thanks for the trumpet lessons. I use the trumpet in my act, Pa, and the people love it."

I have to risk now, to walk over to a closed person and say, "Hey, man . . . I love you."

If my dad were alive today, I'd love to take him to see *Gandhi*. My dad looked so much like him—slight, bald, little round glasses that hung over his nose, he even shuffled along like Gandhi! The only difference is that my dad shouted words of vengeance: *"Fuck 'em!"*

And poor Gandhi's wife. How she followed him—worshiped him, apparently. The movie didn't say much about her. My mom, too, followed in the footsteps of her husband, and in her way was much more like Gandhi himself.

Her kindness and caring were known throughout the neighborhood. She gave to everybody—without Hyman ever knowing about it, of course.

If a poor person or a bum came into the store for a handout, my father would always chase him out. It was then I'd see my mother sneak out the back of the store, through the alley to find the person and give him some money or food. The fear that Hyman instilled in my mother could not faze her belief in the goodness of others. So many times she had to swallow her pride after being lambasted by the ruler of the house. And so many times she would corner me and tell me of this or that neighbor and what a wonderful person she was. Those were the lessons that stayed with me.

Elvis was a very generous man. In fact, his generosity was about the only way he could show people how much he appreciated them. It was obviously difficult for him to come to you directly and tell you that he liked you or enjoyed your work.

The Warm-up

Among the entertainers Elvis really admired was Redd Foxx, who was playing the lounge at the International while we were there. Now Redd, to my way of thinking, is a truly funny man, but he could also do something with an audience that Elvis could never do—and that was to tell the audience, Go fuck yourself. Nice guys who are entrapped into being nice—guys who were very dependent on their mothers, like Elvis and I were—don't say that. So for this special ability that Redd had, Elvis gave him medallions, gold rings, and chains worth thousands of dollars. It not only was Elvis's way of saying that he liked someone, it was another way to say that *he* was a nice guy. And Elvis admired strength and needed the inspiration given by others who had struggled and made it to the top. So one night, when Sammy Davis, Jr. was sitting ringside and enjoying Elvis's show, Elvis took off his black star sapphire ring and gave it to Sammy. The ring was worth fifty thousand dollars.

The summer of '71 was our third year at the Hilton. I could see that Elvis was not quite himself in some ways anymore. He seemed bored, he was starting to gain weight, and his shows were not the same. He started fooling around with his musicians onstage, spitting water at them while they all laughed and got silly—which was fine, except it meant Elvis and his group were now just out there to please themselves instead of the audience. By now my shows were fantastic, while Elvis often had trouble getting in gear. But I didn't know how to approach him—perhaps nobody did—and say, "Elvis, what's bugging you?" For one thing, I still felt that I was fighting for my life out there, no matter how well I did. I was drinking more. And most of the time I was working in fear, waiting for the day when the Colonel would tell me, "That's it, Jew boy, you've had it."

But I think Elvis had an inkling that I cared about him. Around two-thirty one morning I was sitting alone in my dressing room with my door open. My open door was my plea for some kind of company, flattery, attention. All the people who came down to see Elvis would have to notice me first. Maybe somebody would tell me how funny I was, maybe some girls would stop in with me instead of next door. Sometimes I felt like I was running a bus stop. The nights I did the best, I kept the door closed because I didn't feel the craving for recognition. Then I felt, let 'em come to me if they've got anything to say. But most of the time, my door was open like a hungry mouth.

The excitement of our previous years in Vegas had worn off and now the feeling was that everybody was more or less just phoning it in. I think the fading glory was beginning to bring out the conflicts in Elvis.

It was hard for people to appreciate just what Elvis was until after his death. When a great artist dies, he becomes famous and special. Elvis was supremely famous, of course, but few people realized just how special he was. Few saw that little boy inside, crying so hard, trying so hard to get out and find his mommy. And he was indeed a mama's boy. He rarely used profane language, always, "yes, sir" and "yes, ma'am." One thing I could always understand about him was that we both had overpossessive mothers—mothers who believed we could do no wrong—who trapped us with their overpowering need. Sure, it's great to be needed, but being *possessed* leaves you unable, for the rest of your life, to do the things you need to do for yourself. It left Elvis with an emptiness inside that he was helpless to fill.

Early that morning in Vegas, when most of the people had left Elvis's dressing room and were heading up to his suite for the usual party, I was getting ready to leave, too.

But standing in my doorway was Elvis—chunky, pallid, with a shade of the look of death on his face. I was taken aback by his presence here, although many times he would stick his head in to say, "Hi, Brother Sam," or some other meaningless pleasantry.

"Hi, Elvis," I said. I was thinking—I couldn't help it—that he was here to tell me, in his very nice way, that it had been nice working with me, but he and the Colonel wanted to try someone new.

"Can I come in?"

"Sure, Elvis—can I get you some water?" He loved Mountain Valley water in bottles.

"Yeah, ya got any of that stuff?"

"Got a six pack. I drink it, too—except I put it in my Scotch." I kind of laughed. "Makes a healthy drink."

"I just want to sit on the floor here a moment."

I was kind of puzzled at him coming in and wanting to sit on the floor. "How are things going?"

"Not too good . . . I just had to get away from all that bullshit. I just can't be alone for a minute. If I go take a pee, someone is there watching me."

"It's not easy being where you are," I said.

"I don't know what's happening to me, Sammy. Every night I go out there I'm either bored or scared . . . like maybe the people won't dig my music anymore, that this will all end."

51

He was so vulnerable right then, I was in awe. I told him how I had many of the same feelings.

"When I'm home and not working," Elvis said, "I don't know what to do with myself. Maybe the guys'll come over and we'll play paddle tennis outside, then come in and watch TV. But I can't even leave my house and just go for a walk—people won't let me be.

"It's really hard on Priscilla. She's so young and full of life, she just wants to go out and do things, be with people . . . walk in the park, take a bike ride . . . go have a dinner by ourselves in some nice little restaurant with candlelight . . . hold hands, go to a movie . . . all the things that are really important. And I can't do it—too much at stake. But I want all that, too, Sammy. I'm just a country boy, really, and I like the simple things in life. Like I miss taking walks with my mama, going shopping with her sometimes, sittin' out front just talkin'.

"All we do now after an engagement is fly back to Graceland to be locked up there for a couple of weeks, till we get bored and back to LA, then Palm Springs to be a recluse in the desert. Seems like all we do is shuttle from house to house."

I told him a little about my own feelings of emptiness anytime I wasn't being applauded onstage. One difference between us, I said, was that I still craved the recognition that he wanted to avoid.

Just then there was a knock at the door and a voice. "Sammy, is Elvis in there?"

"Yes, I'm in here," Elvis said. "I'll be out in a minute." He stood up. "Let's keep what we were talkin' about to ourselves. I really enjoyed talking with you, Sammy."

"Thanks for your trust, Elvis. Feels like we're brothers."

He put his arms around me before he left. "Amen, Brother Sam."

The next night Joe Esposito, Elvis's road manager, came into my dressing room and handed me a small package.

"What's this, Joe?"

"Open it up and you'll see." He darted out.

Inside was a beautiful green suede box, and inside of that there was a gold necklace with the initials T C B, for "Take Care of Business." And in another box was a gold ring with a beautiful green stone and a card: "Thanks, Elvis."

I understood that he cared for me and this was his way of telling me—the only way he knew.

3

SHECKY AND SHAKY

It was the third week of my initial Vegas engagement with Elvis and my self-confidence was at a peak, or as near a peak as I ever got. So I decided to do something that ordinarily would have terrified me: go over and say hello to Shecky Greene. I had known and dreaded Shecky for a very long time, long before he became a huge success as a Vegas lounge comic. Now he was working at the Riviera.

I walked into the hotel casino and immediately spotted him at one of the crap tables, shouting and screaming. That was Shecky, all right. He looked like he'd had a few, and he could be very ornery when he was drinking.

I walked over to the table and waited until he had finished rolling his dice.

"Hi, Shecky, how ya doin'?"

"How am I *doing*?" He did a mock double take. "Folks, look who's here! Sammy Shore in person. He's a star now, working with Elvis—wouldn't even come by to say hello."

"I'm here, Shecky. I came by to see how you're doing. I wanted to see your late show."

He looked at me for a moment. It turned out he was saving up strength for yelling. "You fucking asshole! You been in town a fucking month and you waited this long to come by and see me?!" He hauled off and shoved me to the floor. "I don't need your goddamn support! Get the fuck out of this hotel!'' He was all over me, and a couple of the dealers had to grab him and pull him off.

I was shaken all the way through, but not really shocked or surprised. I knew he didn't know what he was doing, that Shecky became impossible when he drank. Shecky was always angry at everyone in his life, it didn't really have anything to do with me as a person. He and I went back a long way together, and that meant I was in for abuse.

Actually, the event was liberating for me. Shecky had always had a terrible hold on me, but now that he had completely lost his cool, I could relax. He wouldn't torment me again.

It's an overcast day in August 1949, at Oakton Manor Resort, Wisconsin, about ninety miles north of Chicago, in the middle of nowhere. This place is the Midwest's answer to Grossinger's and the Catskills circuit. For me, it's heaven. And it's my first job in show business.

Lou Pollack owns a men's clothing store in Chicago, and until this summer I've been working there as a salesman and unofficial store clown. But Lou thought I was better suited for something else. I hated to agree because I needed the job.

"The customers only come here to laugh," Lou said. "Look, Sammy, I'm going to do you a big favor. I know the owner of a resort. I think you belong there."

Now that I've been here for a while, I can't agree more. Just sitting on the bus and looking at all the beautiful scenery on the way up was marvelous for me: the trees, cows wandering around the fields, I really didn't know this other world existed. And everything here is great—the fresh air, the greenery, and a room of my own that I know my dad can't possibly rent out. I do everything; I practically run the place. Social director, swimming instructor, counselor for the kids, sometimes a desk clerk and, best of all, emcee and comedian for the shows. The entertainment here consists of Manuelo and his Rhumba Band, dance instructors Pepi and Louise, and me.

I'm really not that funny in my first job. When you're kidding and entertaining people all day as they participate in the activities, you don't have much left for the stage at night and you also don't need much. When Manuelo shouts in his Mexican accent, "And here's ower o-wen *Sam*-mi Sho-o-re!'' all I have to do is come out and imitate Mrs. Cohen playing shuffleboard and I'm a smash.

54

But today the Greyhound bus down at the end of the road delivers my first professional bad news. I just know that the short stocky man walking toward the lodge from the bus stop is Shecky Greenfield.

Shecky Greenfield is all I've heard about this summer from some of the guests from Chicago's North Side. They don't think I'm so funny because they've seen better—their boy Shecky. "You know Shecky Greenfield?" they start out. "Funniest guy I've ever seen. He's always at Rogers Park Beach with a big crowd of people, makin' 'em laugh all day. That guy never stops. If he's not on the beach he's in the delicatessen throwing corned beef at the owners. . . . I thought sure you'd know him, you being a comedian." Every time I hear his name my stomach gurgles.

"Hey, kid! Where's Sid Schinderman's office?" It's the man himself, cocky as can be, like somehow he already knows he's going to be my lifelong nemesis. "I'm Shecky Greenfield, he sent for me." Emphasis on "sent."

"His office is over there in that main building." I've got the shakes; I just hope I can give him the right directions.

"Thanks, kid. Love your sweater. Looks like a Hudson seat cover."

I want to run after the Greyhound bus and go home to Ma, where it's safe. Why was he sent here? And here I'm just beginning to relax for the first time, away from my father.

Just a few moments later the loudspeaker is booming from the top of the main building. *Sammy Shore . . . report to Sid Schinderman's office . . . on the double!*

I've got to pull myself together. I don't want Sid to see me trembling and nervous. I just can't fathom why he sent for Shecky. I thought he liked me. I know the guests love me, and I'm doing a good job. Maybe he wants Shecky to do the shows at night and for me just to take care of everybody during the day.

I'm feeling sick as I enter the main building. "Hey, Sammy," someone shouts from across the lobby. "Who won the shuffleboard tournament?"

"No one yet, they're still playing."

"Samela!" a woman's voice bellows from in back of me. "How's my nice Jewish boy? Oy, you're such a dollink." I turn around and get pinched on my cheek.

"Oh, I'm fine, Mrs. Weinberg." I feel like throwing up right on her. Always the nice little boy. I'd like to say, "Leave me alone, you old hag, and go shove your diamond rings." But most women just remind me of my mom. Now I've got to go into Sid Schinderman's office, where Sid and Shecky wait like two fathers.

I knock lightly on the brown door marked SID SCHINDERMAN in big tan letters. The door opens and the first thing I see is the smirk on Mr. Schinderman's face. He's short, fat, and ugly, with a dark thin moustache. He's wearing a pair of shorts that come down below his knees. His stomach protrudes over a tight belt, and every once in a while you can catch a glimpse of a buckle monogrammed ss. If ever there was a human modeled after the Goodyear blimp, he's it. But I know he likes me, or at least I've always thought so until now.

"Come on in, Sammy," he says as he wipes the drippings of a Coke from his moustache. "This is Shecky Greenfield, a very funny comedian."

Is that so, I think to myself.

"My brother and I saw Shecky last week at a B'nai Brith function in Chicago. He was hilarious. So I thought I'd hire him."

Sid is smiling all over me like this is the most fun he's had in weeks. I'm wobbling, sweat is pouring down my sides, and I think my tan must look like gangrene.

"Hi, kid!" Shecky says, extending his hand. Boy is he smug. I shake his hand, but mine is like jelly.

Sid finally decides to let me off the hook. He and his brother just love practical jokes, especially ones that turn people inside out.

"To be honest with you both," he says in a tone like now he's the nicest and most reasonable man in the whole world, "I invited Shecky up here to meet you, to see how you two would hit it off.

"I want you to get together as a comedy team—another Dean Martin and Jerry Lewis! You can use this resort to try new material, and I'll be getting two comedians to keep the guests laughing. You guys could become stars out of here—like a lot of comedians do up in the Catskills. . . . What do you guys say?"

I look at Shecky and know he's not too thrilled. But I know he wants the job and the opportunity.

As for me, I don't feel any better knowing that I don't have to leave. The idea of being Shecky's partner makes me turn a new shade of white. Right then and there, I hate him. And for the next twenty years, he's the monkey on my back.

Sid takes us into the dining room for lunch and to introduce the new team. As soon as Shecky finishes eating, he jumps up on a chair and goes into part of his act. Everyone's screaming; they love it. They're shouting, "Hey, Sammy, tell a few jokes too!"

I can't even open my mouth. Lockjaw. I tell them I have to go get a gin tournament started, and I run out to my room and cry.

Working with Shecky later, it seems like he never wants to rehearse, he just wants to go out there and ad-lib. I feel like I'll never keep up with him. But we become a successful act—people are flocking to the resort to see us, business is booming.

Shecky just never gets enough, he always wants *more*. We finish our show and five minutes later he's out there again, doing twenty minutes all by himself. He's always got people around him—at the pool, playing baseball—always. Never enough.

He's hard to work with, and he always fights with Manuelo, the band leader. One weekend it blows up. Manuelo says he'll no longer play for Shecky when he sings and that if Shecky stays on, he's quitting. "That fucking spic," Shecky says. "I ain't gonna work with him, I'm leaving!" He turns to me and tells me I can take this resort and shove it.

Sid tells me I've got to work the show alone. I panic. "Sid, I can't work by myself anymore."

He tells me to do what I always did before.

And I do. The crowd, restless to see Shecky and Sammy, perplexed at first because Shecky's not there, warms to my act. My confidence comes back to me. They're really laughing, and at *me*, not Shecky!

Just as I'm finishing my act, out walks Shecky, and the people start to applaud him. He grabs the mike and says, "Wasn't Sammy great, folks?" They all applaud. Then he whispers, "Let's do the opening."

> *We're the boys from Oakton*
> *And we've come to say*
> *That Oakton treats you in the finest way . . .*

We do our act and get a standing ovation.

Shecky never thought I could stand out there alone and get that many laughs. He just can't handle me doing it without him.

He grabs me in the kitchen. "Hey, you were pretty funny out there. Where'd you get those bits?"

The Warm-up

"That's what I was doing before you showed up."

Shecky lets me know he thinks we're a great act, he doesn't want to break up. He even apologizes to Manuelo.

Our partnership, soon known as Shecky Greene and Sammy Shore, lasts less than a year. Working with Shecky is, for me, horrendous. He's so talented, so spontaneous, so fucking funny. My jealousy mounts. How can one man have so much talent? Sometimes it's all I can do to remember my lines.

> *There was a boy,*
> *A very strange enchanted boy,*
> *They say he wandered very far . . .*

Shecky is singing the strains of "Nature Boy" as I jump up on one of the tables, naked except for a towel wrapped around my groin, chewing on a head of lettuce, wearing a fright wig. I jump off the table and prance around Shecky, mumbling incoherently. It's our biggest and funniest routine.

Another Martin and Lewis we are not.

But a very wealthy lady guest at Oakton Manor thinks we're even funnier than Dean and Jerry and she's got fantasies of being the manager of a smash comedy team. She knows absolutely nothing about show business, but that does not make a dent in her tremendous ego.

Through her money and contacts she gets us a showcase in New York City at a place called the Rathskeller. It's not the Copa, but many well-traveled performers work there. If you're a New Yorker, it's a good place to get in a few weeks when you're home. Unfortunately, we open and close the same night. Instant flop.

The New Yorkers who frequent the place are just not interested in seeing someone come out half-naked eating a head of lettuce. To them, this is just not funny. In fact, it seems to be repulsive to them, along with the rest of our act. Our rise to stardom as a team is doomed. Shecky's pissed at me for flopping, and I'm angry at him for dragging us away from the resort to New York, a place I dread. I'm happy at Oakton, Shecky wants to be a big nightclub star, and our partnership folds.

The same lady who brought Shecky and me to New York introduces me to a singer by the name of Joe Silver. He's got a big baritone voice, so we team up as a sort of poor man's Martin and Lewis.

SHECKY AND SHAKY

We're billed as Sterling and Silver. (Thinking about it today, I'd like to throw up.)

Joe's at least ten years older, married, and has been knocking around the joints for years. Even though we're doing a few jobs together, he also has to work at a department store to make ends meet. One day he calls me and asks me to meet him down at work because he wants to talk to me. I know something's wrong.

"I think you're a terrific kid," he tells me that day, "and you've got a lot of talent."

Uh-oh—the kiss of death.

"But I'm a lot older," he says, "and I've got a family to support and I feel I need a partner with more experience."

Oh well, I think to myself, that's pretty much what I expected. It hurts, but it's not too bad.

Joe looks at me with a little smile. "So, Sammy, what I'm gonna do is team up with Shecky Greene."

What!

I'm in shock. And I hate Shecky more than ever.

As the years pass, the monkey on my back becomes an ape. I just can't get away from Shecky Greene. We're traveling pretty much the same circuit—Des Moines, St. Louis, Kansas City, Minneapolis. If a city has a club, we work it.

It seems like every time I'm about to open a club the owner tells me, "You ever hear of Shecky Greene? He was just here a couple of weeks ago, killed the people. Did the biggest business we ever had. . . . You work like him?" That's all I have to hear and I'm practically finished.

Eventually I head farther south and west, through Louisiana and Texas. I know he won't follow me here. He just loves the joints around Chicago and the Midwest; he identifies with those people.

As for me, I love the Texans. Houston and Dallas become my stomping grounds for a few years. One of my mainstays is Abe's Colony Club in Dallas, a milestone in southern show business because it's both well respected and a strip joint. Abe Weinstein, the owner, loves me because I'm such a rarity in Texas—a Jewish emcee working a strip club.

Next door to Abe's is the Carnival Club, another strip joint owned by a Jew. Only this Jew is Jack Ruby. I finish my second show at Abe's and head over to Jack's. He always tries to fix me up with one of his strippers. If they're busy, he takes me out to breakfast across the street at the Adolphus Hotel's coffee shop. Jack is so American, so proud to be living in this country. Many nights and early mornings he rambles on about his heroes, like Truman and Roosevelt, and how lucky a person is to have the opportunities of taking part in the country's growth. In all the months I know Jack, he never says anything derogatory about anyone or anything official and governmental. He's politically star-struck.

How sad, years later, when I see with my own eyes Jack Ruby shooting Lee Harvey Oswald in cold blood. Looking again and again at the bizarre television replays, I just know what Jack was feeling and how he must have worshiped President Kennedy. And to this day I do not believe that Jack died in his cell of a malignant disease. I believe that Jack Ruby committed the shooting on his own but then was used and murdered.

Nineteen fifty-five is a great year for nightclubs, and nowhere more than in New Orleans. Louis Prima has his own club, Pete Fountain and Al Hirt are just coming into their own, and so am I. I'm booked into the Preview Lounge. Al Hirt has the band in there, and I'm going to be the first comic to try working a room that has been strictly for Dixieland jazz. The owner, Bill Gruber, wants to try something different—jazz and comedy. I'm booked for four weeks and come out a smash, the talk of New Orleans. It's another Oakton Manor for me. With my trumpet and Al Hirt with his, we drive the people wild. Every night it's standing room only. So for the next year I'm in and out of that wonderful room.

One night Bill Gruber comes to me and says, "Sammy, I just don't know who to bring in here after you leave. No one else can do the job here. . . . Paul Marr, the agent from Chicago, told me about a comic named Shecky Greene. He said you knew the guy."

My stomach goes into its familiar free fall. "Yeah, I know him, and he's really funny . . ."

I just can't deny his talent.

Shecky follows me in and does fantastic, as I expected. The next month I come back and I can't follow that ghost. Shecky comes back and stays two years. I never come back, and I'm soon forgotten.

As the years go by, Shecky becomes bigger and bigger. The entire industry is talking him up as the comedy find of the decade. He becomes the lounge star of Las Vegas, he's heralded as another Danny

Thomas. I try to avoid him whenever possible. Until I finally start to make it with Elvis and pay him that friendly visit at the Riviera.

I was really hot coming off the Vegas engagement and tour with Elvis. Diana Ross, who had just left the Supremes to go out on her own, wanted me to warm up for her at the Frontier in Las Vegas. Frank Sennes, the Frontier's entertainment head, offered me a twenty-week contract to go into the Frontier lounge as well, at seventy-five hundred dollars a week. I told him I couldn't because I didn't want to leave Elvis.

But I did go to the Colonel and ask him if it would be all right for me to work the three weeks with Diana Ross. "Sure, boy," he said. "Grab the money and run." He told me I had a lifetime "contract" with Elvis, that he'd be looking for me to start again with his boy when he opened again in January. What more could I ask? I had my cake and ice cream, too.

The Diana Ross engagement went by in fine shape, then another opening with Elvis, and I was driving everybody crazy, nobody more so than myself. There were more new jokes, new clothes, more drinking and, despite all the success, more anxiety than ever. The idea that I had to go back to Vegas and do it all over again always stopped me cold. Will I be as funny as the last engagement? Will Elvis and the Colonel still like me? Will I still be Alex Shoofey's boy? There were no answers.

After some attempts to patch up our "therapeutic" relationship, Dr. Wiggins was out of my life. He had cried when I told him I didn't think I needed him anymore, so I kept on for a while. It was like trying to talk your wife into a divorce. Finally I had gotten away. I considered getting a new doctor, but put it off. And since Dr. Wiggins was no longer a part of my life, he became part of my act.

Everyone today has a psychiatrist. I got one too. Only mine's black. He said to me, "Sam, remember, we're all brothers under the skin. I'm your brother and you're my brother."

And when he found out I was three payments behind, he said, "Listen, cousin."

He said, "Sam, ya gotta find yourself." I said, "Where do I look?" "I don't know, but not in my neighborhood."

The Warm-up

He's really great. I recommend him to anybody. In fact, the first year he was so good, he made me feel I was black! But I don't believe that anymore. In fact, just the other day I said to my son, "Leroy . . ."

Then one night changed the course of my show business career. I was finishing my third Vegas engagement with Elvis and everything was going fine. My wife, Mitzi, and I were having dinner at the hotel's Continental Restaurant with Alex Shoofey and his cronies, along with some weird mind reader. The new contract I'd signed with the hotel stated that at my discretion, I could appear in the lounge four weeks a year.

Alex was encouraging me to pick up on that option. "Sam," he said, "if you want to work in the lounge, go to it, and you can still work with Elvis."

There was quite a bit of money to be made working the lounge. Lounges have since faded in importance in Vegas, but then they were great places to work and wonderful places to see a star-quality act without going to a dinner or cocktail show in a main room. They were like smaller versions of the main show room. If I went in there I would no longer be a warm-up, I'd be carrying the ball and would need a longer, stronger show.

I considered Alex's suggestion for a moment. I said to Mitzi, "What do you think about going into the lounge for four weeks?"

"Sam, you're not a lounge act. Stay with Elvis as long as it lasts." Rarely did I ever listen to her when it came to my career.

That was good advice, but I wasn't level-headed enough to take it, particularly when my agents were insisting that I try the lounge, that I couldn't depend on working with Elvis forever. Of course, what they didn't mention was the fact that there was a lot of commission in it for them if I hit it big there.

I accepted the offer, and *then* I approached Colonel Parker. I was afraid of confronting him with it. I found him at the hotel's health club, where he was shaving in front of a long mirror. We were both clad in white towels.

"Colonel," I said, coming to a halt at every other word, "the hotel wanted to know if I would work the lounge for four weeks."

Parker eyed me with his best blank look. "Are they paying more money than in the main room?"

"Yes they are, Colonel, a lot more."

He said, "Well, okay," and it was one of those okays that just isn't.

And that was it. He never said another word about it, and neither did I. It was a very uncomfortable situation, and the fault was all mine. I was too scared to go to the Colonel beforehand and ask him, like a man, "Colonel, how would you feel about me going into the lounge for a while? Would that jeopardize my working with Elvis?" I presented him instead with an accomplished fact and hoped for the best. I was thinking, well, Alex Shoofey's the president and he's the one who signs the checks whether I work the main room with Elvis or the lounge by myself. As was often the case in my career, I could neither resist nor confront anyone.

I hired the Sweet Inspirations, the singing group that backed Elvis, I had a large gospel-revival tent built right in the middle of the lounge, and Shoofey spent a lot of money promoting my opening. He had a huge billboard at the airport with my picture and the message, BROTHER SAM IS GOING TO HEAL YOU! . . . AT THE INTERNATIONAL. He wanted his boy to be a big star and did everything to help make it possible. He even put my name on the marquee nearly as big as Elvis's had been.

I was getting fifteen thousand dollars a week as the star of the lounge. But I needed more than money or publicity or opportunity. If you don't have it going for you on the inside, all those things can't make the difference. The situation was too much for me to handle. I took my Brother Sam character, a tambourine-wielding preacher, which was five minutes of my regular act, and tried to do a whole forty-five minute revival meeting. It was just too long. Brother Sam started to wear thin after only fifteen minutes. After thirty minutes he was bad news.

One day during my ordeal in the lounge, I got a call from Joe Siegman, my publicity agent, who claimed he had "great news" for me.

"What is it, Joe?"

"I just got finished talking with John Gregory Dunne about you."

"Who the hell is John Gregory Dunne?"

"John Dunne's a well-known writer. He's written books, movies. Believe me when I tell you he's an important man. He's doing a book called *Vegas,* all about the inside story of the town—the whores, the

cops, the underworld, who really runs the town—and he's very interested in doing a story in there about a comic.''

"Why me? Why doesn't he do it about Buddy Hackett or Shecky
or Don Rickles?"

"I'll tell you why you. He doesn't want a big star to write about,
he wants someone on his way up, someone that's working a lounge
. . . and I told him all about you, and he'd love to do your story.''

It sounded fantastic. To my flattery-prone heart, it seemed like a
dream come true. Somebody wanted to write a book about *me*. It had
to be the break of the century.

Joe said that Dunne wanted to spend a couple of weeks with me.
My only mixed feelings were due to the fact that I was doing such
an indifferent job in the lounge. It was a big room, just a smaller
replica of the main room, seating seven hundred fifty people. I thought,
what the hell is John Dunne going to see? I wished he could have
seen me with Elvis.

The night he called me from his hotel and I started explaining how
he'd recognize me in the bar of the International, he said he'd seen
me with Elvis. I was so psyched up about impressing this writer that
this little bit of information came as a great relief. At least he'd seen
me when I was funny.

I got up from the phone, went to the mirror, fluffed up my hair,
put on cologne, put on a black blazer over my white turtleneck. I
wanted to look sharp. I felt like I was getting ready to meet a girl on
our first date.

As I walked through the casino, the feeling just wasn't the same as
when I was appearing with Elvis. All the pit bosses knew I wasn't
doing well in the lounge, and all they cared about was how many
people you brought in. All I got from them was absentminded nods.
I very seldom came to the casino now. During the Elvis engagements
I had been up and around the casinos nearly all night. When you're
a winner in Las Vegas and doing business, there's nothing you can't
have—everybody wants to shake your hand or have you tell them a
joke. When you're bombing, even the waiters and busboys who were
so friendly turn against you—because they're not making enough tips
and it's all your fault. Even Alex Shoofey was starting to avoid me—
no more fun in the restaurants after the shows, he was always tied up
in meetings.

John Gregory Dunne was a man of medium build, five foot eight, with glasses, and when I met him in the bar, he was wearing a short-sleeved sport shirt and plaid slacks that looked like the flag of some new country. His unimposing appearance helped put me at ease. We each ordered drinks—something we'd be doing a lot of in the next three weeks.

"I want to spend as much time as possible with you, Sammy," he said. "Wherever you go, whatever you do, I want to be there so I'll be able to write the real story of a Vegas comedian."

I told him that was no problem, I'd love it. And so for the next three weeks I couldn't even go to the john without Dunne being there.

A year later, when *Vegas* was published, I was stunned. In the book my name was Jackie Joey "the Vegas comic," but of course everyone in the business would know me from the descriptions and the circumstances if they didn't already know after a year of my bragging about being in the book. Dunne made a big deal of how I was bombing in the lounge, said I was involved with hookers, even described a night when a girl came into my dressing room to give me a blow job, which he said he witnessed. If that was true, and if I were his friend, I would have shared her. He literally crucified me.

I could not believe that any author would do what he did to me in that book. The part that was really hard to take was my disillusionment with Dunne personally. He had really befriended me, or so I thought. I was fond of him after spending three weeks doing absolutely everything together, and I thought he genuinely liked me. Now I understand that almost all performers are insecure, and comedians are the worst of the lot. We have an insatiable need for approval and applause, a need to believe that people love us. Without that drive we could never put up with the roller-coaster unpredictability of a show-business career. So I was all too willing to believe that whatever Dunne wrote would be like literary applause, and I took his act at face value.

Were his reports accurate? Probably, although the fact is I was drinking so much I really couldn't say. My alcoholism plunged me into many different kinds of craziness and left me unable to recall most of it. Whatever happened, I not only probably enjoyed it thoroughly, chances are that Dunne did too, since he was part of it, and as I reflect back, I remember that we did double-date a couple of those showgirls, each time Dunne leaving, happily, with one of them at night's end. I guess John's after-hours escapades didn't rate a chapter in that book.

The Warm-up

When Mitzi read the book, our marriage was already in trouble. *Vegas* clinched it. She cried for two days, and I have never forgiven John Gregory Dunne.

Ten-thirty on the night of April 10, 1972, comedy-nightclub history was about to be made in a little room adjacent to the once-famous Ciro's on the Sunset Strip in LA. The place seated about 125 people and had always been used mainly as a cocktail lounge. A few people had tried opening nightclubs there, but they always failed. Tonight the room was jam-packed with celebrities, producers, writers, and other show-business people. No one knew what it was going to turn out to be. It was the birth of The Comedy Store, the club that changed the comedy business across America.

'Seventy-two had been a down year for me. My work with Elvis had ended. It turned out that the Colonel didn't want an act opening for Elvis if it was also a lounge act, and especially if it was a lounge act at the same hotel, and most emphatically if it was a lounge act that had bombed. So when it came time for Elvis to return to the International, about two months after I closed in the lounge, my agent called the Colonel and got the bad news. I even went to Jerry Weintraub, who booked Elvis nationwide, to appeal my sentence, but it was no good. I never spoke with the Colonel or Elvis after that day in the health club. Elvis came back to Vegas with a new comic and did bigger business than ever. Everyone forgot about Sammy Shore, the "guy who used to work with Elvis."

Also in '72, my marriage was slipping away and I didn't want anyone to know—I didn't want to know, myself. I didn't know what to do next.

"Why don't you take over that little room next to Ciro's?" Frank Sennes, Vegas producer and owner of Ciro's, was having lunch with me at Scandia, the famous restaurant at the upper end of the Strip. I had just finished performing for the Vikings Men's Club there and had been a hit.

"What would I do there, Frank?"

He was ready. "Open up a comedy room. Invite your friends, all the people you know in the business . . . call it the Sammy Shore Room." (Later Mitzi came up with the name The Comedy Store, and my writer friend Rudy DeLuca came in to help me run things and define the concept of a club for "comedians.")

"I won't charge you any rent," he said, "till you start making some money. It's all free. Just go have some fun."

I had previously met Rudy in New York. He was a comedy writer, and he started writing for me. Rudy seemed like the only writer I had met in years who captured my comedy style.

We became close friends, and I asked him to come to California. He did, and for a while he lived with us, although Mitzi didn't approve of him. Of course, he was replacing her in helping me with my act. And when I finally got the opportunity to open The Comedy Store, Rudy contributed so much to it that I made him my partner.

There was no place to move in the room. It was elbow to elbow, filled with laughter, smoke, hand-shaking, the sound of drinks being served, and all the talk you hear among comedy people.

"What's happening, Joey?"

"Oh hi, Dave. I'm up for a pilot for NBC. I read for it yesterday and I'm going back tomorrow."

"Hey that's great, Joey. I open in Vegas next Friday at the Tropicana—with Abbe Lane. I'm really excited, it's my first Vegas booking . . ."

When the time came to open the first show, I gave the word to Larry, my piano player, to hit the stage lights, and he started pounding out "Everything's Coming Up Roses." Larry was gay, and he was crazy about that song. I looked around the room for one last moment, taking in all the work that had gone into it—all the painting, hammering, installation of lights, and shifting around of booths—just so I could go up there and get another chance to be seen.

"Good evening, ladies and gentlemen, welcome to The Comedy Store! I'm Sammy Shore, maybe you've seen my picture on the cover of *Watchtower*." I always started with that line. Everyone laughed and applauded.

It was a nightclub solely for comedians. Many of them performed that night, and just about every night that followed it got better and better. Many comedians came there. It was informal, and often a Redd Foxx, Don Rickles, or Richard Pryor would jump up and do a few minutes, but basically it was for unknowns looking to be seen by TV, movie, and club producers. The Store was becoming the talk of the town and the gig that could give a new performer a springboard to a national TV audience. The talent coordinators for the Johnny Carson,

Merv Griffin, and Mike Douglas shows were almost always there, along with casting directors from each network. Talent buyers were always asking me to put certain comics on when they could check them out. One night, for example, I got a call from TV producer Jimmy Komack asking me to schedule a new comedian who had been working for the Store so Jimmy could see him. The comedian was Freddie Prinze and the rest is history. Gabe Kaplan and David Brenner are just a couple of others who were discovered at The Comedy Store. Many of the new comics appearing on the tube would be introduced as coming "direct from The Comedy Store."

The more successful the Store became, the more desperate I was for recognition. Every night before I introduced the new acts, I'd try doing a few extra minutes of my own, hoping producers would like *me*. But no one seemed to want me for any TV shows. I wound up being the warm-up comic in my own club.

I didn't know it then, but what I was really doing was warming up the club for Mitzi. She really wanted it badly, a place she could call her own.

As the months progressed, Rudy and I had our differences about running a nightclub.

There were nights when we were literally at each other's throats. Rudy not only had me to contend with, but his job included getting twenty-five to thirty comedians a night on and off the stage.

Then one night Rudy and I really went at it. We were married to that club, and the inevitable happened. He told me to "take the club and shove it" and left. Our longstanding friendship had ceased.

Rudy took a job as a writer on *The Carol Burnett Show* to keep his sanity. What started out to be comedy became tragedy, as far as we were concerned.

Now Mitzi could make her move. "Who's going to take care of the Store and watch the money while you're in Vegas working?" was her cry. "Let me take care of it."

After a while, though, it looked as if my luck would change again for the better. A VIP finally took note of me at The Comedy Store. Art Stark, former producer of the Johnny Carson Show, was looking for a comedian to host a late-night talk and variety show for ABC. He came to The Comedy Store to see some of the new kids, but I did my whole act and happened to be very funny that night. Stark and his head writer, Danny Simon, both were impressed and thought I might be the guy they were looking for.

When they talked to me after the show, I was in seventh heaven. They were going to surround me with a new "family" of talent, I was going to be a TV star. We went into rehearsal right away at the Store and in rehearsal halls, hired writers, auditioned talent, and finally put together a show that seemed tight. We did it live at a studio with the ABC brass in the audience. The show came off well and I of course thought it was a smash, but ABC didn't buy. It was fine for one ninety-minute special, but it lacked the ingredients for a night-after-night affair.

I know now that it wasn't the writers or the people we hired who were to blame. It was me. I was funny doing my act and various bits, but a whole show was too much. I didn't have an overall personality or attitude that would tie everything together. I hardly knew who I was or what I was doing; how could I possibly have a consistent attitude?

So it was back to The Comedy Store. Now my marriage with Mitzi was really coming apart. She got into therapy and after a while felt that we should be separated, so I dutifully agreed and moved into an apartment in Hollywood. It was kind of a strange separation, because every weekend I'd stay at the house and we'd live together and sleep together like nothing had ever happened, then Monday morning I'd go back to my apartment—as if the weekend had never happened.

Then one day I got an important call from my agent, Freddie Moch, at William Morris. He'd gotten me back to Vegas. It was the new lounge now called the Hilton.

"I got you twelve weeks the first year," Freddie said, "and if you do well, they'll give you sixteen weeks the second year."

Sounded fantastic, just the break I needed and exactly when I needed it.

I still discussed all my career moves with Mitzi. I hoped the news would impress her—maybe she'd want to get back with me. But she was merely disappointed that I would try a lounge again.

"You had a bad experience working the lounge at the Hilton, that nearly ended your career," she pointed out. "You're not a lounge act, I don't think you should take it. . . . Just wait for another opportunity to open for a star in the main room."

I couldn't stand realistic advice, especially from Mitzi. I wanted to make this work. I couldn't possibly turn down any opportunity. I would go anywhere, anytime to struggle for an audience's approval. Picking my spots was impossible because my craving reduced me to a man without judgment.

"But this is a very small lounge," I protested. "It only seats about a hundred fifty people. I'll be able to tumult and ad-lib with them."

"You're not an ad-libber like Rickles or Shecky. You do a good act, but only when the situation is right for you. . . . Go ahead and do what you want, I would just hate to see you go back to Vegas and not do well. It'd take you another five years to get back."

I accepted the engagement and now was the time for Mitzi to make her move into the Store. I really didn't want her to get more involved, because we were just not making it in our marriage, but there seemed to be nobody else on hand since Rudy was gone. I knew she was waiting for the day when she could become more involved in the Store. She'd always suggested many ideas for improving it, but I'd tried not to listen. Now I showed her what she had to do, how to book the comedians, how to run the register, and I hired an emcee. She was ecstatic. I began to calculate that offering her this position might be the thing that would get us back together.

I was always trying to make her a part of something—although not too big a part. I'd sent her to art school, opened a business called "Shady Touch" Personalized Window Shades, had her work with me in a company called Four Star creating comedy shows, opened a business across from The Comedy Store, a boutique called the Pickle Barrel, for her and our daughter, Sandy, to run. That had lasted six weeks. I knew that she had special talent, but she couldn't find a handle for herself until the Store. Up to this point her identity had been wrapped up in me and my all-consuming career.

Business at the Store was starting to drop. Before I left for Vegas, while I was training Mitzi and working on my act, I was getting totally insane. My drinking stepped up; I was mushrooming as an alcoholic. I was terrified of Vegas and anxious about the Store, which increasingly seemed too big and troublesome for me to handle.

There seemed to be no one to turn to. I got into therapy again, but it was with a female psychologist who didn't associate with me outside of sessions like the good Dr. Wiggins. She was strictly business, and I wanted a nursemaid. I wanted to call Dr. Wiggins, but I found out he was in worse shape than me, having suffered a heart attack and virtually lost his practice. It was like he had never existed, and I had gained nothing permanent from him or anyone else who had ever tried to help me.

The Hilton lounge was dubbed the Vestal Virgin Room. It was so pretentious and silly, with the decor done completely in silver, like the inside of a jumbo Reynolds Wrap dispenser with chandeliers. The room was supposed to conjure up visions of dancing vestal virgins with the gods in attendance. They were, in fact, in the audience when I opened—Baron Hilton and Henri Lewin. Lewin was vice-president of the hotel, which Baron Hilton had purchased from Kirk Kerkorian for fifty-three million dollars.

The hotel was changing drastically, and the fun was going out. It was becoming another typical chain hotel with the Bible and Hilton's autobiography in every nightstand drawer.

I hated the lounge and it hated me. All I had was a piano player, a Japanese fellow who didn't think I was very funny. I didn't do any business. I was unhappy and so was the management.

To make matters as painful as they could possibly be, Elvis came to work the Hilton's main room while I was in the lounge. I felt like shit. Not too many months ago I had been working with the biggest star in show business, in the world's largest nightclub, and now here I was in the Vestal Virgin Room trying to entertain the hookers who could be seen every night hanging around the lounge bar. Some nights I was busting my ass trying to get laughs from fifteen people. None of my so-called friends who worked for Elvis came by to see me; they could not have cared less. I finished my four weeks and couldn't wait to get back home.

This time when I flew back to LA there was no one to greet me at the airport. Always before there would be Mitzi and our boys Peter and Pauly, and that was a nice feeling.

Now I headed for my apartment through the evening traffic, dumped my bags, unpacked, on the bed, and went straight down the street to The Comedy Store. I walked in and could hardly believe that it was packed—not a table was free. I felt unwelcome somehow, uncomfortable that the club was doing so well without me. And when I saw Mitzi I knew something wasn't right.

I headed for the bar while Mitzi pounded away at the register, not even noticing me. I walked up behind her like the scared wimp I was and tapped her on the shoulder. "Hi, Mitzi, how's it going?" She turned and looked at me like I was in the wrong place.

"Oh hello, Sammy. When did you get back?"

"I just came straight from the airport."

"How did it go for you?"

"Not bad," I lied. "It's a horrible lounge to try to do comedy in."

I started to sit down on the ledge next to her. She said, "Sammy, do you mind sitting in the back of the room? You're crowding me here at the register and I can't do my work."

I said, "Okay, I understand," and headed for the back. I was starting to feel like shit. I felt like I was being moved out of my own club. I noticed all the comedians fussing over Mitzi, hugging and sweet-talking her.

"What time do I go on, Mitzi baby?"

"You're on at nine-thirty, Kip."

I was annoyed as hell. She was doing everything—running the money, lining up shows, and loving every minute. This was not the quiet little girl from Green Bay, Wisconsin. She had grown a set of iron balls. I just sat in the back of the room watching all the young comics, some of them completely new to me, all of them funny. After closing time, I asked Mitzi if she'd like to go out for coffee or go over the books.

"Not tonight, Sammy, I'm really beat. I just want to go home and get some sleep. Call me tomorrow and I can show you all the money I deposited in the bank."

She took the bag full of money. "Come on, Sammy, I have to lock up."

One of the comics walked her to her car and she left. It was like I was interfering with her newfound life.

I went back to the club door, unlocked it, walked behind the bar, and poured myself a drink. I gazed around the room at the pictures of all the old-time comedians—the Marx Brothers, W.C. Fields, Eddie Cantor, Fanny Brice, Laurel and Hardy—and next to the bar, an even less current face, Sammy Shore. I wondered when my picture would be coming down.

In the next couple of weeks I came in almost every night and occasionally jumped up onstage to do a few minutes, which Mitzi didn't like because it disrupted her lineup. I felt very uncomfortable and resentful about working there. I was pushing Mitzi. I knew I was being obnoxious, but I felt helpless to stop it.

Then one Saturday night when I'd been drinking quite a bit and was no longer feeling any pain or any trace of guilt, I went on the offensive.

It was getting late, and I convinced myself that the other comedians wouldn't mind if I got up and did a few minutes. So when the guy onstage was finishing his last bit, I grabbed the emcee's arm. "Greg," I said, "I'm gonna go up and do a few minutes. Take a break."

I was up in the lights. "Hi there, everybody, it's nice to be back."

Many people started to applaud and whistle. "Do the black leopard bit, Sammy!" someone shouted. That's all I had to hear. Someone remembering my black leopard routine, which was always one of my funniest. I became this black leopard in a zoo. Pacing back and forth, slouched over, sounding like a cat. Looking out at the people watching me pace.

Whatcha' lookin' at, boy? Ever seen a black leopard before? Ya like my coat? It's mohair.

Then I would point to a bald guy sitting ringside.

Got mo' hair than you got!

Ooh, look what someone did in the cage. Oh, that's the food. Well, what they feed you here you could hardly tell the difference!

Got to split now, it's mating time. Got me a RHINO . . . a horny white one!

I was having a ball, doing more parts of my act, and after twenty-five minutes the audience yelled for more. "Do Brother Sam!" someone yelled.

As I walked off, I felt like I'd just finished walking off in front of Elvis. I was flying.

I knew I had disrupted the room. I was working like I was in Vegas. I knew the young comedians couldn't follow that, and it was downhill for the rest of the night. It was like somebody had dropped a bomb in the room. I could see Mitzi was pissed, but I told myself I didn't care. I couldn't keep down the anger and resentment and the need to prove that I could at least make them laugh in my own club.

Later, as everybody was leaving and Ron, the bartender, was congratulating me on my performance, Mitzi spoke up.

"Sammy," she said, "can I speak to you for a few minutes?"

"Sure," I said, knowing something was coming. I could feel our anger filling up the room.

"Why don't we sit here, Sammy." Mitzi motioned toward the register.

"I'd rather stand," I said. We were already getting defensive. I leaned over the bar and had Ron pour me a J&B on the rocks. To Mitzi, I said, "Want a taste?"

"No thank you," she said. "Sammy, what you did tonight was uncalled for. Two of the young guys couldn't go on because of all the time you did. Don't you work enough that you have to come here and fuck up my schedule?"

I stood there with my stomach boiling. "Hey wait a second, young lady—"

"Let me finish!" she said. "I was supposed to run this club when you were out of town—and I can't tell you how wonderful it was when you were gone."

I couldn't believe she was saying this. "Well, I'm back, so what's your problem?"

"I've had no problems with anyone. All the comics are happy with the times they go on—"

I couldn't deal with this, I tried to snub her. "Pour me another one, Ron, and give Tony and Joey a drink." These were two new comedians who had just stopped by at the bar.

"Why don't you just let me run the club," Mitzi went on, "and when you want to work, just tell me and I'll put you on the schedule. I've doubled the money since you've been gone—that should make you happy. You'll be going out of town again, so we can't keep switching back and forth about who's running the Store." She had to press her advantage. "Anyway, I don't have your ego problem, I don't have to get up on the stage to feel accepted—"

"You fucking cunt!" I was shouting. "I just knew something wasn't right when I walked in here. How dare you say those things to me— I know you don't give a fuck about me now!" I was exploding, "You're a fucking cunt!" as I slapped her across the face. The bag of money flew out of her hand and bills were scattered all over the floor. "Get out of my club!"

Ron, the bartender, came between us as she tried to get me back. "You're old," she cried. "You're a has-been, and nobody wants you!" I lunged at her, but Ron and Tony grabbed me first. She went running down the front stairs, crying and wailing. Ron followed her out and I just stood in silence. I couldn't believe I had actually hit her.

I stayed away from the Store for the rest of the week. On Friday morning I was lying in bed feeling totally depressed when I got a call from my man at the William Morris Agency.

"Sammy, this is Freddie, your wonderful agent. I got good news for you. You open with Diana Ross at the Sahara in Tahoe over Christmas and New Year's . . . how about that? I got you two weeks . . ."

That was wonderful. I decided now was the time to go over and apologize to Mitzi. I drove through the rain and the winter ugliness of LA only to find that my keys no longer fit the lock on the front door. I had to ring the doorbell.

I ended up in the kitchen listening to Mitzi tell me how our marriage was hopeless. She was not impressed by my apologies.

"I think that did it for me," she said. "When you hit me, whatever feelings I had for you were gone."

"But I'm really sorry."

"There's nothing to be sorry for, Sammy—as far as I'm concerned the marriage is over. . . . That's why I had the locks changed. I don't want you walking into this house anymore.

"For twenty-one years I've lived my life through you, and for all that time the only really important thing to you has been your career. Your kids always came second, and so did I."

I tried everything, including telling her that without my career she wouldn't have had what she had—the house, The Comedy Store, the money, things for the kids.

She was willing to admit that I was "a good provider"—"But I didn't fall in love with 'a comedian' or 'success.' I wanted Sammy Shore, but you never realized that."

"Sounds like you've been suffering for twenty-one years."

"No, Sammy, I haven't been suffering, but I've been living a lie—and that hurts."

I shouted, pleaded, cried, and told her about the wonderful date I'd gotten in Tahoe with Diana Ross, and couldn't she think it over during the holidays, and when I came back we could talk further—

"There's really nothing to talk about, Sammy. If we talk about it anymore, it's really going to get messy and we're both going to start crying."

The Warm-up

"What am I going to do now?"

"Go back to your career like you always have. You got Diana Ross, I'm sure you'll get more work in Vegas. . . . When you get back from Tahoe, I would appreciate your taking all your clothes out of here. . . . I really don't want to see you anymore. . . . And if you want to see the kids, call me and I'll make arrangements for you to pick them up.

"Stay well, Sammy. I have to make dinner for the kids. I wish you would leave now."

I started crying like a baby on my way to the car. I felt like I was completely abandoned. I was at a complete loss. I didn't even know where to go. I was too humiliated to go back to The Comedy Store as the word was out that I had hit Mitzi. And of course, as the story was told, the slap turned into a punch.

No longer were the weekend visits at the house available to me. No mom to run to. My real one was already gone. For years Mitzi had replaced her. Always telling me, "Everything's gonna be all right." Combing out my curls sometimes before I went on. Only now they were somewhat gray. Always helping me with my act. Taking care of the kids. A real *balaboost*—a real homemaker.

My mom would have sure fixed it for me. She worshiped me. She was always cleaning me up, fussing over me, holding me . . . combing out my long golden curls. I guess I was her pet.

By the time I was eight years old, I knew my ma wanted a girl. There were already three boys—Morris, Phillip, and Bernard. I'd been the last chance. That was why my ma kept me in long golden curls and knickers well into the third grade. Because of those curls, the James A. Sexton Grammar School became a kind of valley of death, where at the end of every school day I'd have to charge home through battalions of the enemy.

"Here comes the sissy."

And since I was also pudgy—"You sure you're not a girl, Fatso?"

"The queer is here!"

"I bet Fatso don't even have a dick. Let's see if he pisses sitting down!"

Sometimes I'd dodge past them or they would not quite be up for the kill, but many times they'd catch me by my curls. On those days I had to fight my way home. Dirty and bruised, I'd run to my mother.

"Look what they did to me, Ma, look!" I'd sob, and she'd throw her arms around me.

"Oh, my God! What did they do to my Semelah? Look what they did to your *curls*!" That, to her, was the worst. She'd clean me up with a wet towel and soap, then carefully comb out the curls, promising me she'd tell Pa and Pa would go to school and tell the principal, which fortunately never happened.

The day my mother knew she had to cut off my curls was like the end of the world for her. She would rather have been sent to the electric chair for killing Pa. But it was going to be either the scissors or a gradual nose job from all the beatings I was getting.

Every curl she cut off was like a shot to her heart.

"Oy, Sammy, you won't look the same. . . . My poor Semelah, no curls . . . you'll be bald like Pa."

She finally seemed to realize once and for all, after the curls were off, that I was truly a boy, not the girl she so desperately wanted and never had. But she kept the curls in a box, and every time a new neighbor came into her life, out would come the curls. "My Semelah's curls," she'd sigh. "They were so beautiful."

Thirty years later, after my mother's death, I was going through her pictures, jewelry, trinkets, and memorabilia and found the little silver box she had cherished. I opened it and there were the golden curls still intact, like the memory of a longing that was never fulfilled.

***

She's got heart and soul. She's what Jewish moms are made of—always trying to keep it together in an insane household. It looks like it ought to be physically impossible for her to do all the things she does, because of her stature. She's four feet nine, weighs 190, and her breasts just about come down to her knees. It's like when she's scrubbing the floor she's just too topheavy to get up. My father likes it that way; it's the only position he can see her in. What could she be doing standing upright? What is she, a model? A model he knew she wasn't. She's got the knees of a goaltender for the Chicago Blackhawks—if she weren't such a great scrubber, she'd be a great goalie.

My mom, to me, is an exceptional woman, the essence of patience, a self-denying, family-dedicated, old-fashioned European. She's the only person who can take care of the bundle of nerves named Hyman. She's got so much love to give, and Hyman doesn't want it, so she gives it to me. Always telling me, "Sammy, you know Mr. Tonelli, where you always get candy, he told me what a wonderful woman I am. But Pa doesn't appreciate me."

"Sure he does, Ma. He just doesn't know how to show it."

He must like her. How else could she have had eleven pregnancies?

But she works so hard that she has miscarriages and some of them die at birth—only four of us survive.

Never in all the years I've lived with them have I ever seen Pa say a kind word to Ma or even touch her. But once there's an unforgettable exception. I come home late and I don't hear them so I figure they must be out walking around the rooming house. I open the door of the dining room, which is the master bedroom—with twin beds yet. I turn on the light and there they are *in the same bed together*! In panic, I stand there apologizing.

"Pa's not feeling well," my mom says. "He must be coming down with a cold—I just rubbed his chest with Vicks and I'm trying to keep him warm."

I shut their door and I'm shaking. I don't understand. I'm almost fifteen, but I still don't get it. All I ever see is him screaming at her. Why would he be in her arms? And I still think babies are made in heaven, sex is a taboo subject. All I know is that Pa works in the store and Ma does everything else and that's the way it's supposed to be.

Ma holds her true feelings inside and never responds to all the abuse she takes from Pa. That's why she cries a lot and always to me. The worst is when I'm thirteen and I come home from school one afternoon before I have to go down and help in the store. I put my books away in my room and head for the kitchen to get a glass of milk and a piece of the plain yellow cake my mother turns out like a factory makes tires.

Just as I open the refrigerator door, I hear sobbing from the dining room. Naturally, I know who it is. I open the door and my mother is lying on the bed. I've seen her cry all my life, most of the time over something Pa has said or done, but I've never seen her on the bed in the daytime!

"Ma, what's the matter, Ma? Please don't cry. Was it Pa?"

SHECKY AND SHAKY

Her cheeks are wet and shiny. "I just came from the doctor, Sammy, and he said I have to have one of my breasts removed. I have cancer. Hold me, Sammy. I'm scared."

Of course, I'm terrified.

"If I have to go in for an operation, who's gonna cook for Pa? He's so mad now, he won't come upstairs to eat his lunch. I made some nice chicken soup with kreplach, he loves it, but he won't come upstairs. And he locked the door downstairs so I can't bring it down, he's so mad that I was so long at the doctor's."

All I can think of is my ma is dying—MY MA IS DYING—and all she can think of is Pa is too mad to come up and eat!

"Go downstairs, Sammy, and tell him to come up and eat. The food's getting cold."

There's nothing in the world I want to do less. "Why is he mad at you for going to the doctor?"

"It took two hours and I didn't tell him where I was going. I didn't want to worry him. I came home and he was screaming at me, 'You sonofabitch, where you been? Fooling around with some man?' I told him I went to the doctor. 'Doctor, my ass,' he says. 'Two hours you've been fooling around with the doctor? Two hours I've been waiting here in the store and she's out fooling with the doctor,' he says. 'I don't want your goddamn lunch. I'll go down to Dugan's bar and buy it!' "

I'm wishing I could be God long enough to strike Pop dead with lightning, only first I'd make him realize what an incredible s.o.b. he is.

"I've never seen him so mad at me, Sammy." She drags herself out of bed with a sigh.

"Where are you going, Ma?"

She picks up a rag she left on a chair and starts for the bathroom. "I've got to clean the toilet and the tub before Pa comes up. It's Friday and Pa's going to want his bath tonight."

"Mom, rest. I'll do it."

"No, no, Sammy darling. Go down and tell him to eat his lunch. All they have at Dugan's is corned beef and cabbage and he hates that. Please go, Sammy."

I headed down those bleak stairs that lead to the back door of the store. Locked, as Ma said. I knock. No answer. I'd love to believe that Pa's closed the store and is already at Dugan's, but I know my father won't close the store now, at three-thirty, if the Messiah is due at three forty-five.

I knock louder. "Pa, are you in there?"

"WHAT THE HELL DO YOU WANT?"

"Pa, please open the door. I got to talk to you about Ma. She's sick."

"SICK, MY ASS!" His voice shook the door. "She was gone all afternoon. Fooling around with the doctor. Can you believe that sonofabitch?"

I'm swelling with outrage. I bang on the door, leave my feet, shriek, "Pa, open the door! I gotta talk to you!"

A moment of silence. Then footsteps, the door opening, and there's Hyman Shore looking at me like it's my fault.

"This story better be good."

"It's no story, Pa. Mom went to the doctor and he told her she has to have one of her breasts removed." I would never normally be able to say the word *breast* to my dad, and especially in connection with Ma, but now the sky's the limit.

My father's face is almost purple. "What is that sonofabitch doctor talking about? I like both of them right where they are. What kind of a crazy sonofabitch—"

"MOM HAS CANCER!" It's the first time, as far as I can remember, that I've ever really yelled at my father. Now he looks like one of the actors on the screen at the local cinema when the film gets stuck in the projector—paralyzed, with his mouth and his eyes stuck open.

"Hah?" he says.

"CANCER!" I scream. "And if she doesn't have the operation, she's gonna die!" It's the first time I fully realize that I've grown as tall as my father. I get a twinge about how small he really is.

"Hah?" He's turning pale.

"Cancer!" I beat him with it. "And all she asked me to tell you is to go upstairs and eat the chicken soup she made for you. You know how upset she gets when you don't eat."

He's staring at me. I can read what's in his mind like it's printed on his forehead. She's going to die, he's thinking. How could it happen to her, she's so strong, she cleans, she cooks, she scrubs, she works so hard, she never complains about anything? How could she die on me?

He's looking at me for the first time like he's looking for help, but he's not going to get it from me.

"I called her such dirty names," he says in a hoarse voice.

"Go upstairs and eat her soup, Pa. Treat her nice. It'll be good for her cancer."

He doesn't really hear me, he's concentrating on something else. "That sonofabitch doctor doesn't know what the fuck he's talking about," which is strong language for Pa to use without yelling. He marches upstairs still talking about sonofabitch doctors.

He doesn't stop yelling at Ma, but his yelling doesn't have any bite. He finishes eating and grumbles, "You've cooked a lot better than this,"—unheard-of praise. Then he starts a new habit, which I can't believe the first time I see it. He picks up his own plate and puts it in the sink!

Then he starts staring at Ma when he thinks nobody's looking. When it comes closer to her time to go into the hospital, he's muttering about sonofabitch doctors almost nonstop, and once when I'm waiting outside the bathroom door, I hear him saying something as he's flushing the toilet, but the words sound funny. It's not English. I strain to hear and suddenly realize it's Hebrew, and the only word I can understand is *Lena,* said several times. He's praying for my mother in Hebrew because that's the only language God knows, and he's flushing the toilet so nobody but God will hear him.

Ma is planning—after she makes breakfast and packs lunch for us—to take the streetcar, by herself, to the hospital. Pa not only insists on accompanying her, but hires a taxicab to take them. As Ma gets into the cab with her shopping bag containing nightgown, toothbrush, and other necessaries, her words to me are, "Make sure Pa eats when I'm gone." She means "*while* I'm gone," but the words kill me. She's made a week's food for us; all we have to do is heat it up.

In school that day, the day of the operation, the tears finally overflow and I'm excused early. I run all the way to the hospital and burst into the waiting room to see my father sitting, elbows on an end table, hands over his eyes, face wet. I've never seen him cry before. My heart stops, and I stagger over to him and pull his hands away from his face. "Pa . . ." I'm choking.

"Ma's okay. That sonofabitch doctor made a mistake. It wasn't cancer, it was a tumor, a little nothing tumor they cut out, but her breast ain't gonna be cut off," he says as matter-of-factly as if he were talking in the store. Then his voice breaks and the tears start again. "When they wheeled her out," he says, "the first thing she says to me is, 'Did you have lunch?'"

After the operation Pa goes right back to his old ways, complaining constantly about how much the operation and Ma's recovery is costing him. The doctor is a crook, the hospital is a den of robbers, and what the hell is Ma doing laying around in a hospital bed for *five dollars a day*?

Then he comes up with a scheme to help make up for the hospital expenses. He'll manufacture bootleg liquor in the basement.

While he's waiting for Ma to come home, my father thinks about how he'll put her to work in his new operation. He and Ma will make the whiskey, he'll be putting the basement storeroom to better use, and he won't have to pay taxes on that money. Phil, the cop, will get Mom a job with his bookie friend, making sandwiches for the guys who frequent the bookie joint and selling them her and Pa's whiskey. All this will start as soon as Ma gets out and will be on top of her usual daily routine of cooking, cleaning, and schlepping for Hyman and sons. It will compensate him for all the money the hospital stay is costing and bring in a nice income besides. So now Pa can hardly wait for her to be out of the hospital and on her feet. It's a terrible attitude and a dubious scheme, but it does help me get started in show business.

It begins with my visits to Ma in the hospital. To take her mind off being in that room with three other ladies, all of them white-haired and feeble, I show off the one trick I have ever done that's gotten the attention of my friends in school. I pull up my shirt and undershirt and make my naked stomach gyrate. It's a big success. Ma forgets all about her pain and claps her hands in delight.

"You're so talented, Sammy!" Her voice is full of happy surprise. She makes me do it for the other three patients, over my weak objections. Even the oldest and most pathetic of the three women is roused from her stupor and drools and screams with amusement at my performance. It's my first glimpse of the idea that I can make people laugh. My mother is telling her roommates I'm bound to take this great stomach talent all the way to Hollywood. I'm embarrassed at her lack of judgment.

"Ma," I tell her, "in Hollywood you need real talent, like singing or playing the piano."

SHECKY AND SHAKY

"Is that what you want, my darling? Sing and play piano?"

The other women are listening to us, every word. I don't get many chances to be center stage and show off, and I'm rising to the opportunity. "No, Mom," I say loud and clear, "I want to play the trumpet."

It's true. I once saw a movie—I can't remember which one—where an orchestra was playing and a handsome musician stood up and put a trumpet to his lips. Everything went dark except for a spotlight on him and the shining horn, and all the time he played I had goosebumps. When he finished and the audience in the film applauded, I applauded too, and from that moment I've wanted to play.

"Then you'll have lessons, Semelah." I look at my small fat mother in her hospital bed and wonder if she's delirious.

When she gets home and tells Pa she wants me to have lessons, he screams bloody murder. And I'm sure if it weren't for the extra money from the sandwiches and whiskey, he'd never go along.

4

WOMEN, RIGHT AND WRONGED

Mitzi and I had been separated about two months, and there were still some months to go before the changing of the locks. Not long before the separation I had bought a twenty-two-room mansion for us after our twenty years of marriage and four kids. I had thought this house would cement our relationship, because I knew Mitzi wanted it badly. For me, it was hard to believe that I, Semelah, having grown up in a room no bigger than a closet, was living in the place Dorothy Lamour had when she was a big star. The place had seven bedrooms, a fireplace in the master bedroom that was all marble, a full-size bar in the den, which was good for me, old peg-and-groove floors, an enormous kitchen, and a dining room that could seat twenty-five people. In the basement was a walk-in safe that Lamour used for storing her furs or perhaps contemplated using as a bomb shelter.

Outside were forty-foot Italian cypress trees and a sunken swimming pool with statues of swans flowing water from their mouths into the pool. My closet was a special room with mirrored walls. Our bedroom was a private wing, and on the other side of the house was the kids' private wing, with their own kitchen and separate entrance. Just to reassure us that we had moved into the right neighborhood, our next-door neighbor was Andy Williams. Californians are fond of exclaiming over their skyrocketing real-estate buys. I like to shock people by telling them I bought the house for $140,000 in 1971, and today it's worth $2,000,000.

Now I was living in a small one-bedroom apartment. I spent a good deal of time sitting there and feeling like the world was coming to an end.

One night I answered the phone and it was Mitzi.

"How've you been doing?" she asked.

"I'm getting through it," I said. "Why?"

She told me she'd been thinking about our situation, that the younger boys, Peter and Pauly, had been feeling my absence, that it might be nice—if I wanted to—if I spent the weekend with her at the house. All of this was proposed for the benefit of the boys, not Mitzi. "I think it would do them some good to see us together and friendly."

I was elated. I thought, Maybe it's an excuse and she really wants me back. I jumped at the invitation and we agreed we'd see each other that coming weekend.

When I hung up, I just sat there stunned. What a surprise. I'm going "home."

We made love. She kissed me and said she'd never felt so good before. I couldn't help noting that she'd never opened herself up to me so much.

Of course, I knew the reason. She could never trust me. She always traced that back to her father, who had been a traveling salesman and brought venereal disease home to her mom. He was a handsome guy and must have had a lot of girls. The tragedy was that when he gave VD to his wife, she had to have her female organs removed. That helped explain why, every time I came off the road and we had sex, she'd examine me for any sores. A few times she said, "I just never will trust a Jewish man." Her father was one, I was one, and we were both unfaithful.

Now she was telling me it didn't matter whether she trusted me or not. "To be honest," she said, "I really don't care anymore."

I couldn't believe she was saying this just a moment after letting me make love to her.

"But I really love you," I said.

"Bullshit!"

I needed her desperately, but at least she was right about that. I had known from the beginning that it really was bullshit.

The Warm-up

"Sammy, I'm pregnant," the scared, meek voice is saying over the phone. It's my girl friend, Mitzi. I'm gripping the phone so tightly, it feels like the thing will shatter. I wish it would.

"I'm pregnant."

I've heard that pleading sound once before, two years ago, also over the goddamn telephone, from a girl named Gale.

I had spent the summer as social director at Breezy Point Lodge in Minnesota. It was my second job in show business after Shecky and I broke up.

Breezy Point was in Brainerd, the northern part of the state. It was rustic as hell and seventy-five years old, with all the charm of, say, the Grand Hotel in Mackinaw, Michigan. It attracted mainly vacationers from the twin cities of Minneapolis and St. Paul, and many of the summer helpers were kids from the University of Minnesota.

Gale was one of the cuties from the university that I banged that summer. She was working as a child counselor. She was very bright and was going for her degree in psychology. And she loved to fuck. We did it in the woods, on the lake, in the lake, behind cars, on the volleyball court and, one night, even on the stage of the hall where we did our shows. I was having the time of my life. No more Shecky— I had the place to myself. I had a little experience now, too, and my shows were going very well.

My mother and father even came up that summer for a few days and saw their Sammy in action. I even saw my dad smile at me while I was doing my show. I played my trumpet for him—"You Made Me Love You"—and I did impressions of Harry James, Clyde McCoy, Henry Busse, even Louis Armstrong. They were both proud.

When the summer ended, I hated going back to that dreadful rooming house, but at least I could go back there with some respect. Having played the trumpet so well for Pa, I could now even leave the door open when I practiced.

I was upstairs in the apartment one September afternoon when the phone rang. Whenever it rang, it sounded down in the store as well as the apartment. And every time it rang I thought it might be an agent offering me a job.

No such luck. The voice at the other end said, "Sammy? This is Gale calling, from Minneapolis."

I could hear muffled voices on the line—my father listening in, as he always did, from down in the store.

"Yes, this is Sammy. How are you, Gale?"

"I'm getting ready to go back to school next week," she said, "and . . . and I just don't know how to tell you this . . ."

The blood started to rush through my body in preparation for bad news. "Uh, tell me what, Gale?" I thought of my father listening.

"I'm pregnant. I just don't know what to do," and she started to sob. I heard the rustling of the downstairs phone. Holy fuck!

"I found . . . there's a doctor," she said, "who'll give me an abortion for two hundred fifty dollars."

That was almost all the money I'd saved during the summer. "Are you sure you're pregnant?"

"Yes, Sammy. I just came back from the doctor. I'm four weeks' pregnant."

I tried to figure—four weeks ago. Right in the middle of August. I was screwed. Then and now.

"Please, Sammy, send me the money. I'll be eternally grateful to you. And you know I can't tell my folks, my dad being a minister and all. It would kill him. Please, Sammy, I beg of you."

The worst part about it was that I knew she was banging the band leader and the German cook as well as me. How could I know it was my Jewish come that was to blame? I was hooked. She knew I probably had some money, since I had bragged constantly about how I was going on tour after the summer. And, I figured, Gentile girls are ingrained with the idea that Jews have money, especially when the girls come from a place like Minnesota.

"Don't worry, Gale," I said, sighing. "I'll send you the money today. . . . What's your address?"

Amazingly, my father didn't say a word to me—not even about the thing that would be uppermost in his mind, the two hundred fifty dollars. In fact, he even seemed cheerful that night, in his way. I think he was happy that I was a "man."

Now I'm in Toledo working at Kin Wa Low's Chinese Supper Club. Owner Charlie Wong, behind the bar, calls me over in his accented cadence, "Sammy, you-got-a-call, long-distance . . . Chicago." He hands me the phone over the bar.

The band is playing dance music as they do every night before the first show. The club is popular—the best Chinese food in town, and you can always see a good floor show. It's a good place to work, too, because if Charlie likes you, he always has you back.

The Warm-up

"Is this Sammy Shore?" the operator says.

Mitzi breaks in, "Sammy, it's Mitzi. . . . Thank you, operator." I can hear her faintly through the commotion and music coming from the show room stage, just twenty feet away.

"Sammy, I'm pregnant." She starts to cry.

"Did I hear you right? You're pregnant?"

"Yes, Sammy, it's true. What am I going to do?"

Once again I feel like the victim, a stupid one.

I had been balling Mitzi all summer long at Pine Point Resort, Elkhart Lake, Wisconsin, ninety miles north of Milwaukee. The resort was the kind of safe place I'd been looking for after working for a while in Texas. Just a bunch of Jewish people who would love Sammy—no pressure. Mac Stein, the owner, was in real estate in Chicago, a typical nice, warm Jewish man who loves people. He was married to Roz, a typical yenta—precocious, mouthy, a Jewish Zsa Zsa Gabor. Mr. Stein hired me as social director. Sometimes I thought summer social director was about as far as I was going to get in this business—it was my destiny.

Mitzi Lee Saidel was Mac Stein's secretary, twenty-one years old, petite, sweet, Jewish, not pretty, but built nice, from Green Bay, a student at the University of Wisconsin, working for the summer. She did everything for me this summer—typed my jokes, followed me around like a puppy dog telling me what a great comedian I am, what a nice guy. I like her a lot, but I've never had strong love feelings for her. Mitzi is just nice and comfortable to be with, always sitting out there in the audience. And some nights, when it didn't go too well at Pine Point, she'd say, "That's all right, Sammy, they were just tired. And remember—you've been playing games with them all day, so you can't expect them to always laugh at you at night. . . . Anyways, tomorrow you'll get a whole new group."

She's amazing; she loves me. She's like a replacement for my ma. After the summer, she wanted to move to Chicago to be near me. Then she stayed with me in my room in our family apartment. My room is right off the kitchen, and my mom and dad sleep down the hall in the dining room. It was quite a strange setup, but neither of my parents have ever once said to me, "It's not nice to bring a girl into your room to stay overnight." The subject is taboo.

I was never too happy about Mitzi wanting to move to Chicago, but I just didn't know how to tell her. I'm thinking she ought to go back to Green Bay to finish college—I'm not looking to settle down at this point in my life. I'm still flying around getting my feet wet, along with other parts. Until Pine Point and Mitzi, I was bringing new girls home every chance I had. Whatever club I was working, there was always a singer, dancer, a novelty act—I dragged 'em all home to meet my mom. Even my father liked some of the shiksas I hooked up with.

Maureen O'Reilly, for example, was a tap dancer I worked with at a club in Warren, Ohio. It was a sleazy place—Club Libido— with a couple of strippers on the bill. This was one of Maureen's first jobs in a strip joint and she was scared. These pit stops always had a novelty act or a dancer of some sort to open the show, and it never failed that the owner would try to come on to something that was as new and fresh as Maureen. She was nineteen, and looked like Virginia Mayo. I liked her a lot. After we finished our week's run, I asked her if she'd like to come to Chicago to meet my mom.

One thing I never had to do was call my mom and tell her I'm bringing home a shiksa. Ma loved the excitement of somebody new, so she could do her thing—cook matzoh ball soup and really fuss, just to be appreciated.

Now, Maureen was from a strict Irish Catholic family. She'd heard about Jews but had never actually seen one before me. This gave Ma a chance to make an even bigger impact—a kind of surprise attack of Jewish cooking.

If Ma wasn't cleaning, you could always find her at her stove cooking or baking. She always made her own bread, like challah, a twisted white bread that looks like a couple of brown snakes who got lost. She would roll that dough with her tiny hands and beat it—it was a work of art when she was done. There was so much love in all the food she made, but it seems it was never appreciated, except by me and the friends I brought home.

"Oy, she's such a beautiful girl!" Mom said when she saw me walk in with Maureen. Mom grabbed her and pulled her deep into her bosom for a squeeze. I saw Maureen's face turn red. Jewish mamas hug like they're holding on for dear life. My mom never got it, so she was just dishing it out to all who wanted it, and sometimes also to those who didn't.

My bags weren't even in my room yet when my mom grabbed us both and sat us down at the kitchen table for the beginning of the onslaught. Ma was a very robust woman, but when it came to that stove, she moved around it like a ballerina. Plates came flying out of the cupboard—the good china, not the everyday stuff—then silverware, napkins, glasses, and the feast began. She didn't even ask if you were hungry. This was her opening night!

"Sammy, look. I made you kreplach soup." Then, looking at Maureen, "She's so *skinny.*"

Food came pouring forth, and Maureen sat and ate in amazement.

After a couple of days of all the food and affection that my mom dished out, the little shiksas wouldn't want to leave. It wasn't because of me that they stayed—they could hardly move from the weight of all that food. And they fell in love with Lena!

"Jesus Christ, Mitzi . . ."

I feel so guilty. I did use her all summer; I've been using her since. She's always ready if I want her, and me, I'm just plain condescending. But I don't love her, I don't even know what the word or the idea means—it's something I never saw in my house. Even when I left on this tour, I was so happy to get away that I couldn't even say to Mitzi, "I'll miss you." I started out, ecstatic, on the first leg—New Orleans, Shreveport.

"I'll call you, Mitzi, and let you know where I'm staying." That's about all I said. We've talked on the phone, and I've kept thinking that any day now I can tell her I really can't see her anymore, and then I can look up that girl in Texas . . .

I'm petrified, frozen, anxious. Mitzi is not just another girl, but a nice, a *very* nice Jewish girl who loves me like only a mother could, and who am I to say no to that?

"Don't worry, Mitzi. You come to Toledo and we'll get married."

"Really, Sammy? You want to get married?"

I'm dying inside, at the same time feeling relieved—it's over; I've done it; it must be the right thing. Or am I blowing it? I could have told her not to move in with me in Chicago; now I could suggest an abortion, some alternative. I just never know how to say, "no, sorry, it ain't working."

When I hang up the phone, it's time to work.

"And now, ladies and gentlemen, here's a very funny guy from Chicago—let's hear it for Sammy Shore."

***

WOMEN, RIGHT AND WRONGED

The summer at Breezy Point, a year before Mitzi, is the spring-board for my first real taste of show-business pressure. Milt and Dolly come into my life that summer. Milt's in the stock market and is sort of a financial tycoon. They both take a liking to me and want to help me become a star, just as that lady had done with Shecky and me. They feel I've got great potential. I think I know better. Sure, what isn't there to like? I'm young, I've got tremendous energy, I play trumpet, sing a little, and I've got a good personality out there. But Milt and Dolly are at the resort having a good time; they don't realize these resort audiences are pushovers. Where else are they going to go? They're stuck with me. Put the same people in a nightclub, and they can be animals.

The summer ends, and Milt and Dolly keep their word. They get me a tutor to help me with my English, they buy me clothes and a comedy writer. Milt's trying to make me a gentleman and not a kid from the streets of Chicago. That's not Sammy, but I'm doing what I can.

Milt's got some influence in the East and knows Harry Kilby, head of nightclubs for General Arts, the big entertainment agency. He calls Kilby and raves about me. Claims I'm going to be another Danny Thomas. He pressures Kilby to book me in the eastern clubs.

I really don't want to go any more than I wanted to go to New York with Shecky. I start to get tremendous sinus headaches. I simply feel that I don't have the awesome God-given ability of a Shecky Greene.

Kilby books me—six weeks of his clubs. He keeps reminding Milt that he's going out on a limb. Milt just tells him not to worry, I'm fantastic, Kilby will have the credit of discovering me, "we'll have a star on our hands."

Most comedians would be excited as hell. I wanted to go back to Breezy Point or, better yet, Oakton Manor.

My first date is in Philadelphia; Milt has to go to New York and wants me to meet him there after I knock 'em dead in Philly.

It's a neighborhood joint in a Philly suburb. I just know I'm in trouble. A strange city, with different types of people. These people do not look like they've ever been to a resort. They're rough and very Italian-looking.

I'm not funny when I go out there. I work a few more nights and don't do well at all. From the bad reports out of that club, Kilby cancels the rest of the engagements. Milt's disappointed and doesn't sponsor me again.

Back to the rooming house and the store in Chicago and a job at the sleazy Rainbow Gardens. The place even has sawdust on the floor and furry little animals scurrying about that closely resemble cats. From there MCA discovers me and books me in Danville, Illinois, where they need an emcee.

Now picture this: my first night in Danville, first show. I start to introduce the stripper and two guys begin arguing at the front table. One guy pulls out a .45, shoots the other. I keep talking. The stripper won't come out. So I pick up my trumpet and play Clyde McCoy's "Sugar Blues." The police come and take the guys away and the show goes on as if nothing ever happened.

Finally, I get a job in a mini-musical comedy with Eddie Howard and Orchestra at the Blackhawk Restaurant in downtown Chicago. The Blackhawk's really an "in" spot, the show runs sixteen weeks, I'm a hit, and that gets me going all around the Midwest. A taste of freedom and success until the summer, Pine Point, Mitzi, and marriage.

I got through my opening with Diana Ross in Tahoe like the pro that I was, but I knew I wasn't funny. I was mechanical. I could always make the excuse that the audience was down, but who could be more down than I was, locked out of my house and on the brink of divorce. During the rest of the engagement I was just okay. My son Scotty was with me for the first week and tried to tell me how funny I was, how the audience loved me, but I couldn't buy it. I tried skiing, tobogganing, getting out into the fresh winter air, but I couldn't shake the lonely, abandoned little-boy feeling.

When Scotty left for home, it was worse. Now it was me, the mountains, and the snow, Diana Ross and the joyous people filling her dressing room with laughing, drinking, smoking and, most of all, music blasting through the walls. It was the holidays, and everyone was having a marvelous time.

My next gig was the Playboy Club in Atlanta. The Playboy clubs were in sharp decline, so the booking was appropriate for me. I was going back almost to the level where I had started. The Atlanta club was in the middle of a section of downtown that had decayed, and the club was doing no business at all; it was located in the heart of an area that had seen a recent rash of murders and robberies. One night it was pouring rain and I had to walk out at eleven-thirty and do my second show for perhaps two dozen people plus employees.

I noticed a table of four guys who were very boisterous, and I knew I was in for trouble. I was introduced: "The comedy star of our show, the guy who worked with Elvis Presley, let's hear it for Sammy Shore."

I did hear it. As I started to get into one of my bits, a voice from that table said, "Hey, Jew boy, when you gonna get funny?" It sounded like Colonel Parker was back in town.

I ignored him and continued. Again he shouted, "What you do for Elvis, wipe his ass?"

"If you worked for Elvis, what you doin' here, Jew boy?"

I couldn't stand it. I'd been heckled many, many times, but never quite like that. There was also something about the loneliness and misery of the situation, the fact that I was sliding downward in my career, the fact that it did hurt me to think that I had been working with Elvis and was now working here. I was seized with anger and frustration.

I picked up the mike stand and hurled it toward the table. "You fucking bigot!" I yelled, and I walked out of the club to my hotel next door. I sat on the edge of my bed and cried. I felt as much like suicide as I ever had in my life. I knew I had to do something.

I got myself together and went back to the club. It was about one forty-five in the morning, just before closing. I apologized to the manager, who said he understood and that he'd picked up that party's tab and asked them to leave just after the incident.

Then I said, "Bob, I want to cancel the rest of my engagement here. I just can't work anymore. Can you get a replacement for me?"

"Gee, Sammy, I really don't know. I'll call Chicago and maybe they can get someone."

I thanked him. I felt too sick to go on. The next day he gave me a call and told me they had someone, and I was on my way back to Los Angeles, looking for someone, something, to fill the gap.

What filled it was a siege of incredible back pain, a diagnosis of two disintegrated discs, and a hospital stay in traction with the possibility of surgery.

In the hospital I was visited by the few friends I had left, and my daughter, Sandy, whom I hadn't seen in months.

"What happened to you?" she said.

"Oh, my back just went out on me. I'll be okay again in a couple weeks. How have you been, how's school?"

She said everything was fine.

The Warm-up

As if to disprove it, I said, "You know, Mom and I are getting a divorce."

"I know," she said. "Mom is really mad at you. She even said that's why you're in the hospital, because God punished you."

My breath was knocked out for a second. "She doesn't mean that, Sandy," I said. "She's just angry about what happened when I hit her at The Comedy Store."

Sandy wanted to know why I'd done it, and all I could say was I blew up because I felt like I was being treated like a nobody, that I had tried to make amends with Mitzi, but Mitzi wouldn't accept it. Sandy left feeling very confused about the divorce. It was not a good time for her.

Meanwhile, child that I was, I was really enjoying all the attention from the hospital staff. I was the lying-in warm-up comic for the fifth floor. After some of them got off work, they'd come by to have a drink and be entertained by the crazy man in traction.

One night, during my third week in traction, I got a call from Alan Lee, talent booker at the Tropicana Hotel in Vegas. We had never met, but he had seen me with Elvis and wanted to know if I'd work the Tropicana with Abbe Lane—starting next Thursday, for one week.

I was so excited that they wanted me back in Vegas in a main room that I assured Lee I'd be fine, the back was no problem, and when the call was over, I reached down beside the bed to take a few slugs of J&B straight from the bottle.

I called my doctor, who agreed to the idea and arranged for me to have a special brace. I asked Dennis Klein, a writer friend, to help me with my act. He came to the hospital and we wrote jokes about my back. I also called my close friend Stan Christo, an Oakland musician and nightclub owner, who agreed to come to Vegas with me and help me get around. I knew I couldn't make it by myself.

I was insane to think I could go to Vegas hardly able to walk and still be funny. I just had to do it; I had to prove myself; I couldn't wait and pick a better time or depend on the good chance that Lee might have something else for me later.

When I was introduced at the Tropicana, I was backstage in a wheelchair. At the right moment I got up and hobbled out front. I started talking about my back brace and did some hospital jokes, but no one really cared that I'd gotten out of a hospital bed to open for Abbe Lane. In fact no one seemed to care about either me or Abbe

Lane. My act was twenty minutes of torment, and the whole thing was stupid because my comedy has always been very physical. I have to jump around. Physical inhibition on top of all my other problems was a killer.

When the week ended, I decided not to go back to LA. For what?

"Pick him up and take him to my room," she said to a couple of guys at the party. I heard her from what seemed like the bottom of a well. I was lying on the floor completely bombed. Booze and pot had annihilated me.

I was living with the woman who gave the order. She was Rita Alexandra, a top show girl in the Folies Bergère at the Tropicana. We'd had a romance going for weeks, and I was thinking of living in Las Vegas. Certainly it had been wonderful living with Rita. About all I did every day was go pick her up between shows. We'd come back to the apartment, she'd have wine and grass, I'd have my J&B, and we'd talk about our future, when we would travel around in a van, me working some clubs and her being my old lady. I had always fantasized that someday I'd have a beautiful blond lady who'd come with me wherever I wanted to go.

Things were mostly okay until the night of the party. Up until then, we'd spent almost all of our time together, just her and me. We'd take our nightly baths together, I'd rub her feet and massage her back and she'd be in heaven. She'd take care of me completely. The problem was that I was becoming more and more possessive and uptight about Rita's beauty. I knew she had dozens of admirers, and within a few weeks we were already having little spats about it. Nothing serious, I thought.

Then Rita gave a party for some of the cast in her show, and her friends became more and more lasciviously interested in her as the night progressed. I was extremely jealous. I tried to drink myself into an agreeable coma, and then there was pot, and then there were those distant words I heard Rita saying, and I woke up the next morning in Rita's bed with all my clothes removed except my shorts. My head was spinning, I felt utterly sick, and Rita was not in the bed but was downstairs waiting to talk to me.

To make a long story bearable, she told me that she found my jealousy and drunkenness disgusting, and she kicked me out. If I was going to live in Vegas, it wouldn't be with Rita.

The Warm-up

***

As exciting as Vegas is when you're doing well, that's how lonely it is when you're not making it. You can stand in the middle of a crowded casino with hundreds of people milling around, gambling, shouting, and laughing—and nearby, dozens of people checking in and out, other dozens standing in line for the dinner show—and you can be more alone and isolated than in almost any other place on earth. Afraid to walk over to a pit boss you know and say hello. "What ya doin' in town, Sammy? Ya workin'? Haven't seen you around in a while."

"Just came in to play around for a few days."

Bullshit!

When you're not making it in that town as an entertainer, people don't have time for you. And when I called people in my post-Rita phase, I found that to be out of work *and* living in town qualified me for a special kind of reaction.

"When'd you get in town?" they'd say. "Where ya gonna open?"

"I'm moving here."

"Oh." A pause. "Call me when you get settled, maybe we can play some tennis."

All bullshit. No tennis was played. How much money you're worth, how much power and prestige you command, those are the keys to Las Vegas. I had some money, but I was low on the coin of the realm.

The old camaraderie of Vegas is now gone. The friendly relations between the hotels, the personal relationships that held things together, even the greeters to welcome you—they're gone. Only the high rollers are treated with anything approaching the old aplomb, and even then it's calculated. Unions have taken over, strikes have struck, Ticketron will spew out a computerized slip that is your ticket to a show at Caesars Palace. Jackpots are ridiculous—over $250,000. Years ago a $2.50 jackpot on the nickel machine could be exciting. A floor manager would walk over and congratulate you, even offer to buy you a drink. For five dollars you could see a cocktail show starring Nat King Cole.

Yes, we know that inflation is partly to blame. But the real caring is gone. Vegas has become dehumanized and processed through computers. Inside of twenty minutes the casino can get a reading on your worth, using your name, city and social security number.

No one stays up late anymore, at least not in the stylish way people

96

did before. The exciting hotel lounges are no more, where at two-thirty in the morning you could walk in and for one drink see a lounge star, rising stars like Louis Prima, the Mary Kaye Trio, Shecky Greene, Don Rickles—where all of us entertainers could go and hang out and heckle or jump on stage and do a few minutes. You didn't go to bed until the next morning and you loved every minute. One entertainer would say, "Hey, go catch Louis Prima and Sam Butera at the Sahara, we're all gonna be there at the late show." On any given night, in the audience for Don Rickles you might find Frank Sinatra, Dean Martin, Tony Bennett. Everyone who was appearing in town would make a last stop in one of the lounges, and all the hotels had them.

Now they're all keno parlors where castaway Oklahoma grandpas, Chinese men and women, and little old ladies in their babushkas sit and pray for the winning numbers to come in. The casinos let the people come in with their shorts on—what the hell. The class, the big-time feeling, has nearly evaporated.

In its place: volume. Volume, domination by computers, accounting systems and impersonal greed, these explain how the architects of the MGM Grand, where I appeared in 1979 with Donna Summer, could decline the fire department's request that they install sprinklers in the casino. After all, the hotel was up to the old building code. No additional safety measures were legally *required*, so none were taken. Profit margins were maximized. All very rational. Nothing personal intended. Except that eighty-four people died in a horrible fire.

"We're up seventeen percent over last month," the manager of a hotel's casino might report to the vice-president at the monthly meeting. His words are what it's all about.

"Atlantic City is starting to hurt us," another executive tells his colleagues. And indeed, Atlantic City represents the coming of a new era in gambling. When I was appearing at the Caesars Boardwalk Regency Hotel in the summer of 1980, revenues for the month of August were $22,600,000. Poor people were taking their paychecks and throwing them away on the machines. I said in my act that they even had a slot for food stamps: if you were lucky, you'd get three lemons.

The most bizarre and insane bunch of people I'd ever seen was flocking to Atlantic City, completely wacked-out on gambling.

"Here," they seemed to say, "take my money. Please show me how to lose. I just want to learn."

97

The Warm-up

People were standing in line to get into the casino and gamble.

The East Coast had never had the concentrated frenzy of gambling; they'd always come to Vegas. All the big-time gamblers were from the East. Now their pit stop is Atlantic City.

By 1985 there will be more than fifteen major hotels in Atlantic City—a place the Vegas operators swore would never happen. "Atlantic City? That's a joke," they'd say. "If those people ever want to know about big-time gambling, they're gonna have to send for us."

But the stars have faded in Vegas. Only the MGM Grand has kept alive the policy of featuring major stars. What are the other hotels featuring? Animals and feathers. Revues. Five-thousand-pound tigers that disappear and elephants that fall through a trapdoor to the bottom of a revolving stage, where they shit all over the tigers and the stage crew. It's wonderful, this new show business. The cozy attitudes of the Mr. Know-It-Alls who once said, "Who needs 'em if they don't gamble?" have disintegrated. Now they're saying, "What *happened*?" and are even paying plane fares and offering rooms at unbelievable discounts.

People are tired of being shoved around and used. They're dollar-conscious. Yes, entertainment is essential to our survival—to get away for a few hours and have some laughs—but it's no longer worth going into debt! Between breakfast, lunch, dinner, room and a show, two days in Vegas, before this drought, would have cost a couple nearly five hundred dollars. And that doesn't even include being able to go to a table and gamble. Yet for twenty to twenty-five dollars you can see any major star on any given weekend, in the Casinos by the Sea.

Hundreds of buses a day roll into Atlantic City with the little old ladies and men, *and they're welcomed.* Given ten dollars to gamble with and a free lunch, these folks have found a new life for themselves. Some of the little people will take their roll of quarters and pour it into the slots. Others will take the quarters, eat the hotel's free lunch, get back on the bus, come back on the next trip, get another ten, and make a nice living from the hotels and buses. But that's okay by the hotels. The revenues they've recouped from slots alone would be enough to keep many entire nations in food and clothing. And much of this also comes from those bus people who cash their pension checks, and even their savings, hoping to win the big million-dollar jackpot.

For the bus people it's a way of life that beats the typical handling given to the elderly. It's not so bad, falling asleep in the lobby and knowing the security guard will wake you when your bus is leaving, knowing that you're welcomed. It's wonderful—every day is like New Year's Eve. In fact, on some slow weeknights, some hotels allow the bus people to come in and see a show—free!

Meanwhile, in Vegas, unemployment exceeds eleven percent. One-time dealers seek employment as waiters. In Atlantic City the jobs are plentiful. Although Harrah's Hotel sits in an isolated area called the Marina, away from the busy boardwalk, it will net over fifty million dollars this fiscal year. By the time you read this, there'll be another Harrah's on the Boardwalk. Virtually every major hotel will be adding a sequel, while in Vegas, the party's over. There, the collapse of the peso has been another in a series of blows, because it cuts out affluent Mexican gamblers who comprised a small but steady market.

But, as they say, you can't keep the good guys down. And I believe the pros will come back. I foresee a whole new evolution in Vegas, reaching out to the people and making them feel welcome with the return of things like the $1.25 chuckwagon and the $10 cocktail show.

As Vegas settles into the sands, at least for the moment, and Atlantic City emerges as the hottest game in town, we seem to lose sight of the city that made it all possible.

Reno, Nevada. Still calling itself "The Biggest Little City in the World." Named after General Jesse Reno, a Civil War hero. This is the little town where the gambling all began.

Reno wasn't much of a town until the turn of the century, when it started to gain a reputation as a villainous, corrupt little place filled with gambling dens, dives, and whorehouses. Every known criminal migrated to Reno, it seemed, for refuge from the authorities in other states. A Reno mayor gained election during Prohibition on a platform of "A Whiskey Barrel on Every Corner."

Who could have foreseen that after 120 years the little city of Reno would be a modern metropolis of medical centers, a good university, skyscrapers, luxurious hotels. And a train that every morning at two-thirty comes chugging through the center of town, blowing its goddamn horn, reminding us of the trains that came through here in the 1880s.

On any given night a cab driver can take you out to Reno's Mustang Ranch—a legalized whorehouse. And in the summer of 1982 was born Reno's first annual Gay Rodeo, a gathering of gay cowboys.

" Have you ever roped a calf?"

"No, but I've touched a few."

Working to an eastern audience, like one in Atlantic City, is much different than working to people who live on the Coast. The West Coast audience is more relaxed and casual. You can have a conversation with them. They're laid back, and why shouldn't they be? They just finished smoking a joint in the bathroom. So there are certain jokes I use for a Coast audience.

Everyone's into Quaaludes. I won't take anything I can't spell!

A girl asked me, do I take drugs? Sure, I said—Maalox and Di-Gel!

I had a date with a beautiful girl, and I was going over to her apartment. She said, "Be sure you bring over some COKE!" Carrying that case up the stairs, I nearly broke my back!

You can always talk to people from the West about health food:

Women are so skinny here in California . . . 'cause they're all into health foods—alfalfa, oats, barley. When they say let's hit the hay, they mean breakfast! I dated a vegetarian. . . . Got her hot, she wilted!

But those jokes are just not funny to an eastern audience. In general, they could care less about health food and diets. Sometimes I think their whole life is food, especially for the ladies. In one sitting they'll eat a lobster and steak, mashed potatoes, gravy, bread, cake, and pie, then turn to the waiter and say, "Excuse me, ya got any Sweet'n Low?"

Now that joke is funny to an eastern audience. They can identify with it.

People in the East are very impatient. They want it now! They want to hear the jokes come at them fast. Like a machine gun—so they can run back to the casino and gamble.

They holler and scream in the casino like they're back in their old neighborhood.

"Hey, Boojie, look at that, another seven!" He starts blowing on the dice. And after a minute he says, "Gimme another set of dice— these are wet!"

In Vegas, if you get boisterous, a security guard will gently tap you on the shoulder and say, "Will you kindly hold it down, sir, or you'll have to leave."

In Atlantic City, the louder the better. I've seen guys play and jump and shout at a crap table for over ten hours. I did my two shows and they were still there! And the smell is horrendous—they won't go to the room to freshen up. They want to lose it all. They know the casino is going to close at four A.M. for cleaning and they'd have to wait until 10 for reopening.

I recently ran into two guys from New York who proudly told me their saga. They'd driven to Atlantic City in the early afternoon. They gambled most of the afternoon and lost all their money except for a check, but the casino wouldn't cash the check. So they both got into the car and drove back to New York, got some cash, drove right back to Atlantic City, and lost it all again.

Yes, Atlantic City has really changed. In fact, I was mentioning that to my cab driver tonight, Bert Parks.

That's the type of humor they like in the East.

Only the brilliant minds that work here have really turned this city around. Basically, they've taken a slum and turned it into an eyesore!

The gaming commission in New Jersey consists of a group of men and one woman who control the gambling licenses for all the hotels. Sometimes I think they're ex-Gestapo agents. The Nevada gaming commission are teddy bears compared to them. If you're going to open a new or refurbished hotel and casino in Atlantic City, you even have to get your color scheme approved. In fact, Caesars Boardwalk Regency was getting ready to open and the woman on the commission decided she didn't like the color contrast in the rooms. So Caesars spent almost a million dollars to redo the color combination, just so they could open. And I can't tell you how bad some of the color schemes in these hotels are. As I say in my act, the colors in the rooms are so bad, the people get sick and run out of their rooms to gamble.

New Jerseyites are a special breed. As Bill Cosby says in his act: "You ask somebody where they're from and they say, 'New Jersey,' and you ask them what city, and they tell you, 'A city in New Jersey,' and then you say what city is that near, and they tell you a city that is not even in that state."

***

101

The Warm-up

In the early days of my career there was no such animal as a "talent buyer." Your agent would go directly to the source, the guy who owned the club. The impresario, the entrepreneur. He knew his club and he knew the type of act that would please his customers. So if the club was in a heavily Italian neighborhood, and the owner was usually Italian himself, he'd lean toward an Italian singer and a comedian who could do a lot of Italian shtick. The Jewish owner was pretty smart, too. He'd always bring in a black singer, one who could do "My Yiddishe' Mama"—and the black performer always knew a few Yiddish words to throw in. The Jewish audience loved it. And of course, since most comedians in those days were Jewish, the club owner had his pick of those.

That's how the many clubs and dives operated—until television became bigger and more sophisticated and the entertainment industry became more centralized. Then the oncoming stars were not only recording artists but were fast becoming TV stars. And Las Vegas became the entertainment capital of the world.

In Las Vegas, the hotel operators were preoccupied with gambling and didn't have time to book their entertainment talent. They were concerned only with their casinos—that was their show. Enter the "talent buyer," the "house booker," the "entertainment director." Those titles once had a great deal of meaning, for these were men with tremendous theatrical background: former nightclub owners, producers, former entertainers.

Jack Entratter was talent buyer for the once-famous Sands Hotel in Las Vegas. Jack got most of his training under Jules Podell, of New York's Copacabana, and booked the Copa's shows. The training you got under Podell was irreplaceable. He was the image of a club owner. Tough and hard, but honest. His word was God, and he ran his club with a very strong arm. If you were a customer and you were getting out of line, you'd be told, very politely, to please shut up. If you persisted, four waiters would come by, pick you, and sometimes also the table, off the floor, and calmly carry you out into the street. If you had worked for the Copa and decided to leave for greener pastures, you knew your craft.

That type of talent buyer, in that special Vegas heyday, had the power to pay the star under the table, in cold cash, to get him or her to work his hotel. The star got the stated salary, but buyers like Jack could make it very sweet besides. The gamblers ran that town, and when they wanted somebody, they didn't care—just get 'em!

WOMEN, RIGHT AND WRONGED

Bill Miller, who first brought Barbra Streisand and Elvis to Vegas and gave Tom Jones his first engagement at the Flamingo, had been owner of Bill Miller's Riviera in New Jersey. He always had a great eye for talent, and knew exactly how to handle stars. There were many others like him. Once they told you you had a deal, you had a deal. They never tried to back off or screw the performer in any way.

Then came the advent, in Las Vegas, of Howard Hughes and of operations run coldly and efficiently by computer. The talent buyer for all the Hughes hotels was Walter Kane, elderly and long-time friend of Hughes who did have a background in show business but who was thoroughly out of touch with current happenings. He was hard of hearing, and an agent would often be horrified to sit with Kane during his client's act and see Kane doze off. Of course, not all of the new breed were that bad, and the personnel in the empire created by the late Bill Harrah are so good they're legendary. But the arrival of Hughes in Vegas was the beginning of the end of the fun, and Kane was the first in a line of no-talent entertainment buyers.

Now things have gotten so bad in Vegas that the hotel owners are taking over the reins as bookers. This may be a very good thing, like going back to the days of the local night club. Except what's so creative about an owner who can only protest:

"What? Wayne Newton again?"

I was so weak and helpless when I looked for a place of my own in Vegas that I would have done anything anyone wanted me to, and did. I ran into Norman Kaye, former entertainer who now had a very successful real estate company, and he told me I ought to buy a condo at the new Jockey Club. He showed me a two-bedroom apartment on the tenth floor, overlooking the city, with private tennis courts, pool, even a private club. I was hooked.

Norman was not to blame, my fantasies were. I visualized going to my own private club to impress the girls, with lots of people around so I'd never be lonely. This was going to be it; this place would really impress. I was so frantically obsessed with these thoughts that I not only moved in the same day with six thousand dollars as my ten-percent down payment, but I had them give me a condo that was completely furnished down to dishes and sheets. This was my new front. I had it made. Until I realized that no one really cared that I had a condo at the Jockey Club.

I was just plain alone. I'd been no good at holding on to Mitzi, my security blanket, and I was no good at following my real needs and desires. I'd always been hung up somewhere between the two alternatives, so I could blow both of them.

It's the summer that Mitzi—still Mitzi Saidel—is staying with me in my room in Chicago. I'm constantly thinking, am I stringing her along, should I tell her to go home, do I want to marry this girl, how can I avoid it? I don't know what to do about the situation. I don't know how to say, "The summer's over."

I have no eyes for Mitzi. I'm really crazy about a girl I met in Dallas before I ever came to Pine Point. She's the one I'd be with if I could: Phyllis Lightenton, the ideal Texas girl—built like a brick shithouse, with a beautiful face and a thick Texas accent, which I love. I've always been crazy about southern girls, something about them I adore.

I met her not long after the previous summer, when I started working in Dallas at a private Jewish club. Danny Leventhal, a rabbi's son and one of the town's swingers, caught my show and loved it.

I was kidding the audience about being Jewish in Texas.

Howdy, pardner, I'm from Tukus, Texas—that's the county seat. Y'all know what halvah is? That's an OH HENRY dipped in cement!

Well, I was a hit. Danny took to me and he introduced me to his date, Phyllis Lightenton. It was my first personal confrontation with a beautiful Texas lady, and I couldn't take my eyes off her. I knew Danny liked her a lot and I didn't even think of attempting to see her on my own.

As the months passed, I became a favorite in Dallas, and every time I worked there I'd stay with Danny and his family. We became very fond of each other.

His romance with Phyllis eventually ended. He knew how I felt about her, so he gave me his blessings. And bless my soul, she was ecstatic when I called.

When a Texas person likes you, whether the Texan is male or female, they take your interests to heart, their home is yours, and it seems they just can't do enough for you. I was invited to her home to meet her family, which included a sister who looked just like her, and then Phyllis gradually showed me that Texas hospitality and romance were an unbelievable combination. We kept in close contact all through the months leading up to my summer at Pine Point, and I really fell in love with her, or whatever those feeling are. On my last trip to Dallas I invited her to Chicago to meet my folks. We traveled across the Midwest together, and I felt like I was on a honeymoon.

My folks loved her too. Even Pa took a liking to her because of her Texas accent. After Pine Point I was supposed to go back to Texas to work and be with her. Except that's not the way things turned out.

Just before the summer she called and said she was confused. She was involved with someone. She really wanted to be with me, but being apart, she simply met someone new. She wanted to keep in touch, she said, and cared a lot about me, and maybe when I came back to Texas things would change back to the way they used to be. I was heartbroken. I said I understood. Then I had to go to Pine Point, and now here's Mitzi.

With most of the other girls I've brought home, Ma has known that I was just having fun with them, that they'd stay a couple of days and be gone. Maybe the only difference with Phyllis was just how *much* fun and excitement we had. Anyway, Mitzi's different. She isn't the flashy type—she's very plain, simple, and Jewish. It's amazing how a mother knows. She's had the feeling after meeting Mitzi that Mitzi is going to be serious about me and that I'm going to be vulnerable to her.

In fact, a few days after I brought Mitzi home my ma approached her.

"Mitzi," she said in her thick Jewish accent, "can I talk to you? Come with me into the bathroom.

"I just want you to know that Sammy doesn't want to get married and I hope you're not getting too serious about him."

"Oh no, Mrs. Shore. I like Sammy a lot, but I don't want to get married either. I want to go back to college."

"That's fine, it's good to finish school first. . . . You know, Sammy's just crazy about the show business, and he has to travel, and for him to get serious with someone wouldn't be good I'm sure you understand."

Mitzi, as both Ma and Mitzi later reported to me, said she did understand.

Then one night about two-thirty Mitzi and I are sleeping in my room and the phone rings. I jump out of bed and run to stop it from ringing anymore and waking up my dad. My door is still open behind me as I grab the receiver.

The Warm-up

"Hello."

"Hello, Sammy?" A woman's voice, long distance.

"Yes, who's this?"

"It's Phyllis. I hope I didn't wake you up, but I just wanted to talk to you. It's been such a long time."

I'm holding the phone in my hand; I'm speechless—and petrified, realizing Mitzi is just in the other room. I whisper into the phone, "Hi, how are you, how've you been?"

"I really miss you, Sammy. I want to come to Chicago to be with you again. I realized after being away so long that I really love you."

I don't know what to say, so I whisper, "I miss you too, and I love you," which is exactly how I feel.

"When can I come see you, Sammy?"

"Maybe in the next couple of weeks," I say as low as possible. "I'll try and work something out. I'll call you tomorrow. I can't talk now, my mother and father are asleep and I don't want to wake them up."

"I love you, Sammy."

"I love you too."

As I hang up Mitzi comes to the doorway, crying.

"You love who?" she says. "I heard everything you said to that girl. Who was she?" I'm standing there speechless. "I thought you wanted to be with *me*," Mitzi cries. "And how do you think I feel sleeping in your bed every night and you're telling some girl on the phone you love her and want her to come here? Why are you doing this to me?"

I don't know how to say to her that I feel just awful but my heart isn't really for her. I want to be with Phyllis.

"I really love you, Mitzi," I say. "That was a girl I met in Texas almost a year ago. We're really good friends—in fact, before I knew you I brought her here. I love her as a friend. She had such a good time here with my mom and dad, she wanted to come back—really, Mitzi, you're the one I want to be with . . . she's not even Jewish . . ."

I'll say anything to stop her crying—it's worse than Ma. I know I'm committing myself now, I'm going down with the ship. I even manage to convince myself that I'm telling the truth, and she's satisfied. Mitzi was special, and I didn't want to lose her.

I never call Phyllis back.

WOMEN, RIGHT AND WRONGED

***

I decided that living in Vegas wasn't going to make it for me. I started thinking about going back to LA. What made the decision easier was Charlene, a beautiful twenty-one-year-old girl I'd met in the lounge of the Jockey Club. She wanted to move to LA too. So one night, not long after we'd met, I simply asked Charlene if she'd like to come to LA with me. "I'll get an apartment for us," I said, "and try to find you a job."

"Gee, Sammy," she said, "that sounds terrific."

Terrific. Instant relationship. I felt wonderful—a beautiful girl more than twenty years younger than me, maybe this would be the one.

I had my XKE in town—the same one I'd driven to the Elvis opening, only now it was falling apart, just like I was. I packed it up with all my stuff plus Charlene's and headed west. I found a beautiful apartment on Doheny, seventeen floors up, overlooking Sunset and most of Beverly Hills and Hollywood.

I stood on the balcony that first evening back, looking at the city. Charlene was in the other room unpacking our clothes. Through some trees I could vaguely make out the mansion where Mitzi and our two little boys were living, and where I used to live. Why did I want to move so close? Maybe I'd run into her, maybe the kids could just walk over to my apartment, maybe everything would revert to the way it used to be and she'd take me back. Yes, I knew it was crazy. Mitzi already had a young comedian living with her, a guy I'd first put on at The Comedy Store. Now he was sleeping in "my bed," in the house that I'd paid for.

It was a beautiful clear night. The lights on Sunset were so bright they seemed to pop. I could see Gazzari's across the street, and opposite that, Scandia, where The Comedy Store had been conceived. A line was starting to form at the Roxy nightclub-theater, underneath the neon-lighted rocking *R* of the Rainbow Room. Another line was crowding the sidewalk outside the Celebrity Club, the night spot run by Pat Collins, the "hip hypnotist." Next door was Turner's, the liquor store at the corner of Sunset and Doheny where you could always run into other entertainers and where I'd already made my first alcoholic purchase of the season. I followed the curve of the Strip up to the east and north, to Mirabelle's and all the other spots that were just rooftops among the bright showbiz billboards but that I knew intimately: Butterfield's, Art Laboe's, the Continental Hyatt House, Dean

107

Martin's restaurant Dino's, and The Comedy Store.

I realized I couldn't stand being secluded in Vegas but I also couldn't stand the thought of going down into all that action on the Strip when I had nothing going for me. How wonderful it was to stroll along Sunset when I'd just come back from working with the King and people would stop me. "Hey, Sammy, saw you with Elvis. You were great." They'd ask me for an autograph. Maybe now I could relive some of that past, get something back, like my confidence. People could see me with a beautiful young chick. "Hey, Sammy, that's some nice lady you got there." That would be my new fix.

But there was too much that needed fixing. I was desperate for Charlene to prove to me how young I still was, how wonderful I was, how successful I still could be. That first night she froze up on me when I wanted to make love; she even got out of bed and slept on the couch. One night soon afterward I came home and Charlene was nowhere to be found. Her clothes, her stereo, all her things were gone. There wasn't even a note.

Welcome back to LA.

It seems that when it comes to women I'm always hung up between the homey Jewish security of Ma and Mitzi and flashy, sexy excitement. I can't choose; I can't do either one right.

In the couple of years leading up to the Elvis opening I'm really on my way for the first time. I'm exploding. I open in front of Trini Lopez in Vegas and I'm a smash. I repeat the same thing a few weeks later at the Grove in LA in front of John Gary. I'm even getting TV offers, and I take a week guest-hosting with Della Reese on her own show.

I'm getting ready to do my first show with Della. I'm putting on my clothes and getting nervous, and there's a knock on the dressing room door. I'm thinking it's the stage manager, but the door opens and no stage manager ever looked like this.

It's Debbie. Oh my God.

A friend of mine introduced me to Debbie a few months ago, when he brought her as his date to one of my shows. She had knocked me out then, but there wasn't anything I could do about it. She was twenty-two years old—long blond hair, fantastic body—from Dallas, Texas. It was Phyllis all over again, except now I was much older.

It seems that all middle-aged Jewish men gravitate toward that Nordic shiksa-bombshell look. Sometimes it seems like I'm trying to set the pace for all of them. I'd managed to put Debbie out of my mind, but here she is again.

"Debbie, what are you doing here? I don't believe it's really you."

"I work here, Sammy. I work for the production company that does this show." She's positively twinkling at me. "When I heard you were going to be on the show, I got all excited."

Oh Jesus.

"I've really thought a lot about you," she says.

"Gee, Debbie "—I always say "gee" a lot around beautiful girls, I guess because they make me feel like I'm about thirteen years old— "I'm flabbergasted. How long have you been working here?"

"Just a few months—since I came here from Dallas. Wanted to get into some form of show business. I just love all the people. They're all so friendly and want to help me."

Sure they want to help you, honey, I'm saying to myself. They all want your pretty little body. I guess I'm no different.

I start to kid her about her accent. I'm always trying to be funny for a beautiful girl. Maybe then they can't see how scared I am. Laughter covers up everything.

"Howdy, ma'am! I'm foreman of the LBJ ranch—my friends call me Ringo Bird. . . . And this here's God's country. 'Course he's just renting it from us."

Hardly great stuff, but Debbie is really laughing. She tells me I'm adorable and wants to know if she can stand in the back and watch me tape the show.

"I'd love it, Debbie. I'll have the stage manager put you in a seat. I don't want you standing in the back, you're with me."

"You sure I won't be in your way? I know you're busy. I just want to see your act and then I've got to go."

Of course I'm such a generous guy, I tell her it's no problem. She suggests maybe we can go out for coffee after one of the shows this week. I tell her I think I can fit it in.

I feel like a little kid. I get so excited just looking at her. I still think that a beautiful girl with those all-American looks and that incredible figure can always fix it for me, can eliminate whatever unhappiness I'm having at home. The internal flutters and excitement and obsession brought on by a girl like Debbie can wipe out entire families.

109

The Warm-up

I'm always looking for that kind of girl—Miss Right! I've never once had any of these kinds of feelings with Mitzi. And the last time it's felt like this was with Phyllis.

I'm already married eleven years and have two kids. I'm always fantasizing that someday I'll just tell Mitzi it's over and I'll run away into the mountains with a beautiful blond Texan and live happily ever after. I keep thinking the thing that stops me is the money—how can I afford to get divorced when we own the duplex and there has to be support for the kids and since it's California, she'll get half of everything. I keep thinking that I'll think about getting free when I start to make it and I can afford it. But I've always been so guilty toward Mitzi that I let her control everything—the bank books, the checking account. It's not till years later that I realize money is the least of the reasons why I'm hanging on to Mitzi. Like I said in my act: Everything's in her name—the house, the car, the bank books. You know what's under my name? *Her* name.

I think, Debbie's going to be my savior. She'll take me away with her. She'll show me how to live. I've always thought that pretty people have no problems, if you're physically beautiful you've got it made. I feel I'm ugly, and now this beautiful girl is crazy about me! It's a miracle. She's perfect—until the insanity starts.

I start seeing her practically every day. I go pick her up at her office for lunch. I'm completely obsessed; all I think about day and night is Debbie and how I can sneak out of the house to see her. She's got absolute power over me and that's what I assume love is. How foolish I became.

When I finally get my big break with Elvis, one day Debbie takes the unprecedented step of calling me at my house. Lucky for me I pick up the phone.

"I want you to come over," Debbie says. "There's something I have to tell you."

Feeling apprehensive as I arrive, I open the apartment with my own key, and she's sitting on the couch looking very pensive. My stomach jumps with anxiety.

"Hi, Deb, what's up," I say like an idiot.

"Sammy," she says, "I don't know how to tell you this, but I've got to know where I stand. We've been seeing each other a year and a half and you keep telling me how much you love me, how much you want to be with me—"

"But I do love you," I break in. "I take you wherever I go—Vegas, Palm Springs—I see you practically every day, don't I?"

"That's just what I mean, Sammy. Why can't we be together *all* the time? I've devoted all my time and energy to this relationship and I've always been wherever you've wanted me to be, and when I couldn't be with you, because of Mitzi, I've understood, I've gone along with it. I played second fiddle to someone you don't even love. Isn't that true?"

"Yes, that's true. You've been really supportive no matter what, I can't deny that. But is there something wrong? I thought everything was going along just fine."

"Well, it isn't. Sammy, I've been waiting for you to make a move like you always told me you would—that someday we'd be together."

I'm acting stupid, only it isn't an act. I say, "But aren't we together? We've been together practically every day."

"I don't mean that kind of together. I want us to *live* together. I've made up my mind. You're going to have to tell Mitzi about us and end it with her. So at least I know where I'm at.

"I love you and I want to be with you," she goes on. "Am I asking too much?"

All I can do is stand there. It's like Mitzi and the phone call from Phyllis all over again. I need time to work this out—to work out of this.

"I told you I was going to tell her when the time was right. You know I've got to go back with Elvis in the next couple of weeks." I'm pleading. "It'd be too much for me to split now."

"Bullshit! I want to know now. I want you to go tell her tonight. And if you don't, I never want to see you again, and I mean that. I have to start planning my life. I don't want to keep chasing you all over and hiding in closets. I want to be a lady and I want to be introduced as your old lady, not just your 'friend' and 'secretary to your agent.' "

I know she means it. I've never seen her like this.

"Tonight, or never. We've talked enough. I'll wait for your call, or just drop by. I want to know one way or the other."

I head back up the street. I'm really screwed now. I can't go on without Debbie, I'm crazy about her. But how can I tell Mitzi? We've not only got two kids, there's now one more on the way.

111

The Warm-up

I don't get back to Debbie that night. I try calling her at her office the next day to explain that when I got home Mitzi was sick and throwing up and I had to help her, so how could I tell her, but Debbie doesn't answer my calls. I'm in panic. I run to her office; she won't see me. I come by the apartment that night; she doesn't show. The emptiness of the place, the void without her, makes me go crazy. I leave flowers in the apartment with an eloquent letter pleading with her just to let me explain.

The next night I go back to her apartment, knock on the door for twenty minutes—no answer! I just stand there crying; the pain is horrendous. It's happened again: I've had a chance to be with someone I love, but I just don't know how to get out. My mama's-boy need and my Jewish guilt will never allow me to leave Mitzi and the kids. All I can do is play around and make everybody miserable.

It takes me months to get over Debbie. She filled a neurotic need I had to be validated by a kewpie doll. In another few months my son Peter is born. He's gorgeous. Now I have three, while I wait for the day when I can get up enough balls to say to Mitzi: "Hey, look, the summer's over. It's been great, but I gotta split. See ya around."

Mitzi comes to Toledo with her whole family, and we're married by a rabbi in Kin Wa Low's. I'm unhappy and scared and when I say "I do," I know it's the end of my freedom. I've got to walk out there that night in front of her mother, older sister and brother-in-law, and older brother and sister-in-law, and try to be funny.

When summer approaches we go back to Pine Point. Our son Scotty is born in a small town nearby. He's beautiful, but the three of us are staying in a single room and it's driving me nuts. That's when I first discover the power of alcohol. I want something to take away the anxiety. I have my first Scotch one night before I walk out to do my show and it feels fantastic. I become completely relaxed and all anxiety leaves—until the next day. So at age twenty-four I'm on my way to becoming a steady daily drinker.

After the summer, I take Mitzi and Scotty back to Green Bay to be with her family. I get some out-of-town dates, but soon Mitzi insists that she and the baby join me. They come out on the plane to Cleveland, where I'm working the Skyway Lounge.

I hook up with a manager who helps us buy a house in Detroit, where I'm working. Another summer at Pine Point and then Mitzi

112

and Scotty come along on tour with all our stuff, even a TV set, packed in our station wagon. We go to Pittsburgh, Erie, Columbus, Dayton. Montreal and Toronto in January, with chains on the tires. We are like gypsies.

Mitzi's always in the audience watching me work. She's trying to help me with my act, although many times I resent her when she's right about my routines.

"That bit doesn't fit you, Sam, it's too jokey. You're not a joke-teller—stay with your characters." She has that natural, intuitive knowledge. Some nights she even goes to the rival club in town and writes down jokes she thinks I can use.

How can you repay someone like that, someone who's always there for you, helping and sharing and waiting hopefully for maybe one day when I'll turn to her and say, "I *love* you."

After a few years in Detroit, we move on to Miami, where I become a popular comedian on the Beach—not *too* popular, since I only rate thirty-five dollars a show. My break comes at the Americana Hotel, with J. P. Morgan and her brothers. On opening day I take Miltowns and drink and run around the Americana's beach trying to make the fear disappear from my gut.

I do okay and get stronger as the nights go by, but when Bullets Durgom, Jackie Gleason's manager, comes in to catch me, I'm not so good. I question myself insistently: When is it going to leave me? Why can't I just go out there and enjoy myself? Miami is where I start going into therapy.

Ten years in Miami and it's time for us to make a move. I go out to California on my own to see if it has anything to offer; I work the Playboy Club in Kansas City on the way out.

We settle in a nice duplex in Beverly Hills, since Mitzi wants the kids to go to a Beverly Hills school. I'm doing club dates around LA, San Bernardino—stag shows, anything, seventy-five dollars a show. Living upstairs is Jimmy Burns, a small-time show-business manager, and his family. Burns is pushy, with the guts of a raging bull, and his wife and kids drive us crazy with their noise. Mitzi's always complaining about it, but I can't even get up the nerve to mention it to Jimmy.

Then Jimmy gets me a job as the warm-up on Regis Philbin's TV show. I warm up the studio audience before the real show, at $139 a week. Here I am, fifteen years in show business, trying to make little old ladies laugh so that all my comedian friends can come out and appear on the tube.

Mitzi mounts a crusade against the noise upstairs. I've got to stand up to Jimmy. It's incredibly hard for me to get up the nerve. I don't want him to think I'm not a nice guy and I'm not grateful. On top of the fear, there's my resentment at Mitzi for "making" me face him.

The night Mitzi tells me I've *got* to do it, I take a full glass of Scotch, straight. Fear still comes over me as I go up the front stairway.

"Hi, Jimmy, how's it been going?"

"Just fantastic," he says. "Got a new girl singer. Hey, there's something I was going to tell you. I got you a shot at *The Steve Allen Show* next week! Finish your warm-up for Regis, then run down the street to ABC and do Steve."

Now my anxiety is a triple whammy. Fear of Jimmy, fear of Mitzi, fear of *The Steve Allen Show*. I just stare at Jimmy for a moment.

"That's great, Jimmy, what a break for me."

I just can't mention what I came up for.

I head back downstairs, give Mitzi the good news. She's happy. But then back to the subject: "Uh, did you tell him about all the noise with his kids?"

No, followed by excuses.

She turns, walks into the bedroom, slams the door. It's such a small thing, this vendetta she has about the noise, but it's also everything— her frustration, my failures.

Doing *The Steve Allen Show*, I know that if Steve likes me I'll be able to do more of his shows. I go in there obsessed with the future: maybe I'll become a regular, maybe I'll be a hit, maybe I'll die.

Out there on camera I feel like I'm bombing. It's hard for me to get the words out; my mouth is dry, I'm sweating.

"Thank you, Sammy." Steve Allen has a look on his face like he's wondering what the hell *that* was all about.

I take a few hours' worth of detours in bars on the way home. Finally, when I get home and Mitzi asks how it went, I just walk past her, sit down on the couch, and cry. She sits down beside me, reassures me that it might not be so bad when it's aired, tries to pick me up. It never occurs to me what a barrel of fun I am for her.

In fact when the show is broadcast, it isn't so bad. It just isn't so good.

114

WOMEN, RIGHT AND WRONGED

Then one night, having tried cheapo psychotherapy with an intern from Cedars Sinai Hospital, I meet Dr. Wiggins. I'm working a little club in the Fairfax area of LA, which is predominantly Jewish. The club used to be the spot for new talent like the young Buddy Hackett and Joey Bishop. But now the business is mainly a few wandering Jews in search of a ginger ale. I'm sweating my ass off hoping somebody will notice me and praying my check won't bounce at the end of the week.

There was never any question of quitting the business. My ambition was fixed—to become a nightclub comedy star. I didn't want to be like my brothers or my father. I had that insatiable thirst to make people laugh, and through all the years of torment, never once did I doubt my innate ability to be funny. And even then I knew that the day I stop is the day I die.

This night I come off the stage and head, as always, for the bar. Sitting nearby is a very distinguished-looking black man, about thirty-five, handsome, tailored black mohair suit, white shirt, gray striped tie.

"Very funny show, Mr. Shore. You're very clever. Bright and inventive. It's nice to see a comedian who can do so many things and not just tell one-liners. Very refreshing to see."

He introduces himself as Dr. Timothy Wiggins. "It's an honor," he says, "to meet such a talented man."

I'm amazed at his praise; I tell him how appreciative I am. "What kind of doctor are you?"

"I'm a psychiatrist."

My brain lights up. What a unique man. A black psychiatrist. I tell him I'm in therapy and ask if he knows my intern. No, he doesn't. Well, I don't like that guy anyway.

It feels so good talking with him, makes me feel very comfortable. In a few minutes I'm getting into my problems, my fears, my opening nights. I walk with him to his car. It seems like I've covered more ground in two hours with Dr. Wiggins than in three months with the intern.

As he's getting into his car, I tell him I want to be his patient. "I feel you know where I'm coming from."

"Yes I do, Sammy. It's a shame such a talented man as you has to put up with those problems. I'm sure in time I can free you of at least some of your opening-night fears."

The Warm-up

That's all he has to say. I'm hooked. God has sent me a Messiah—and a black one yet!

I tell my doctor I'm quitting; he thinks it's a mistake, that we're just starting to make headway and I need a lot more therapy.

I'm too impatient. I want it fixed *now*. I'm obsessed with Dr. Wiggins. He's the one. In the ensuing months we spend a lot of time together. He's not just my psychiatrist, he's my buddy. After a session, we go out for coffee or to a bar. I love it—all that free therapy. What a bargain! He comes to some of my shows and it's amazing, I feel very relaxed just knowing he's there.

Soon I get my key break, the one that gets me to Vegas. I'm working the LA Playboy Club and the entertainment director of Harrah's in Reno notices me. That gets me on the bill with Trini Lopez at Harrah's. It's no accident—I've known the guy was going to be there, and the only thing that gets me through is seeing Dr. Wiggins three times that week. But it works, and I'm on my way; the team of Shore and Wiggins is headed for Reno and then Vegas.

I've replaced Mitzi with Tim. My career's on the upswing, the witch doctor is working his magic, and Mitzi and I are growing very distant.

I can see it now, as if I'd actually been there. The year is 1905 and a freighter, maybe Russian but more likely Greek, Italian, or French, is making its way through the Atlantic on the long journey to America. On board are many Russians and Eastern European people who have left their homelands for what they hope will be a better life. Many of them already have relatives in the United States.

One of those on board is Hyman Schinder, a nineteen-year-old from the Romanian side of the Russian-Romanian border. He's thin, bespectacled, small, with blond wavy hair, and he's really very handsome. When he gets to New York, the immigration officials will "help" him change his name from Schinder to Shore.

He's been an orphan for most of his years, shuttled from family to family until there was nobody left who wanted him and he was encouraged to look up a certain cousin who lives in a place called Illinois.

Hardly anyone aboard ship would speak freely. They were all treated like cattle and they were afraid.

Also on board are Sonja and Lena Nestrofsky, two sisters from Kiev, Russia. They are from a well-to-do family of a widely known Russian judge, known largely because it is rare for a Jew to hold an official position of importance. Sonja is twenty-five, Lena is fifteen. They are both very buxom and plain-looking. They've had a wonderful life, with much caring and loving paid to them, but with the recent death of their father, the family has become afraid for the future of young Jews in the turbulent land of the czar. They, too, are being sent to find relatives in America.

One day during the voyage a storm is brewing and the ocean is getting rough. The people who are standing on deck go back down to their quarters, which are little more than a few filthy bilges. Hyman trips and falls on the dilapidated stairs. Sonja and Lena are coming down behind him and help him up. They start to talk.

Hyman is shy, Sonja is stern and straightforward, and Lena hardly ever says a word. Sonja gets the idea that Hyman would make a good match for her sister. Some marriages were made in heaven; my parents' was made in steerage. Hyman marries Lena within a few weeks after they arrive in America.

The way I think about it now, what was Hyman to do? He was lonely. And here were these two women fussing over him. It occurs to me, in the light of my own experience with marriage, that maybe Hyman really didn't like her that much. Maybe that's why he was always so pissed at her—maybe he didn't want to be there. What was he going to say—"Give me a few weeks to think about it"? And once he got into the marriage, what could he do then? Go into therapy? What? Therapy was a two-by-four upside the head. And divorce—what was that?

Maybe it was just like with me and Mitzi. My mother dedicated her life to Hyman, to prove to him that she was worth something, just as Mitzi did for me. And the irony is that in both cases the women only became themselves after they were rid of their husbands. For her ten remaining years after my father's death, Ma became a total person. She delighted in wearing a mink stole, jewelry, and lipstick, had her hair and nails done regularly, and most striking of all, became quite a conversationalist and the center of attention wherever she went. She blossomed, just as Mitzi would when she got away from me.

After Pa's death, I took my mother on the road with Mitzi and me to all the clubs around the country. She really enjoyed herself. It seemed to me she was kind of relieved that Pa was gone. Now she could stand up and be counted.

The Warm-up

Everyone fussed over her. The club owners couldn't do enough for Lena. Any place she walked into, her hands were always reaching out to touch, to feel, to share the love that she was in such dire need of receiving. She would always tell me how they all loved her, and they usually did.

Then it's 1968 and we're living in LA and so is Ma. We take her to the hospital because she's complaining of chest pains. Actually, Mitzi has to take her because I've got an interview in Hollywood. That's always the way with me—reluctant to spend time with my family or Ma because I'm afraid I'll miss out on something—an opportunity, a phone call.

Later, the doctor says she has an enlarged heart but that with rest and medication she should be okay. On her ninth day in the hospital, I'm trying to feed her and she keeps spitting the food out of her mouth.

"You got to eat, Ma, you need your strength."

"I don't want to eat anymore," she says. "I got to go. Pa is calling me. I talked to him last night and he said he's waiting for me and what's taking me so long?"

"Oh, Ma, you're not going to see Pa yet, you've got plenty of time to visit him. And anyways, he'll probably want you to bring him a sandwich." I'm trying to cheer her up, but she just stares at me. She does look like she wants to die, like there's nothing keeping her here any longer. But I can't believe it, even though she's eighty-three years old.

I'm going to visit her the next morning, but I decide I've got to read a play instead. A movie producer wants me to read it and think about starring in it. I'm nervous that if I don't read it right away, I'll lose a chance. I can go to see Ma in the afternoon.

Except the hospital calls about ten-thirty that morning, a Sunday, to tell me she's just passed away. I don't believe it—she really was serious about Pa waiting—and I'm standing with a phone in one hand and this goddamn play in the other.

"What happened, can't you save her?" I'm screaming into the phone. "Try again, don't let her go—please try!"

They tell me they tried everything and she didn't respond, that she died peacefully, even with a smile.

I cry and hold on to Mitzi. "She's gone," I tell her, "and I wasn't even there with her."

I didn't take the chance I had to say good-bye. And now, thirteen years later, it still feels like part of me has never really been able to let her go.

The Horn was a little neighborhood club in Santa Monica where new acts showcased and veteran acts broke in new material before appearing on TV engagements or going on tour. I always used it before going into any important room, especially one in Nevada.

Months after my "break-up" with Charlene, late of the Jockey Club, I was getting ready for another try at Vegas. I was to open for Connie Stevens in two weeks at the Flamingo. It was a chilly December weeknight and there weren't many people in the club, mostly middle-aged folks who'd come by to catch the local talent. I was excited, happy, and anxious as hell to be going back to Vegas after it looked like I might be washed up for good.

Everybody knew me at The Horn. Jack, the bartender, automatically poured me a J&B on the rocks when I came in the door. He knew how nervous I was from the way I was pacing. I always paced before going on, but now I was galloping. I even bumped into Kathy, one of the waitresses, and almost knocked over a drink on her tray.

I told her I was sorry, she asked me if I was okay. "A little nervous," I said. And I told her about the Connie Stevens job.

"I'm sorry I interrupted your thinking," she said. Sweet girl; she actually meant it.

"You didn't interrupt my thinking. I don't believe in thinking. If God had meant for comics to think, why did He give us agents?"

Kathy laughed, and that made me feel good.

"That's in my new routine," I told her. "Think it's too inside?"

"I'm sure it's funny. Sammy, you're funny without trying. You've always been one of my favorites."

I felt confidence rush through me. All I needed was a pretty girl telling me I was funny and that was adrenaline, security, hope. It was enough to let me go out there.

I always came on to the waitresses at clubs I worked before I hit the stage. It was like my own warm-up; if I could make the waitresses laugh with some of my lines, then I knew they were funny, because the waitresses see every comic around and quickly become jaded.

As the singer on the stage started into her last song, I had Jack pour me another J&B. I loved that shit. Getting the okay from the girl and the booze was all I needed, except I needed it all the time.

119

The Warm-up

I was sipping my drink and noticing a middle-aged to elderly lady, heavyset, in a cheaply tailored black dress with a floral print, as she made her way into the club. She looked odd, like she didn't belong here, but I didn't pay much attention. I kept on with my drink as the singer wound up her act.

I stepped away from the bar toward the stage. I heard a lady behind me say, "Is there a Samuel Shore working here?" I glanced back; it was the odd lady. I stayed where I was, near the stage. I heard Jack laughing. "Samuel Shore? If you mean Sammy, that's him over there."

I felt a tap on my shoulder and turned around to face the lady.

"Are you Samuel Shore?" She was extremely polite.

"I do remember that on my birth certificate, last time I saw it. Samuel, as you know, was one of the closest to God, so if you've come to ask Samuel for a loan, God will punish you.

"Just kidding, having a little fun," I added, since she didn't seem to appreciate the humor. "I'm a comedian, I have to go on here in a second."

"I know, Mr. Shore." She took out a snapshot and showed me a picture of myself. "Is this your picture?"

"Yes," I said, "maybe you've seen it on the cover of *Watchtower.*"

Not a smile. Christ, this lady was all business.

She quickly took a sealed white document out of her purse and put it in my hands. "You are served," she said.

"I'm what?" I was confused.

"I'm the process server for the attorneys of Cohen and Kravitz, your wife's lawyers. Your wife has filed for divorce." She gave a smug little smile. "Have a good show," she said, and then she bustled toward the door like a good little Girl Scout who had done her duty.

My eyes started to tear. Of course I had known our marriage was a shambles, but there was something about the finality, the secrecy, and the timing that left me in shock.

I looked down at the document and all I could see was

SUPERIOR COURT OF CALIFORNIA
County of Los Angeles
Petitioner—Mitzi Shore
Respondent—Samuel Shore

The typed letters started to waver and wiggle because of the tears.

"And now, ladies and gentlemen—" the emcee was saying—

My head was beginning to spin. I thought, It's not like her to do this.

"—a very funny guy who's appeared with Elvis, Tom Jones, and next week opens with Connie Stevens at the Flamingo Hotel in Las Vegas, let's welcome one of our favorites here at The Horn, Sammy Shore!"

I stepped up onto the stage. I couldn't take the document out of my hand. I took the mike off the stand and just looked out. Already the audience knew that something was off.

"Good evening," I said. My voice was weak. "Maybe you've seen my picture on the cover of *Watchtower*."

Scattered laughs—two, I think.

All I could see before me was Mitzi's face saying to me, I don't care about you anymore, Sammy, take your jokes and shove them. The same thing I knew my mother wanted to say to my pa about the store.

I had come full circle from that night at Kin Wa Low's. Once again, Mitzi got through to me just before the show.

5

NOT MINDING THE STORE

I went to Vegas to work the Flamingo with Connie Stevens and I was doing only fair. I got along well with Connie, and I improved overall as the two weeks of the show went on, but I was drinking more and more heavily and my timing was affected. I could never have admitted it, but I was losing control of myself. The impending divorce had added one straw too many to my load of insanity.

One night toward the end of the engagement I did my second show of the night, came back down to my dressing room, and started my third round of drinking for the night. I was by myself, as I often was, pouring one Scotch after another. Connie was onstage. My head was spinning, I wanted to do something crazy.

So I took off all my clothes, ran upstairs, and streaked across the stage in front of Connie. The whole place went wild. The streaking craze had just started, and no one had done it in Vegas. Within hours, word of my "achievement" shot through the town. The next day many newspapers in the country carried the story, and when I returned to LA I found that my picture, taken from a discreet angle, had been on the front page of *The Los Angeles Times*.

I was the talk of the town, but not because of my comedy. The Flamingo Hilton was upset about the incident, and Baron Hilton warned me that if I ever did that again, I'd never work in another Hilton.

Most people, including Connie, thought the stunt was wonderful, but in the final analysis none of it mattered. I was still going under, with or without publicity. I had no prospects for any shows after the Flamingo, and I was beginning to get the feeling I might be dropped by my agents, William Morris. I was putting together a reputation as a real fuck-up. I was beginning to think more and more about the old days in Chicago, sometimes wanting to go back and change the past so I never would have gone into this business.

Major is my dad's helper; he's been in the family ever since Dad's had the store. He's six feet tall, built very solid, black; to me, he looks a lot like Joe Louis. There's something wrong, some tragedy that must have happened in his life, but I never really find out what. Major's just Major, a mystery. Might have been a prizefighter who got hurt emotionally, or maybe he was in the army—I don't know. There's got to be some reason why he's content to live here with us and put up with Pa's meanness. Pa even has him sleep in the basement, next to the boiler, won't give him a room upstairs, yet Major is so dedicated he'd kill for Ma and Pa and especially for me. Poor Major; when it rains and the basement floods, he's floating around in there with all the furniture, like Noah and his ark, only all the animals are rats and cats. And after the rain, Pa has Major take the wet furniture out to the sidewalk to dry. When the stuff cracks Pa puts up a sign: ANTIQUE FURNITURE SALE.

Finally, after Ma and I have pleaded for years and Major comes down with pneumonia, Pa gives him a room upstairs, with the celebrities.

A few days after my after-school trumpet debut I'm bringing some lemonade to Major in the hallway, where he's replacing burned-out light bulbs.

He says while he's looking up at the ceiling from a ladder, "Hey, by the way, you were really good the other day. You play a nice trumpet."

This gets me all confused because I've been feeling like I never want to see or touch a trumpet again. "Pa thought I stunk."

"Now, boy," Major says, "you know he was only kidding you. You play pretty good, and you know I wouldn't lie to you. I think you got real talent. Just stick with it. All you need's a little more soul."

The Warm-up

"Soul?"

Major gleams down at me from his ladder, then goes back to working with another bulb. "My boy, where have you been all your life? Music is all soul, it's what comes from inside of you. You got to have it to begin with, nobody's gonna teach it to you." He looks at me. "Don't worry—you got it. I'm gonna help you develop it!"

He starts down off the ladder, clapping in a very leisurely way, and then he goes into singing "When the Saints Go Marching In," slowly at first. I start clapping and following him down the hallway. He stops at his room, which I've never seen, opens the door, and says, "Welcome to the French Quarter."

The walls are covered with prints of New Orleans, old pictures of musicians, can-can girls. I figure this must be what a café looks like in New Orleans. I'm overwhelmed.

Major puts his arm on my shoulder. "You ain't seen nothin' yet!" He reaches under his bed and takes out a battered trumpet case, unlatches it, and inside, glimmering like a jewel, is a beautiful old horn. Major takes it out with great care.

"This was left to me by my daddy—ain't she a beauty. He was one of the best jazz men ever to come out of New Orleans. He played with the best of them."

He hands the trumpet to me. "Now play your 'Tisket A Tasket.' "

His horn feels heavier than mine and somehow the brass is softer, like satin, but when I play, it doesn't sound much different than it did the other day.

When I finish I expect Major to laugh at me or tell me to forget about it. But he says, "Not bad, Sammy, not bad. You just got to put your back into it, you just got to let your soul kinda seep through. It'll happen for you, just wait and see."

Then he takes the trumpet and blows a long, wailing note, and slips into "Basin Street Blues." I'm hypnotized, captured from head to foot. I feel like I'm in another world of music and dancing and fun. I know then that I really want to learn how to play. I want music and laughter in my life.

Every day after that I sit in class and stare off into space, daydreaming about someday playing my trumpet onstage and maybe even making people laugh, too. My teacher confronts me about my lack of interest in assignments and my failure to do homework. I like her a lot, but I'm just not interested in school anymore. My new nickname is Satch, and I even have it painted on the back of the truck I drive to make deliveries for Pa.

I've felt before that I want to go into show business, but now I know I can't give up. It's Major who gives me the feeling that I'll never stop.

The alcoholic depths around the time I streaked had me not only reminiscing about my roots in show business—Major, my first club dates, my early travels—but also wallowing in nostalgia. I couldn't help wishing for a time when life was simple and fun, and when I had a real friend.

"What the hell are you doin' here, black boy?"

It's 1944 and Rudy and I have decided to join the navy together, and we're even hoping we can be stationed together. But the chief petty officer at our induction is trying to wreck things from the start.

"I said, what are you doin' here?"

"Standing in my underwear," Rudy said.

"What are you, a comedian?"

"No, sir, but my friend Sammy here is, sir."

I'm mute. I'm shivering. Me being a Jew and Rudy being half black, it looks like we're in deep trouble.

"There's nothing like a smart-ass nigger," the petty officer says. He looks like Charles Bronson after a train wreck. His service stripes go all the way down his arm—twenty years in the navy. The war's almost over, but he's acting like we started it.

He looks Rudy directly in the eye. "Don't you know we ain't enlisting any niggers at this induction? All of 'em are down the hall. You can't miss 'em, they're doing the windows." He laughs and snorts at the same time. "See, I'm the comedian here, and *that's* funny. Now get your ass moving, boy!"

"Excuse me, sir," I say, surprised I have a voice. "Excuse me, but Rudy's not black."

"Who the hell are you, shorty?"

"I'm his friend, sir. We grew up together, went to the same school. He's not black, sir, he's part Indian."

"Just what kind of an asshole do you think I am?"

It comes out before I can stop it: "I'm not sure, sir."

"So you *are* the comedian!"

125

"I'm sorry, sir. I didn't mean anything by it."

But he has me bend over anyway, kicks me in the ass, and knocks me to the floor.

I want so badly for Rudy to be stationed with me; I'm scared to be alone. But it looks like if you're black you go with the blacks, and whites go with the whites. Rudy looks white except his features are those of a black man, including kinky black hair. His skin is tan.

"I knew it," this idiot goes on. "A bunch of niggers and Jews. What's the navy comin' to, anyways."

Rudy steps forward. Nothing ever bothers him, he's fearless. "It's true, sir. I'm part Indian."

"Yeah, I'm part Santa Claus, now get your black ass down the hall before I kick it there."

Just then a young ensign wanders in, looking for the source of the commotion. Wants to know what's going on.

"I'm sorry, sir," the petty officer says, "but we've been having a little disagreement with this colored boy, sir."

"What colored boy, Chief?"

"This ni—this colored boy, sir," as he points to Rudy.

The ensign approaches Rudy. "He doesn't look colored to me."

"Well, sir, you know I'm from Georgia. I know a colored boy when I see one, I was brought up and raised with 'em." He smiles.

The ensign looks straight into Rudy's face. "Are you colored, son?"

"No, sir, I'm part Indian. My father is a full-blooded Cherokee in fact, sir. If you want to look it up in the history books, my great grandfather fought side by side with Geronimo against General Custer."

Luckily the ensign doesn't know any more about Indians than Rudy does. "That sounds very interesting, young man. You know, if you are colored, you're going to have to join a colored platoon—those are the rules of the navy."

"I understand, sir."

"But if you can bring your father down here today and he is who you say he is and he can sign for you and show us he's Indian, we would foresee no problem. Then you can be sworn in with your friend here."

As soon as the ensign leaves and we start to go out, the petty officer reverts to form. "Hey, Geronimo," he bellows. "If that ain't your real redface father here today, I'm gonna shave every hair off your head and all your other hairs, if you have any."

Out on the steps of the induction center, I grab Rudy. "Holy fuck, Rudy, what're we gonna do? You're part Indian like I'm Mongolian. Your father is black as coal."

"Keep cool, Satchmo. You want us to go through boot camp together, don't you?"

"You know I do—"

"Then have faith in me, man. There's got to be some wanderin' Indian somewhere in Chicago lookin' to make a few bucks."

"You mean you're gonna find an Indian in six hours?"

"No—*we're* gonna find one," Rudy says. "And for an hour or however long it takes, he's gonna be Charley Blackfoot Reeves, my father."

So we go up and down the streets looking and asking until it occurs to me our best bet is Newberry Park. That's where the drunks and derelicts hang out. In fact, one of my pa's favorite forms of entertainment has always been to go to the park in his truck, tell a few drunks that if they want some work they should jump in, drive them past his store and then past the corner of Oak and Wells, where Phil would be waiting to turn the fire plug on them. Pretty sick. But now I've got something else in mind, and Rudy knows what I'm thinking the minute I mention the place.

We run up Oak Street and we're in the park. On any given day or evening, so-called communists are standing on their wooden boxes preaching what's wrong with America. It's also a good meeting place for The Salvation Army in its search for converts.

"Hold it, Rudy."

I'm thinking I see our man Geronimo. He's propped up against a tree, holding on to a bottle in a paper bag. He looks dark from here. Maybe it's just dirt. I point him out.

"He's no Indian, he's a bum!" Rudy says.

I point out that we don't have much time left.

"Maybe we can have your dad run him through the fire hose," Rudy laughs. But as we get closer, he does look dark-skinned.

"Hi," I say. "How'd you like to make five dollars?"

His eyes flare up a little. "Sure. What do I have to do?" He's got some sort of accent.

"Are you an Indian?" Rudy says.

"What, are you crazy or something—an Indian? I'm Greek!"

127

He seems pretty sharp even if he does look like a mess. "You're dark for a Greek," I say.

"I'm a dark Greek."

"Well, all you have to do is pretend you're an Indian."

"That's it?"

I point to Rudy. "You also have to pretend you're his father."

"That'll run you another five. He don't look like an Indian."

We agree to his terms, go with him to Rudy's to pick up his Dad's Social Security card and anything else that doesn't list his race, and walk him down to the center. As we enter, I wish we had some Indian feathers we could have put on the guy.

The minute we walk in, the wino takes charge. He goes up to the petty officer and the ensign and says, "I've come to discuss my boy."

Both men are amazed. The petty officer is also pissed. "What's your name," he says, "Tonto?"

"No." This is said with great calm and dignity, like the wino is quietly offended. "My name is Charley Blackfoot Reeves. I'm a full-blooded Cherokee Indian and my great-grandfather was Geronimo, who attacked General Custer."

Then, to Rudy's and my astonishment, the wino breaks into a mysterious chant, shuffling his feet in a pseudo-Indian dance. Not a war dance with shrieks and yells, but a subtle performance. Charley Blackfoot Reeves seems to be far away, reliving his primitive heritage. The sounds he makes seem mystical, the movements graceful and small, like the complete dance is going on in his head and he's just reacting to it with his feet. It's intimidating.

"Let me make a . . . uh—" he seems to be groping for the words, "—let me swear and make an oath about my boy." He looks at Rudy. "He's only half Cherokee, but if he wants to serve in the navy, let me help him."

The ensign tells the petty officer he doesn't want to hear "any more of this darky talk," Rudy and I get sworn in together, and soon we're on a train for six weeks of boot camp at the Great Lakes Naval Training Center.

On August 27, 1974, at eight-thirty in the morning, I was sitting at a table with my attorney, Paul Caruso, facing the judge's chair in a room of the Los Angeles superior court. I kept looking around for Mitzi, but she hadn't come in yet. I felt nothing but a kind of nauseous dread. I knew that Mitzi had switched lawyers four or five times in preparation for the divorce and had finally come up with Marvin Mitchelson, one of the most expensive attorneys in town. Mitchelson handled many of the movie stars' divorces and later would become nationally famous by bringing Michelle Triola Marvin's "palimony" suit against Lee Marvin. Mitzi knew her stuff and went for the best. For my part, I was just lucky to have picked a great attorney whom I happened to know through the Vikings Men's Club at Scandia.

I'd told Paul I couldn't understand why she kept switching lawyers, that we really didn't have that much property to divide. Paul's feeling was that Mitzi wanted The Comedy Store and would do anything to get it. I was befuddled. This did not sound like the woman I had married.

"Don't worry about it, Sammy," Paul had said. "She can't take your business away from you. No judge is going to award a husband's business to his wife."

But I was already thinking of surrendering the Store, though I hadn't mentioned it to Paul. A germ had been working its way through my brain, a germ planted long ago, in effect, by my pa: maybe if I gave up the Store, I could save some cash.

Mitzi came in with Mitchelson and was dressed like she never was when we were together: a scarf around her neck, lots of beads—sporty, breezy, and businesslike all at once. She passed by me in the aisle and looked at me like I was the enemy, like this was what she'd been waiting for through all the unhappy years when she'd never been able to confront me with what she was really feeling.

She sat a few yards away from me, all the while writing on a legal pad and turning to Mitchelson and whispering in his ear. If I'd had a piece of paper with me, I wouldn't have known what to write on it, except maybe HELP. But Mitzi was always prepared. In our family she was chairman of the board. I couldn't even add up my checkbook; all I did was grab a microphone and act funny and send home the money. Maybe I kept fifty dollars in my pocket to spend. God forbid I would keep over a hundred dollars. "Why," she would say, "do you need to carry that much with you?" I always felt guilty if I kept too much; I allowed her to keep complete control. As if somehow that would make up for the fact that I didn't love her and wasn't faithful.

The proceedings began, and it wasn't long before the subject of The Comedy Store began. "Your honor," Paul said, "as you know Mr. Shore is already paying eleven hundred dollars for child support

129

while Mrs. Shore is managing The Comedy Store and earning an income from it.''

Mitchelson objected. He had records to prove, he said, that the Store was operating at a loss.

"Paul," I said, "they're lying."

"Well, you know the nightclub business. You can hide a lot of money. And her attorney wouldn't lie under oath. He's got proof."

I panicked. Mitzi was going to make me fight for The Comedy Store. I got Paul to ask for a recess.

In our fifteen-minute break Paul reminded me the Store was mine and would never be awarded to Mitzi if I didn't want it to be. But all I could think about was lowering my child support. I was thinking exactly like my dad. I was holding on to cash money; I didn't want to spend any more than I had to. In keeping The Comedy Store, I not only faced higher alimony, but also the risk that it might not remain a successful business. I had a deep dread of risking money, no matter what Paul was saying about how I had created something important that could grow in the future. I told Paul I was going to give it up.

He told me the truth: I was being penny wise and pound foolish.

Mitchelson and Mitzi agreed to the arrangement I suggested, except they added, and I accepted, a condition: that I could never open another nightclub in the Los Angeles area and could never again use the name The Comedy Store. Upon securing this agreement, Mitzi hugged and kissed Mitchelson.

Mitzi Shore went on from that courtroom to build a comedy empire. To date she has four Comedy Stores—one in San Diego, three in LA.

What was so bizarre about the entire Comedy Store situation was that even after all the dust had settled, she still in actuality thought that the judge in court, over the divorce, awarded her The Comedy Store.

I gave it to her.

And now the phenomenon that she and I began has become nationwide, and clubs all around the country have copied the Store's formula; you can find a showcase-type comedy club in almost every important North American city. It was an idea whose time had come, and by the time I saw what was happening, the opportunity was gone.

I became the butt of many a joke around town—the guy who gave away The Comedy Store. Who in their right mind gives away a successful business? Everywhere I went people would say, "How come you don't own The Comedy Store anymore? We went by there the other night and they told us you were no longer involved. What happened?"

I just wanted to run away. I felt like I had nothing left. Then a few weeks later I got the call from Freddie Moch, my agent at William Morris. My contract had expired and they didn't want to renew it. I went back to work at The Horn, not to get ready for anything, but just to work. I wasn't even doing well there. I was like someone who had been defeated in a war, except I hadn't even really faced up to the action.

That was not a new feeling for me.

The six weeks in boot camp are dreadful. I just want to go home. Rudy and I and the platoon are getting ready to be shipped out to our camp and then our final destination on some ship heading overseas. The war has already ended, but still I'm in a state of constant panic. I just can't do it; I just can't see myself being shipped overseas.

A few days before we're supposed to go, Rudy and I are playing basketball and I fall and hurt my knee. A blessing. They examine the knee and find a torn ligament. I go to a recuperating hospital in Colorado while the platoon goes overseas. I'm really sad about splitting up with Rudy, but I'm also too scared to go anywhere.

A few weeks later things are getting sticky.

"There's nothing wrong with your knee anymore," Dr. Bloomfield says. He's the hospital shrink. "The orthopedic doctors have all examined it, there's nothing structurally wrong. Whatever problem you had before, it's healed. But you continually complain about how much it still hurts you. That's why they've sent you to me. I want you to be honest with me and tell me what's really going on."

"I'm not lying, doctor," I lie. "It pains me a lot. Sometimes I can hardly stand on it."

He doesn't buy it, says he's going to recommend a medical discharge. "I honestly believe," he says, "that you're a troubled young man and have some emotional disorders that need examining. We don't have the time to delve into your type of problem under these conditions."

I feel ashamed and awful. I know there's nothing wrong physically, that it's something deeper. I'm given a Section 8—a medical discharge of a psychiatric nature. It's honorable yet demeaning.

I'm ecstatic to be going home, but there's tremendous guilt about my knee. I don't feel clean inside, and the feeling seems to stay and even grow as the days and weeks go by. I'm worried about what my family will say and what I'll tell them.

The cab stops in front of 936 North Wells. The cabbie helps me step out, as I'm still walking with my cane. I'm all decked out in my sailor uniform—duffel bag at my side—knee still bandaged inside my left pant leg, bulging.

I open the door and see my dad and mom in the back, moving some linoleums. "Pa, Ma!"

They both drop the linoleum and dash toward me, my mom shouting, "Oy! Semelah's home from the war, I don't believe my eyes!" which are starting to tear as she grabs me.

"What happened to your leg?" she says, almost in panic. She reaches down to touch it. My father doesn't know what to do or say. I know he wants to grab and hug me. Instead, he gets me a chair and helps me sit down.

By their standards I'm wounded, some kind of hero. Wounded? Hero? The war's been over for months! I explain that I hurt my knee in training.

I know that their son is not a hero, but a fake.

One night after my divorces from Mitzi and William Morris, I was sitting in The Horn after my set and talking with Ray, a comedian who worked at The Horn with his wife. He knew I was having a rough time and he was trying to cheer me up.

"Sammy, you were real funny tonight. That was a nice set you did."

I thanked him and told him things seemed to be getting a little better.

"Well," Ray said, "what you need in your life right now is a nice girl."

"That'd be great, but I wouldn't know a good one if I saw one. I can't seem to meet someone who sticks."

"Snap out of it, Sammy. Have I got a girl for you."

I rang the bell to her apartment. I was very apprehensive. Ray had given me her number at The Horn, and here I was just an hour later with a date. The way Ray had described her, she was an impossible combination: beautiful, with a gorgeous body, twenty-five years old, and a naturally funny lady. Also, the way she'd responded so quickly on the phone seemed unbelievable. "You sound cute," she'd said. "You have a sexy voice." Oh Jesus.

She opened the door and *voluptuous* immediately got a new definition. She was a flaming redhead with incredible boobs accentuated by her tight-fitting open shirt that was barely buttoned, and high heels.

We introduced ourselves at the door, and then she—her name was Mercedes—mentioned that Ray had told her I worked in Vegas and was back in town to work on new material. And she mentioned Elvis.

"Yeah," I said. "I worked with him for a few years, but I just decided I wanted to go out and do my own thing. They all came to see Elvis, y'know, and I was becoming just a warm-up for him. I needed to get my own identity."

"I understand, Sammy," she said. "I think you did the right thing. I love someone that's his own man."

I knew I was being totally dishonest, but at that point in my life I'd say anything that sounded good, especially to a beautiful girl with a figure that would put most Vegas show girls to shame. From the moment Ray had started talking her up to me, I'd felt hope and had started thinking maybe this is the one. Just the fantasy of someone waiting for me, as I'd driven over to her place, had started to fix my pain.

"C'mon in, Sammy," she said, "and stop staring at my tits. On the other side of these bazooms is a nice person."

"I'm not just staring at them," I said. "I'm staring at you, you're beautiful."

She thanked me and got me a Scotch and water. She sat down next to me and my heart started to pound.

It was simple: I wanted her so badly, and even more so as the evening went on. She was very funny and made me laugh. I still couldn't get over it: how could there be a beautiful, sexy girl with a great sense of humor? My head was beginning to spin. She's got it all, I thought. I've finally found the girl I've been looking for, and an interior decorator to boot.

At one point she said, "You're so damn cute, Sammy. I really like you and I have a friend of mine who's a comedy writer. He could write a whole new act for you. I'd like to come and see you work. I know with a new act you can get a booking back in Vegas."

133

The Warm-up

I knew now that everything was going to get better. We laughed and joked and flirted for hours until I saw a certain look in her eyes. She wanted me, too. I took her face in my hands and kissed her. Now I was *really* getting excited. She wasn't like all the other flashy girls I'd dated, she was also a nice Jewish girl from a warm Jewish family. She was Mitzi, Phyllis, and Debbie all in one. I put my arms around her.

She pushed my hands away. "Please, Sammy, don't. I really like you a lot, but not the first night."

At that point I reminded myself that she really was a Jewish girl.

She excused herself from the room. I watched her walk away with her hips swaying and I was ready to die.

Ten minutes passed and I was wondering what was taking her so long.

I heard her footsteps along the dimly lighted hallway and as I caught her silhouette, she just didn't look the same. She came out into the dining room where I could see her. She was wearing a sheer black negligee and heels. She was like Playmate of the Century. I was confused; she'd said not the first night. So what was this, the prelude to the overture?

"Sammy, come here." Her voice was so low I could hardly hear it. I got up off the couch and my whole body was tingling. I walked to her like a robot. She embraced me and started rubbing herself against me.

"Sammy, let's go into the bedroom."

She took my hand and led me like a little boy into her bedroom. Candles were burning next to her bed, there was incense, a red antique lamp was glowing; it seemed a bit like a whorehouse. I stood at the edge of the bed and she gently unzipped my pants and undressed me until I was standing nude.

As much as I wanted her—and I was dying for her—I was confused. I always placed women in categories, and I didn't think Mercedes was really like a Vegas show girl. I was out of my depth.

We got into bed and made love through most of the night. When I saw daylight seeping through her window, I wanted to go. As hypocritical as it sounds, I was disappointed. Somehow nice girls didn't do it this way.

But we made love again; the pain and loneliness were gone while we held each other, and she started saying—less than twelve hours after we'd met—how much she adored me.

134

"I love you, Sammy," she was saying. "I have never felt this good before with any man. You're a great lover, you're kind and warm," all this while rubbing my head. I was somewhere between a six-year-old kid and a one-year-old puppy.

"I'm really serious about you," she said.

"I love you, too," I said. I hardly knew her. I always thought that if someone told you they loved you, you had to tell them you loved them too, even if you didn't.

"You just turned me into an animal," she said. "I couldn't help myself. I want to see you again tonight."

"Sure, Mercedes, I'll come back."

"I'll make us a nice dinner."

Here a beautiful twenty-five-year-old girl was telling me she loves me and wants to cook and care for me, too. Holy shit—I had it made. And I was lost. I sensed serious problems somewhere, but she was such an unbelievable replacement for Mitzi that I felt helpless to do anything but go along.

I did see her that night and the next night and throughout the week, and the weeks turned into months. I was almost living with her, even though I knew something was wrong—with her, with me, with us together. She was dependent on her father and I seemed like his replacement.

I didn't want to move into her apartment, even though she had suggested it many times, so she had the idea that I buy a house for myself and get out of my one-bedroom dump. We went looking for one, and I bought a cute two-bedroom colonial, a purchase that was still cheap and easy in LA. She helped me move in and pick out a few furnishings, since all I had was a bed and some dishes.

I got a brief gig in Tahoe with Connie Stevens and called Mercedes one night between shows.

"I've been dying to tell you, Sammy," she said. "The house looks really great, I got you some plants. I was spending so much time over there helping fix it up, I thought I'd feel more at home if I moved over some of my things—like the piano, the dining room set. Uh, also the sofa. I can't keep sitting on the floor. I hope you don't mind."

I minded very much. But what I said was, "Oh, that's all right. If it makes you feel more secure to have your things over, I understand."

"I just knew you would. You'll love the house when you get back—it's adorable."

"I'll bet it is."

"We were planning on moving in together anyway, so I thought now would be a good time to get it done."

"Sure," I said. "We'll live together. You're right. Listen, I've got to do my second show, I'll talk to you later."

I hung up the phone, gulped down a few inches of a bottle of Scotch. I was so angry—why didn't I tell her I didn't want her things in my house, I don't want to be involved anymore? Guilt was starting to pile up between Mercedes and me, guilt over not loving her while I clung to her, and it made me do anything she wanted.

I tried to stall her about getting married, but she gave me an ultimatum: either marriage within a month or I'd have to find her another place and reimburse her for six months' future expenses. She had me on the same hook as her dad! And I went along with all of it.

The day of the wedding was horrendous. We were getting married in the house and her whole family was there, while the only person I had was my best man, Trini Lopez. It was like Trini was ushering me into some alien country where I was going to be a hostage.

Mercedes was a wreck. She'd been hiding from me the fact that she saw a psychiatrist regularly, for problems which she would never discuss with me. She'd been behaving erratically, and some days didn't even bother to go to work. She just stayed in bed. Now, at the wedding, she started to hyperventilate. Who knows, maybe she was just as unhappy as I was. I had to get a paper bag and hold it over her mouth. She was shaking and could hardly stand for the ceremony.

History was repeating itself. When the rabbi pronounced us man and wife and it was time to step on the glass, I felt an impulse to run out of the house. Her family seemed to love me, but I felt nasty; I hated her and I hated them. I guess her father was thinking, Thank God, let this guy take care of her now.

Our honeymoon at La Costa near San Diego was a nightmare. She put on the pink negligee her sister had given her, but I was so miserable I couldn't touch her—such a great distance from the frantic first night we met. It was so sad for her; twenty-six years old and on our honeymoon night we couldn't make love.

I was so unhappy, we left the next day and came home to the beginnings of a marriage of total insanity. Being married made all the problems worse. I could hardly touch her at all. She didn't cook, clean, at times didn't go to work. *And* lost her sense of humor. I couldn't blame her. There was nothing I could give her—I had nothing to give. Meanwhile Mitzi was becoming known as "The Mother of Comedy." Young comics from the Store were showing up every other night on TV, and the more I heard about it all, the more I drank.

And the less I felt for Mercedes, the more I felt compelled to give her something to make up for how little I felt. So I called Paul Caruso and told him what I wanted to do.

"You're out of your mind," he said. "You want to give her half your house? To someone you've been married to for six months? Haven't you learned anything since you gave away The Comedy Store?"

"Yes, Paul, but—"

"She has no rights to your house. You bought it before the marriage!"

"I know," I said. "But she's been complaining she has nothing. What is she getting out of the marriage?"

Once again Paul did all he could, which was advise me against doing it. In the next few days I had quick-deeded the half share in the house over to Mercedes. All I'd needed to say was that I was going to give her half the house and within three hours there was an attorney, her brother-in-law, at the door to make the arrangements. Mercedes had me where she wanted me—by the nuts. It was a painful position for me to be in, and I'd worked hard to arrange it that way.

The house was now starting to fall apart, especially the plumbing. I looked in one of the neighborhood papers for a plumber and I decided to call "REASONABLE PERSONABLE PLUMBING BY FRANCO . . . YOUR MUSICAL PLUMBER . . . LISTEN TO MY MUSIC WHILE I PLUMB." Sounded cute.

Within an hour a battered old station wagon pulled up and out walked Franco the plumber, a short, bald, bearded hippie-looking guy with beads and old denim, carrying plumbing tools and a battered trumpet case.

"Hey, man, are you the Mr. Shore I just talked to? Show me your problem and I'll blow it away."

Nice, I thought—a breath of fresh air. I brought him into the house, introduced him to Mercedes, and inside two minutes I could see she took a liking to him while he laughed at her wisecracks about his trumpet and tools.

The Warm-up

I showed him the problem, and he said we had to go outside and get under the house. Outside, before he crawled through the opening, he pulled out his trumpet and played a little jazz before entering. He got on his knees and continued to blow a few notes as he crept underneath. Then I heard a little banging and he crawled out.

"Hey, man," he said, "I got some bad news for you. A couple of your pipes are rusting away and they got to be replaced. I stopped the leak, man, but your pipes underneath really suck."

So I hired him to repair my sucking pipes. In the weeks that followed, there were more problems with the plumbing and more and more visits from Franco. By now he and Mercedes were becoming really good friends. He'd come in after he finished his work and spend a couple hours playing his horn while Mercedes played the piano. She now had someone to relate to; he was younger and into all kinds of music, and I wasn't into anything but booze.

My daughter, Sandy, was nineteen at this time and friendly with Mercedes. She was spending a lot of time at the house watching me drink myself into oblivion. She and Mercedes started commenting on it.

"Sammy," Mercedes said, "I think you ought to check into Alcoholics Anonymous. One of my girl friends' husbands has been going, and he stopped drinking."

"I could stop if I want," I said. "I'm not an alcoholic. I'll show you—I'll just have two drinks a day and that's it."

I did it for a few days and once again it progressed into a fifth of alcohol a day. My body smelled from it; I was slowly sinking into the bottle. Once I'd had a couple of belts, everything was going to be okay, I was chasing my own tail. Mercedes sent away for the AA literature, so one day I received all these pamphlets on alcoholism. I read them and threw them away. I really thought I didn't have a problem. The problem was "them"—Mercedes, no work, Mitzi, what she did to me. I drank at all of them, until the realization came that I was becoming a very sick man.

I had just come back from one of my afternoon binges scouting nightclubs, and I was lying on the floor talking to Sandy.

"Gee, Dad," she said. "You really smell."

"I just had a couple of drinks, Sandy. I don't drink like I used to. Right, Mercedes?"

"You're drinking more than ever."

NOT MINDING THE STORE

Twenty-five years of drinking and this was the first time that anyone had ever said I smelled. And not just anyone—my own kid.

The next day I called a couple of hospitals and they suggested that as long as I wasn't really sick or having convulsions or blackouts, I should look into AA. Once again I rebelled at the thought. Me, Sammy Shore, who has worked with the biggest stars in show business, a drunk? No way—Skid Row, that's where all the alcoholics are, in the gutters. I still have a career. I work out at the Y. I'm in great shape. But the bottom line was, I could not put the cork in the bottle.

I'll never forget the night. It was Friday, September 30, 1976, a little past seven-thirty. I was sitting in my chair with a Scotch in my hand. I looked at it, got up, walked to the bathroom, and dumped it out. I'd heard there was an AA meeting in Beverly Hills at Roxbury Park, corner of Olympic and Roxbury. Beverly Hills, I thought. They can't be drunks; I'll just go over and take a look.

Mercedes heard me open the front door on the way out. She popped out of the bedroom and asked me where I was going.

"To an AA meeting," I heard myself say. "I'll see you later."

I drove toward Olympic. I was shaking, my anxiety was mounting. I opened the glove compartment and took out my pint. I just couldn't stand the fear; I had to have a drink. I gulped down nearly the whole pint and felt so warm, all the anxiety disappeared. I started to feel good. I started thinking, Maybe AA can teach me how to have just a couple of drinks a day and a little wine with dinner and then I can become a social drinker.

I parked my car on the side street. People were playing night tennis on the courts. I saw the little house in front of the courts, and through the windows as I approached I could see people sitting as in a little schoolhouse. I entered through the back of the room. The meeting had just started.

The room was filled with all kinds of people, men and women all dressed nicely, blacks, a couple of Orientals, young and old people.

At the head of the room was a man in his late fifties. "My name is Pete, and I'm an alcoholic."

Everyone in the entire room shouted, like at a rally, "Hi, Pete!"

"This is the Friday night Roxbury meeting for beginners," he said. "We'd like to welcome you all.

"Are there any newcomers in their first thirty days of sobriety?" A few hands went up, but I was too scared.

"Is there anyone in their first week?" A couple of hands went up

The Warm-up

"How about the first day?"

I just had to do it. I raised my hand. Everyone applauded me like I'd just finished a show.

"Would you stand up and introduce yourself and your disease?"

I stood up. I was petrified. I had never felt so genuinely terrified, even when I'd opened for Elvis. All eyes were on me, waiting. I couldn't even open my mouth.

Then suddenly a warm glow came over me like I had never felt before. It felt as if the glow was telling me it's okay now, you're in the right place. The fear started to leave.

I said, "My name is Sammy, and I . . . I'm an alcoholic."

The place went into an uproar. "Hi, Sammy!" they all shouted.

People in back of me leaned over and said, "Welcome, Sammy. We love you."

I sat down and could not believe what I was hearing. People were going up to the podium and talking about what they'd been going through and how they didn't have to drink anymore. I felt so comfortable. I'd found a place where I belonged; we were all in it together, helping each other stay sober. I'd never been anywhere where people really cared about how you were doing.

The meeting ended and virtually the whole group gathered around me, with the men giving me their phone numbers so I could call them for help, and I was given the AA *Big Book*, the textbook of the program. I went home feeling I had finally found a home, a real one.

Mercedes was waiting on the couch when I got back. "How was the meeting?"

"Enlightening," I said. "I've never felt this good before."

The phone rang. Mercedes answered and handed it to me. "Some guy named Larry," she said.

"Hi, Larry," I said. "Yeah, I'm feeling really good, thanks for calling me. . . . A meeting at noon tomorrow? Sure. . . . That's great, I'll see you tomorrow."

I hung up, and Mercedes wanted to know who was calling me so late.

"That was a guy I just met at the meeting. A real nice guy, he's got five years in the program. Can you imagine that? He hasn't had a drink in five years. I can't believe it."

Mercedes seemed to have mixed feelings. "Are these guys going to be calling here every night?"

"Gee, I don't know what they do. I'll tell them not to call too late."

I opened up my *Big Book.* I couldn't wait to read it.

"Aren't you going to talk to me?" Mercedes said. "You were gone all night, the least you could do is talk to me."

"I'm sorry, but I've got to read this book."

The next few weeks I went to two meetings every day. My phone never stopped ringing. I had more friends in a few weeks than I'd had in all the years of being in show business, and all they wanted from me was not to drink.

Mercedes became very jealous. She would try to fight with me, and I wouldn't get into it. It was partly that I was becoming more my own man, and Mercedes couldn't tolerate it. But also AA was a way for me to escape from the mess I had made with her. And now Franco the plumber was starting to come over more often. "Franco's my AA meeting," she'd say. "He keeps me entertained while you're gone."

I'd had many warning signals to tell me what Mercedes was capable of doing. She'd once broken my glasses during an argument in the car and then thrown them into the street. She'd blame me for the condition she was in and throw plants, dishes, and ashtrays at me. Once I grabbed her and held her so she couldn't throw anything, and when I let her go, she called the police and told them I was beating her. They came over, and when she claimed that I had thrown all those things at her and was insane and always beat her up, they knew they were wasting their time. I knew they just felt disgusted and sorry for us both.

Another time she threw herself in front of my car as I was starting to go to a meeting. She was lying in the street, screaming, "He ran me over, that murderer wants to kill me! Help, police!"

One Saturday night I came home late after a meeting and Mercedes was furious. I had kept a kind of unreal calm up to now, but this time I exploded. "Why don't you get off your fat ass," I said, "and get a job!"

It made her go wild. "What! Now you're really going to get it! I'm going to call Franco and have him throw you out of the house!"

It was one-thirty in the morning, but she picked up the phone and called him. I was scared.

"Franco," she said on the phone, "Sammy's screaming at me, he's driving me crazy—tell him to leave me alone!"

I couldn't believe what I was hearing.

"Here, Sammy," she said. "He wants to talk to you."

The Warm-up

I grabbed the phone. "Hello?"

"What are you doing to that poor girl?"

"I'm doing nothing to her, she's screaming at me."

"Well, you better leave her alone or I'll come over there and throw you out."

I didn't say anything, I just gave Mercedes the phone. For the first time I realized that something had been going on between the two of them.

It started again as soon as we woke up the next morning.

"Franco really told you off," she said. "Just watch what you say to me or he'll come over."

In the light of day this seemed like an unbelievable threat, so I said, "He'd better not or I'll have his ass thrown in jail!"

"We'll see about that," she said. She started dialing his number. My insides were turning to pure liquid.

"Franco, this is Mercedes. Sammy's driving me crazy. Please come over here and tell him to leave me alone. . . . He just keeps hollering at me—help me!"

She hung up the phone. "Now," she said, "you're going to see who's boss around here."

I was incredulous. "What the hell are you trying to do? How can you have a guy that's practically a stranger come into my house and tell me to shut up?"

"Oh, you'll see."

In about half an hour there was a knock at the door. I opened it and Franco was looking at me like I had broken into *his* house.

"What the hell's going on here?" he said.

I was collapsing inside. I couldn't say anything, everything seemed out of control.

Mercedes hollered from the bedroom. "In here, Franco!"

We both went to the bedroom, where she was lying on the bed and doing her act.

"Franco, he's driving me crazy." Indeed she did look crazy, like I'd driven her beyond tears. "Tell him to stop hollering at me!"

"I'm not," I said. "She's making all this up!" I was actually trying to persuade him of my innocence, like I was going to let him be the judge.

"What are you doing to this poor little girl?" Franco looked very strange and obsessed. His eyes were like a crazy man's. "Look at

142

her," he said. "She's so messed up and frustrated, she can't even get out of bed. Now one of us is going to leave this house, and it ain't going to be me. You can go ahead and call the police if you want, but someone is gonna go right through that window. Now you better just go before I get violent."

I wanted to kill him. My head was on fire, my nerves were raw and I was trembling. I was not the bravest of men when it came to a fight. In fact, I stood there in a complete panic. Something was telling me I had to hit him or at least call the cops, but I couldn't. I couldn't stop a goddamn plumber from throwing me out of my own house.

Franco had an eerie calm. I started reciting the AA Serenity Prayer to myself: "God grant me the serenity to accept the things I cannot change, the courage to change the things I can, and the wisdom to know the difference." It seemed to help. I started to relax and suddenly felt, Everything's going to be all right.

I walked over to my closet, took out a couple of suits, got some clothes out of my dresser drawer, walked into the living room, and started to pack. Tears came into my eyes as I looked around the room. I had the feeling I'd never be back.

I walked out the front door, with Franco following behind me, through the yard and out to the street, and I got into my car and left. I was so confused, I didn't know what was happening, but after a while it seemed like God had sent this man into my life to give me a way out from Mercedes. I had already given myself up to her in going through with our affair, then our marriage, then deeding half the house. Now I was just giving up completely. It was the ultimate humiliation. I could only hope that I would now be able to stop looking for a woman to make me feel like a man.

I drove toward Wilshire in the eastern part of Beverly Hills. I wanted a drink so badly to kill the pain, but I knew I just wouldn't do it; I'd been in the AA program for three weeks and had been starting to feel really good without alcohol. And they said at meetings, no matter what happens, don't take that first drink. So I pulled my car over on Robertson, parked, and sat and cried. I had the phone numbers of some AA members, so I went to a phone booth and tried them. It was a beautiful Sunday afternoon and nobody was home. I got back into my car and drove around just thinking about finding someone to be with, and finally, after I stopped again and went back through the numbers, I got a "Hello" at the other end. It was Jim, a young black man I'd met at a meeting.

I told him the incredible story—that a virtual stranger had thrown me out of my own house and I hadn't even put up a fight. I was ashamed and crying, but Jim reminded me that everybody who came into the program was battered and beaten. And he asked me to come over.

His apartment building near downtown LA looked very much like my dad's old rooming house. I walked through the dark corridor to his apartment, and when the door opened, there was Jim with his arms outstretched. As he embraced me I started to come apart completely, crying like a lost little boy.

Jim helped me and talked with me that day until four-thirty in the morning, when I went to sleep on his couch. In the days after that I stayed with Paul Caruso and went to two or three AA meetings a day. I went back to The Horn just to keep myself busy at night. No one knew where I was staying, not even Mercedes.

I was leaving The Horn one night to go back to Paul's and went out the back way into the alley. Franco was waiting for me.

"Sammy," he said, "Mercedes has been trying to find you. She's really worried about you. Why don't you call her and tell her where you are?"

"Call her? You're kidding me. Get the fuck out of my way. She's yours. I hope you're both enjoying my home. You know, I want to thank you for what you did. You saved my life. Now move." I brushed past him, and he started to follow.

"Please, man, just call her. She's driving me crazy."

"You deserve each other."

I got into my car and was on my way. I felt good. I knew I was not to blame for her unhappiness, and that I was recovering. I hadn't known how sick I was until I'd gotten into the program. The woman I had attracted merely reflected me.

I moved into a small garage apartment near West Hollywood. It was tough to leave Paul's house, which was full of warmth and caring people, to set up in an empty place and face living alone. But I knew I had to do it.

***

144

NOT MINDING THE STORE

Each day things seemed to get a little better. I kept going to meetings; I'd buy a plant, a pot, some dishes for my place; I was starting
over again from scratch. After about a year on the AA program I was
starting to feel really good. I was working on my act, with a few
small jobs out of town in addition to working The Horn; my timing
was back; and my attitude onstage was changing radically. For the
first time in all my years in show business I was making people laugh
without any alcohol in my body. I was much calmer; I stopped sweating; I wasn't pushing anymore. People said they were amazed by the
change in my work and my new calmness.

One night while I was working at The Horn, I was standing at the
bar talking to Jack, the bartender who'd always had a couple of
Scotches waiting for me.

"It's really good to see you like this, Sammy," he said. "No drinks
for a while now. How long has it been?"

"Nearly a year," I said.

"Welcome to the club."

"What do you mean, the club?"

"The club is AA, Brother Sam," Jack said. "I've been a member
for twelve years."

"Holy shit!" I said. "*You*, the bartender who's been pouring me
drinks all these years, in AA? I can't believe it, you're pulling my
leg."

He assured me he wasn't.

"Why didn't you tell me," I said. "Why did you pour me all those
drinks?"

"I couldn't tell you, you had to do what you had to do. AA's a
program of attraction. You really have to want it and be ready to stop
drinking and want us to help you. I remember working for you at The
Comedy Store, too, how much you drank. I knew one day you'd sur-
render."

"I really can't believe all this," I said, and laughed. "Give me a
drink, Jack—a Shirley Temple will be fine."

Not long ago—and years after the fiasco with Mercedes was behind me—I was sitting poolside at the apartment complex where I
live, in Marina del Rey. I seldom go out to sun myself, since I have
a balcony that looks out over the ocean, but on this day I felt the need
to be with some people.

The Warm-up

At our particular pool, as you might expect, many of the residents gather to chit-chat. Some of the males will be on the lookout for any new young thing that might have just moved in. A few middle-aged studs have been living at Mariner's Bay since it opened eight years ago, and every weekend, like clockwork, Stan, Bob, Burt, Larry, and David will be lying in the same spot, talking about practically the same thing—the new women, or the old women, in their lives.

They're all nice men—lonely, but nice—just like me. This particular day, I just wanted to be out among the crowd. Not to get involved in any conversation—just lie there with the cattle.

"Aren't you Sammy Shore?" A sultry southern voice was whispering to me just above my head.

I turned and looked up. Her body almost fell out of her swimsuit as she leaned toward me. She moved to the front of my lounge chair, putting out her hand to shake mine. "My name is Creo Levitan. Mind if I join you?"

"Please do." I was quite taken by her physical beauty. "Yes, I'm Sammy Shore. Have we met somewhere?"

"No, I don't think so," she said. "I just know who you are. . . . You're a well-known comedian. . . . You also created The Comedy Store."

I felt quite flattered as she continued to elaborate on my background. Before I could thank her for her praises, she jumped ahead to give me her story, saying that she was an entertainer—a singer and comedienne—that she was from Memphis, she was Jewish, and she was going to make it in this town.

Well. I sat there and just let her résumé pour out. It sounded kind of appealing, with her southern accent and all. A new person always seems to perk me up—and in a case like this, lustful thoughts start crowding my devious mind.

She seemed needy. The more she told me of herself and her southern upbringing, her family down South and the problems she was encountering here in this massive town, the more she reminded me of my second wife, Mercedes. Her flashing red hair, her deep cleavage, her body formation, with flaring hips and all—she was almost a clone of Mercedes, right down to her tiny feet. I became more and more amazed at the resemblance.

But I tried not to allow that horrendous part of my past interfere with what was happening. She was using all her charm to lure me.

146

NOT MINDING THE STORE

I know how I usually am when I'm attracted to a young female. I play the role of comedian and wind up telling her about all the stars I've appeared with and how I have all my shit together—that is, when I'm the pursuer. This was different. I was the pursuee. I had to keep reminding myself that this was not Mercedes. She was Creo Levitan . . . from Memphis, Tennessee.

By now we had both slipped into the Jacuzzi and were sitting next to each other talking. It was Saturday. I had no plans for the evening. I asked her if she would like to have dinner with me.

"Yes," was her immediate reply. "I'd love to."

In all my years of dating Jewish women, I can't remember any of them refusing. They say the way to a man's heart is food. Take a Jewish lady out to a nice restaurant, and your chances of getting her in the sack are phenomenal.

I wasn't completely thrilled to be taking her out, since she so reminded me of Mercedes. But who knows what lurks behind my beady eyes? I was being cool about the whole encounter.

"I'm in apartment three fifty-one, building five," she said.

"Yeah, sure, see you about seven-thirty," I said.

Wait a minute, I thought. Building 5, apartment 351? Jesus Christ, that's Norman's old apartment! Norman is one of my closest friends and moved into my complex a couple of years ago so we could be near each other. But he had just moved recently. Norman knew all about my past, especially all the traumas with my ex, Mercedes.

I felt awkward outside the door of apartment 351, about to knock. What the hell am I doing here? I thought. I don't even like this girl. And having her remind me of Mercedes. . . . Am I still sick—or just horny? I rapped on the door.

"Is that you, Sammy?" Her lilting voice reminded me of Scarlett O'Hara.

The door opened. She stood there with her flaming red hair lying over her right shoulder, lacy white cotton dress, voluptuous breasts squeezed by some unseen bra. She looked, in a word, hot.

"Come on in, Sammy," she said. "I'm on the phone with my mama in Memphis. I'll be off in a minute."

A piano, a guitar, and an album she had recorded were all situated in the center of the living room, her album leaning against the piano leg. I think she was trying to tell me something.

She knew I was not involved with anyone, and she had recently broken up with her boyfriend, so I got the feeling she was making herself quite available—although she said she wasn't interested in getting involved again.

We had a casual dinner at an oceanfront restaurant in Venice, both laughing and enjoying each other's company. She had a wonderful sense of humor. She really was trying to be nice and as open as she could be with someone so new. I started to feel some warmth for her as we headed back to our apartment complex.

It was approaching midnight. I drove around the complex, to her side of the building, and pulled into her parking space. I was kind of surprised that her spot was empty, but she said her car was in the shop for repairs.

As I turned off the ignition, I said to her, "Come on, I'll take you up to your place"—hoping, by now, that she'd invite me in. I started to open my car door, but first something struck me.

"How do you know so much about my past?" I said it casually, not suspiciously. I was more amused than anything else. "It's amazing. You know more about me than my old psychiatrist!"

She smiled. Then she said coyly, "I even know your ex-wife Mercedes."

My stomach fell to the floorboards. I was stunned. I grabbed her by the arm as she started to get out of the car. "Wait. You know Mercedes?"

"Yes, quite well," she said.

"From where?" My heart was palpitating.

"You remember Franco, your old plumber who was involved with your ex-wife? Well he was my boyfriend until just recently."

I started to die, and then fume, as the puzzle snapped into place. The demon was back. The man who threw me out of my own house and, also, the man who set me free. Who knows—without him, I might still be there with *her!*

They say that history sometimes repeats itself. But I really did not want to be around if one day the plumber decided he wanted to come by and fix a pipe in my apartment complex. Creo said that he still came by to harass her and that she had even called the police to try to keep him away.

I sat for a moment of silence and started to stare into space.

"Are you all right, Sammy?" Creo said.

"Yes, I'm fine." I took her hand in mine and said kindly, "I think you're a nice person, and I had a really pleasant time being with you. I just don't think we should see each other anymore. It really has nothing to do with you—but I think you'll understand. And I hope you don't mind if I don't walk you to your door. I feel it would be best.''

She looked at me kind of strangely. I saw a sadness come over her face. "Thank you, Sammy, for the wonderful evening.''

She closed her car door and headed for her building entrance. I started up my car and went out for a ride around the Marina.

I looked up at the bright moon.

"Thank you, God!''

6

NO BUSINESS AND SHOW BUSINESS

Sam Weisbord was the man I wanted to talk to. He was president of the William Morris Agency. It had been two years since they'd dropped me, after I'd been with the agency ten years. I wanted back.

I was nervous as hell as I sat in Weisbord's outer office under the gaze of his secretary. I knew I really had to do a selling job if I wanted to be with William Morris again.

The buzzer sounded on the secretary's phone.

"Mr. Weisbord will see you now. Go right in, Mr. Shore."

I mustered all my confidence as I walked in. Weisbord stood up, extended his hand. "It's nice to see you, Sammy, how have you been? It's been a long time since the days of Elvis."

"I've been doing fine, Mr. Weisbord."

"What can I do for you?"

"Mr. Weisbord," I said, "as you know, the past few years after I got divorced everything went bad for me. I lost everything, but especially I lost me. I was drinking heavily, I gave up, and I really didn't want to live anymore. It's taken me this past year and a half to put myself back together again.

"I stopped drinking, my timing is better than ever, my act is all new. I've never been funnier. In fact, Freddie Moch here, who used to book me in Vegas, saw me the other night and suggested I talk to you about a resigning.

"All I ask is a chance to prove that I can come back again. You know, I was one of the best warm-up comics in the business. Just give me a shot."

Weisbord asked me to stick around while he buzzed Freddie Moch's office to see what Freddie had to say. "Hello, Fred. I've just been talking with Sammy Shore, and he says that you caught him the other night at The Horn. He seems like a changed man and he looks terrific, so what do you think about his potential now?"

Weisbord did a lot of nodding, then hung up the phone.

"Well," he said, "Freddie raved about you, Sammy. Says he's never seen you funnier, and your act is very contemporary. I always knew you had something special since I first saw you with Elvis. I'm going to resign you to the office."

Then one day I was in the lobby at one of the bigger agencies, where I often went to meet a comedian friend of mine. I looked into the other foyer while I was waiting for the elevator and it happened again: Miss Right. She was a receptionist, blonde, very Nordic-looking, and I just kept staring at her. The elevator door opened, but I walked away from it. I just had to test out my new fantasy, to see if she really was as beautiful as I thought, to see if she'd like me.

She was indeed lovely, even more beautiful than Debbie, and that seemed unbelievable. She was also very sweet, and it wasn't very long before we had a lively conversation going. She told me she'd been working there five years. Why hadn't I noticed her before?

"Now that you know I'm here," she said, "maybe you can stop by again and say hello."

"I guarantee you I will. I'll be seeing you soon, Anna."

She looked so together, I thought. Working here for five years with some of these assholes and barracudas, she must really have it together. I cut my visit upstairs a little short so I could be sure and see her on the way out, but I didn't want to seem pushy so I just stuck my head in and waved. When I got in my car, all I could think about was Anna.

By the next morning when I awoke I was obsessed with her. I drove over to the agency and just watched her for a moment from the lobby. Her hair was tied back in a ponytail, which brought out the fine features of her face, including a perky little nose. She was wearing a white turtleneck over her shapely upper body.

I walked over to her and stood in a mock-sexy stance with my hands on my hips, half turning toward her. "Hi, Anna. You're probably wondering what took me so long to come back."

She laughed.

"Well," I went on, "I've come here to take you away from this insanity. Oh, my fair Anna, I shall take you to the top of the mountain to my castle, where we shall live together for ever and ever.

"Oh, what light through yonder window breaks, Juliet. . . . 'Tis I, Romeo, cometh with me-eth."

She giggled. "Sammy, thanks. It gets so boring here, everyone seems so serious, even some of the comedians who come in are so serious.

"What are you doing up at this hour?" she said. "I thought all you guys slept late."

I confessed that I really had nothing to do that morning, that I was thinking about her and wanted to know if she'd like to have coffee. She said we'd take her coffee break together outside.

As I held the front door open for her, I got the full impact of her. She was amazingly beautiful. Her tight tailored French jeans were outrageous. My insides were fluttering. I was starved for any kind of love.

It was a wonderful day in LA because along with the sunshine, there was a cool breeze. We both sat on the brick ledge across the street from the agency entrance.

"Sure feels good to get out of there and get some fresh air," she said.

"Fresh air? You call this fresh? 'I shot an arrow into the air, and it stuck there.' "

I got her laughing and I didn't want to stop. I went through a bit about oil slicks on the ocean and seagulls carrying dipsticks. As long as she was laughing, I was flying.

She mentioned that she had seen me once or twice over the years and that I seemed healthier and more relaxed. That gave me an opportunity to come off as Mr. Health.

"Thanks, Anna," I said. "Yeah, I started to work out and I lost some weight. I'm watching what I eat—you know, sort of a health freak, no smoking or drinking. I guess I've become more spiritual; I meditate and it's helped me."

Beautiful women seem to be enthralled by someone who's into God—Buddha's even better—and who has an aura of spirituality and health. I think the reason must be that they're so messed up themselves, they think *you've* got the answer. Of course at the time, I thought I had it too, because the AA program is very spiritual in tone. When you first come in, you believe anything. And after you've stopped drinking for a couple of months, you're a saint.

Anna was looking at me like I'd been sent from heaven to rescue her. She kept staring at me as I babbled until I decided it was time she told me something about herself.

"There isn't that much to tell you," she said. "I work here as a receptionist. I'm Jewish, as you can probably tell by now."

"Jewish! I can't believe you're Jewish. You look like a shiksa with your blond hair and dimples—and don't tell me you've had your nose fixed!"

She assured me her features were the original. I wanted to ask if she was involved with anyone, and I started to feel very uneasy about the idea.

"Are you married?" I said.

"I was for a short time," she said, "but not now."

I was relieved.

"But I'm living with someone now," she added.

My heart dropped into my stomach. Fuck, I said to myself—all this for nothing. I started to clam up.

"Something wrong, Sammy?"

"No, no, I just remembered I have to meet my attorney at eleven."

"I hope I'm not keeping you," she said.

"Well, no, his office is just around the corner." Then I said, "Who's your boyfriend?" I couldn't help making the question sound cold and bitter.

"Mickey Black, one of the agents here."

"Mickey Black!" I shouted. "He's one of my old agents—I don't believe it. Mickey Black—Mickey never mentioned he was living with someone, but come to think of it, I never asked him."

"It's not all a bowl of cherries," she said, "since he's in and out of town so much, going to Vegas to cover acts. But he also handles all the concerts for rock groups, which is really exciting when he takes me, everybody getting stoned and everything. It's been a wonderful life for me."

She was talking happy but sounding sad. There was a sense of being victimized in what she was saying and a feeling like she didn't know what to do. That gave me new hope, and I started to get back some of my verve.

"I know how you must feel, Anna," I said. "Sometimes show business sucks." Then I managed to hype myself and put agents down at the same time. "When things are popping, there's nothing like the excitement of having everybody fuss over you. Of course, I'm talking about being a performer. But I guess it's a lot different sitting behind a desk and being involved with someone who peddles flesh for a living."

I was about as subtle as a gunshot, but Anna was listening.

"I know some of those agents," I continued, "are really cold assholes and all they can think about is their ten percent. And if they can't sell you, then they'll find someone else on their enormous list. But I don't really know Mickey that well," I said, "so I shouldn't be judgmental." I was disgusting. I was cutting it both ways. And it worked.

"He is one of the assholes," Anna said. "He's really screwed my head up many a night, but I really care about him. Basically he's a nice man, but his ego won't let him alone."

It sounded like she might want to split from him but was scared to try. I was thinking about Mickey—a very strong macho type, into Gucci, booze, and parties, one of the young swinging agents at the office. He was well liked by the older, staunch, semiretired heads of the company because he got great results.

Anna said, "I could tell you some stories about what goes on in this building that would make your hair straighten out."

I wondered why she was being so confessional. I said, "You sound pretty disturbed—sounds like *As the World Turns at the Agency*."

"Well, it's just that we're so harassed here," she said. "Some of these agents, all they want to do is ball you, and sometimes right in their office. And I know of a few young girls who were working at one of the other agencies in town—they were fired because they didn't make it with their agent."

Even I was a little shocked, and I asked her why she wanted to tell me this.

"I don't know, I just don't have anyone I can talk to about this. Mickey knows what goes on, of course, and he thinks it's hilarious, like when an agent is getting head while he's trying to sell a client.

"I've been lucky because everyone knows I'm Mickey's girl. But when I first started here—forget about it! One girl who worked here, she couldn't even type, but she was a nympho. Practically every lunch hour she'd make the rounds, like all the agents around the building were booking her. It's sick."

Anna seemed to feel she could trust me, and I was beginning to feel like her therapist, which I now realize was kind of crazy. But I was loving every minute.

In the next few weeks we kept in touch over the phone and through occasional visits at the office. I kept it very discreet because I didn't want anyone to suspect that I was trying to steal Mickey's girl, which of course is exactly what I was doing. We never met at night, and our relationship was entirely platonic.

Then one night I was attending an AA meeting with a friend who wanted to see what it was all about. The meeting was in Brentwood in a large hall. It looked like more than five hundred people were there when we came in. The hall was filled with smoke and the conversations of alcoholics of every age, color, and persuasion. As my friend and I were heading toward the back to find seats, I noticed someone coming toward me who looked like Mickey Black. And then I knew it was Mickey. He had stopped in an aisle beside Anna and an elderly couple.

I knew Mickey had a drinking problem, and I figured he had joined the ranks. As a fellow alcoholic I was pleased, but as a pursuer of his lady I was not thrilled to see him. Besides, as an agent he'd never once gotten me a job.

"Mickey!" I shouted. "What a surprise to see you here!"

He looked at me the same way I must have been looking at him, like what was I doing here.

"How long have you been a member?" I said as I came up to him.

"Me a member?" he laughed. "You're kidding. I brought Anna, she's the receptionist at our office."

"Hi, Anna," as we looked at each other, perplexed. She introduced me to the older couple, her parents, Mr. and Mrs. Hoffritz.

Anna told me that this was her first week at the meetings, that she'd been going every night and sometimes at noon. We all sat in the same row, and as the meeting ended, I suggested to Mickey that we all go to a meeting together some night.

I couldn't believe that Anna had a problem of that kind. She always seemed so calm and at peace with herself, but then I always interpreted good looks to mean serenity, wisdom, and happiness. I found out later that she'd been taking drugs heavily for years. But in the weeks after that meeting I kept running into Anna and Mickey at meetings and she looked fabulous. They seemed to be getting along and that didn't sit too well with me, but part of me did wish her well even if I couldn't have her. I thought all was lost with me and Anna.

One afternoon I just wanted to talk with her so I called her office as always, asking for "the receptionist's desk" in my most business-like manner. When the voice came on, I said "Hi, Anna!"

"This isn't Anna, this is Laura."

I told her who I was. Where was Anna?

"Didn't you hear about Anna?"

I felt a streak of panic. "What happened!" I almost shouted.

"Well, she overdosed on pills last night at Mickey's house. She's at UCLA Medical Center. She's out of danger. They got there in time and they pumped her stomach. She's coming home tomorrow. Why don't you give her a call, Sammy, I'm sure she'd love to hear from you."

I rushed over to UCLA and as I entered her room, I saw she was asleep, with her parents standing beside her. They knew that Anna was fond of me. Mr. Hoffritz had the look of death in his eyes, like he wanted to blame this on someone.

"That bastard Mickey," he said. "He nearly killed her. She wanted to leave him and move back to her apartment and he wouldn't let her go. He hit her, and she ran into the bathroom and took all the pills she'd been hiding.

"What good did all those meetings do her, anyway?" he went on. "She still took all those pills, and she nearly died."

I told him he couldn't blame AA; he knew she was doing well before this happened.

He looked at me more softly, and I got the feeling he knew I cared. "What do you think we ought to do with her when she comes out?" he said.

I suggested, based on what I knew from AA, letting her stay in a women's recovery home so she could have complete rest and quiet away from everyone. I said it would take her a long time to dry out, physically and mentally, and that if they wanted me to, there was a women's recovery home in the San Fernando Valley where I could arrange for a room the next day, through AA. They agreed to the idea.

NO BUSINESS AND SHOW BUSINESS

The next day when I arrived at the Hoffritzes' house to take Anna to the recovery home, she was so excited to see me that she embraced me as I walked in.

"It's so good to see you," she said as her parents stood around watching. "I'm really sorry to put you through all this. It just seems you're always there when I'm troubled."

I was greedy for every word, but I made it seem like merely the duty of a fellow member of AA. "I don't want to hear about it," I said. I told her she was going to love her place in the Valley.

"Sammy, I don't want to go to any women's recovery home. I want to be with my parents, and you."

I felt seven feet tall. I knew I finally had her. But what did I have? A beautiful face, fantastic body, blond hair, warm personality, Jewish—and really fucked up! And now she was mine. I was inheriting the whole package, including her hard-nosed German mother and passive Polish father.

I was just starting to get my life in order and now was taking on a terrible load. But I needed her; my ego wanted her. Unlike Mickey, I'd do anything to keep her. I knew my "kindness and love" would heal her fast.

She finally agreed to go to the home if I promised to call each day and visit on Sundays. So that's what I did. Every Sunday I'd haul my ass out to the Valley with flowers and love cards and a lot of hope that when she recovered we could have a life together. I could see, as the weeks went by, that she was becoming more and more dependent on me, and me on her. I devoted my full time to her recuperation and through all of these weeks we never had sex. We both were very frustrated. Once we even went back into the bushes behind the recovery home and tried and failed to find a secluded spot.

All this time I was being told by veteran members of the program not to give my life and soul over to this very sick young lady, who, they insisted, was "one of the sickest on the program." They said it would take a couple of years for her to truly recover, and even then there were no guarantees she would be the same because of her many years of drug abuse. And when she finally did recover and started to understand her real feelings, she might look at me one day and say, "What the hell am I doing here? I should be with a younger guy, and who wants to be around show business?"—and off she would go.

The day arrived for me to take Anna home. I was so excited driving to the Valley one last time with the flowers. I really had nothing going on in my life at the time. My little garage apartment was a lonely place, my career was at a standstill. The thought of Anna filled everything up.

When we arrived at my little domain, we could hardly wait to devour each other. Anna had told me that all she did at the home was eat, sleep, and go to the bathroom to masturbate. As for me, I'd become so totally involved with her that I wouldn't even look at another woman. We were both about ready to explode. The anticipation and excitement were so great I couldn't even get the key in the door. When the door finally opened we didn't even make it to the bed, we just started to rip at each other, kissing and feeling.

"Please, Sammy, be careful. It's been so long, I'm scared."

"Don't worry," I said.

We crawled onto the bed, frantically taking off each other's clothes, feeling each other—I was unzipping my pants with one hand and caressing her with the other; she was lying against the pillow, moaning and reaching for me, reaching into my pants. I knelt over her and spread her legs and before I could enter her I came in a great gush all over my hand. Memories of Mary Gufano flashed before me.

Growing up in my neighborhood, I'm surrounded by people of every known ethnic group and denomination. In fact I never did figure out what some of the kids were. And when it comes to talking about getting laid, it seems this motley crew I hang out with is always way ahead of me. I'm so naïve! Whenever the guys expound on the subject, I'm in awe—and I'm busy pretending that I know exactly what they're talking about.

On Sunday, if we're not playing baseball, we stand around on the corner of Wells and Hill streets, laughing, talking, making fun of each other or maybe of some of the people passing by. Me being something of a clown, most of the time I'm throwing out all kinds of remarks and asides about what's happening.

On this particular Sunday, a beautiful new Cadillac convertible makes the turn at our corner. Sitting in it are a gorgeous blonde and a dark, heavy-looking man. As the car cruises past, I shout, *"Pimp!"*

Now, in all my fourteen years of life on this earth, I've never really found out what the word *pimp* means. But it sounds good. I've heard it from some of the guys along the way.

The Cadillac screeches to a halt. The car door opens and out comes this enormous parcel of a man. He's definitely pissed, and he heads straight for Johnny Lee, the only black guy in the group, who's sitting on the curb.

"Hey, you nigger motherfucker!" he shouts. "You call me a pimp?"

"No, sir," Johnny replies. "It was him—Sammy."

The man turns slowly toward me. "You called me a pimp. You little shit. I'll break your fucking legs!"

This looks like the end for me—and some of my so-called friends are starting to disappear from the sidewalk.

"Gee, I'm sorry, mister," I say, blushing like crazy and starting to shake. "I really don't even know what that word means. We were just having fun . . ."

I turn toward the few guys who are left; not a move is made, not a sound is heard. It's just me and Kong. But he seems to believe me and I can see him soften just a bit.

"Well, don't ever say it again."

He lumbers back to the blonde and takes off—and all the guys start coming out from their various doorways and alleys.

But now my troubles are just beginning, because what I've done is open up a can of worms. This is my time to become truly integrated and initiated into the group. So I don't know what pimp means! Or jacking off! Or coming! Or pulling out just in time if you don't have a rubber! I know shit—and now *they know that I don't know*. They all begin to have a feast, especially when I'm forced to reveal that I've never been laid.

They all decide to help. Next Saturday is going to be the night. They know of someone who has taken care of most of the guys and they'll arrange for her to take care of their little Jewish boy, too. Tonelli's Candy Store, nine o'clock, is our initial rendezvous.

The days leading up to Saturday are terrifying for me, knowing that the time has come for me to be a "man" and join the ranks. Late in the week the guys reveal that I'm to meet Mary Gufano—she's the girl who's going to "take care" of me, in the old abandoned bus on the vacant lot. First, Tonelli's Candy Store; then—paradise in the old bus!

Then the night comes that I'll never forget. Saturday; it's raining and dreary. The guys are hanging out in the back of Tonelli's, and I'm a little late because I've had to help Pa in the store and he keeps it open Saturday evenings.

The Warm-up

"Hi, Satchmo," they chime as I walk in. There's a lilt in their voices.

"How's lover boy? Still got your cherry?" That's Mello Vaccarino talking. He's the neighborhood stud—not necessarily because he's a great lover, but because he'll go after anything that moves. He's a small, muscular kid with catlike movements.

Mello turns around and bends over: "C'mon, Satch, shove it in my ass!"

Everybody gets hysterical. I want so much to be like them and just get laid and get it over with.

I know they mean business, and I'm absolutely scared to death. I've got to go through with it.

When we all leave Tonelli's I'm walking in front of them, down the street in the rain. I stop for a moment and turn to the guys and say, "I'm really getting wet."

They all laugh. "Move your ass!" Mello says.

I feel like I'm being led to the sacrificial altar in a Cecil B. De Mille epic. When we get to the bus, I can just make out the shape of somebody sitting inside waiting.

"Hey, Mary!" Mello shouts. "Sammy's here!"

They all stand by the door of the bus and shove me through. And there's Mary Gufano. Skinny, a long nose, pimples, and as flat as Lake Michigan. This is the girl?

"Hi, Sammy," she says, and when she smiles she doesn't look quite so bad. "Give me your hand, let's go to the back."

It's very dark back there.

"We'll have more room," she says.

"Why don't we just sit up here and talk for a few minutes?" I say. I take the nearest seat.

"Fine," she says, and sits down beside me.

"You're really a cute guy," she says. "I love your curly hair. Mind if I run my hands through it?"

She runs her hands through my hair and slowly starts to touch my face, then my chest. My heart is going like a big steam engine. Her hand's on my fly. She slowly zips it open, puts her hand on me, and my cock starts to rise. She pulls it out.

"Oh, how nice," she says. "It's not like the other guys'—it's so clean, and the skin is all pushed back."

Somehow it doesn't seem like the right time to explain all that to her.

"C'mon," she says. "Let's go in the back."

She leads me back by one hand while with the other I'm trying to hold up my pants. She takes off her jeans and panties, then reaches over and helps me take my pants off. I'm standing in my shorts.

"Take 'em off," she orders. "Now come and get on top of me."

I start to climb over her skinny body. My cock is throbbing. When she touches me there, I explode, all over her hand and her legs. I'm so embarrassed.

"Gee, I'm sorry, Mary."

"Don't worry, Sammy. The same thing happened to all the guys the first time."

"Really? You mean it? Even Mello?"

"He was the worst! He came while he was taking his pants off!"

I start to laugh. A freedom comes over me like I'm one of the guys. As we start to leave the bus, I thank her.

"Oh, you're welcome," she says. "You know what—you're the first guy that ever thanked me for it. I'd like to see you again, you're nice."

As I come down the steps of the bus, all the guys are standing there and they start to jeer and applaud. Mary skirts past me and stops in front of them.

"Thank you, guys, for Sammy," she says. "He was the best lover I ever had! If you guys want to see me anymore, you'll have to ask him first."

Anna had her own apartment, but she couldn't stand being alone; she was too frightened. So she practically moved in with me, staying with me every night in my little place. We were totally plugged in to each other. My urgent need to be with her cancelled out any growth I might have experienced through the AA program. We both attended meetings, but I heard nothing. We held hands and went on our merry way, disregarding all advice and warning signs that we were just too dependent on each other. Anna became my God, my program, and my life. Anytime I saw her wanting to spend some time alone or with the girls, I panicked.

We'd been living together for about five months when I got a tremendous break.

Like many men in show business, I'm a member of the Friars, a show business-oriented men's club. Some of the biggest names in entertainment preside over the club. Milton Berle is president. The list of celebrities who frequent the club in Beverly Hills is endless—from Frank Sinatra all the way back around to Bob Hope.

At the Friars Club, just before you enter the dining room, is a billboard that stands by itself at the entrance, with the name of a member who just passed. The funeral home and time of burial are also stated. So before you walk in to have your lunch, there it is: Sid Goldberg passed on. It's very appetizing.

This one afternoon I wanted to go the the Friars because the following week we were going to roast Howard Cosell. All the comedians were looking forward to lambasting Howard because of his loud mouth, and we'd all get a shot at him.

I headed up the stairs to the dining room, saying hello to a few of the members who were leaving. As I entered the dining room I saw no sign up today. Someone got an extra day!

The dining room was filled with loud voices bantering back and forth. I glanced over at Milton Berle's private booth, reserved for him because he is the president of the Friars. It's the place where all the comedians congregate whenever they come to the Friars. Not everyone can sit with Milton, only when he sees you, and invites you.

Milton saw me standing at the entrance and waved to me to come join him.

As I approached the table, Red Buttons, Don Rickles and Danny Thomas were seated with Milton in his booth.

"Sit down, Sammy," Milton said. "You know everybody." I said hello to all and shook their hands as I sat down.

The topic of conversation, as always, was show business—stories that date back to all the beginnings of these men's illustrious careers. I just sat there in awe and listened. Two hundred seven years of comedy legends were their combined ages.

Then the mood and tempo changed. From show business to the coming of Red Buttons's son's bar mitzvah.

Danny Thomas chimed in, "A bar mitzvah? Thirteen years old? Would you believe that come this Friday, Rosemary and I will be celebrating our fortieth wedding anniversary?"

Rickles jumped in, "Big deal! You wanna hear something? Next week, after I close in Vegas, I'm flying to Israel—my son is going to have his bar mitzvah, in Israel. I mean, come on Red, that's Jewish!"

Then Milton started with his wife, Ruthie, and his mother-in-law who plays the horses. It went on for the next hour.

NO BUSINESS AND SHOW BUSINESS

These warm, wonderful family men will in a few days use every filthy word that one can ever think of and spray Howard Cosell. These living legends of comedy will turn into wild animals—loving every minute of it, as Howard slowly sinks into the floor!

As always, Milton Berle was roastmaster. The affair was at the Beverly Hilton, with fifteen hundred men in attendance—a completely stag gathering—all of them patiently waiting for the speakers to really lay it to Howard.

Milton opened the festivities. "Gentlemen, I want to welcome you to the tribute to Howard Cosell. Let's get one thing straight. I am not going to put down Howard Cosell, because he never said anything bad about me—even though he called my wife a yenta, a pain in the ass, and a bad hump. But fuck it, that's her problem.

"As you know, Howard, your co-workers Frank Gifford, Don Meredith, and Keith Jackson wanted to be here—couldn't make it on account of the distance. They're out in the lobby.

"And George Burns was supposed to be here, but he's having trouble with his pacemaker. Every time he farts, he opens his garage door.

"Danny Thomas couldn't be here, wasn't feeling too good. He had a terrible nightmare—he dreamt he died and went to heaven and Saint Jude pissed on him.

"As you all know, gentlemen, Howard is a key man at ABC. Anytime anybody wants to take a shit, they ask Howard for the key.

"He wants you to think he's a sex symbol. He hasn't had any pussy since Morris the Cat died.

"Now I'd like to introduce our first speaker of the evening, Pat Butram, who for years was Gene Autry's sidekick—and who has the only black belt in cow shit—Pat Butram."

"Thank you, Mr. Berle. And you're right, I've been walking in cow shit for years—and that's the reason I don't mind following you!

"I haven't heard words like these since Frank Sinatra kicked Rona Barrett in the balls."

Berle introduced George Allen, former coach of the LA Rams and Washington Redskins, and had him take a bow.

"One night," Milton said, "George's wife said to him, 'That's all you talk about is football, football, football. Either fuck me or trade me!' "

Milton turned to Don Rickles, on the dais, and said, "Don, do you know what a guy with a sixteen-inch cock has for breakfast?"

"No," Don said, "what?"

The Warm-up

"I had orange juice, cantaloupe . . ."

Pat McCormack, one of Johnny Carson's writers, got up and announced, "Usually sports figures get candy bars named for them. Cedars Sinai Hospital just called—they're naming an enema after Howard Cosell."

George Jessel was then introduced and replied to an especially lewd remark that had just been made about Cosell. "I am not in a position," he said, "mentally or otherwise, to talk about Mr. Cosell's associations with the intimate parts of a woman's body—I don't remember any intimate parts of a woman's body."

Berle introduced Don Rickles, who turned to Cosell and said, "Love your nose, Howard. You're either a Jew or a Buick!

"As a boy," Don said, "Howard played with his prick so much he finally became one!"

And on and on.

One night Roger Smith, Ann-Margret's manager-husband, saw me perform at a mixed dinner dance for Friars and wives at the Friars Club. Both Roger and Ann-Margret were in the audience of five hundred, along with many other celebrities and show-business people, and they saw me grab that sophisticated audience and just about knock them out of their seats. I was really hot and everyone there could feel the electricity. It was like I had come back from the dead; I was the surprise of the evening.

Milton Berle, the emcee, stood on the stage after I'd walked off and said, "Ladies and gentlemen, what you just saw tonight was a sheer stroke of a young man's genius. I've attended many of these functions over the years and I've never seen a comedian practically unknown to many of you come out here, disarm you, and totally enthrall you. Let's bring him back and let him know how much we appreciate his talent—Sammy Shore!"

I walked out and to my amazement the crowd stood up and applauded and cheered. I stood on that enormous stage in silence. It was my moment. Uncle Miltie stopped me as I was leaving the stage. He put his arms around me, whispered in my ear, "You bastard, you stole my show," stuck his tongue in my ear, and laughed. He took my hand and once again walked me out in front of the cheering crowd.

"Sammy Shore!" he said into the mike. "Now get the hell out of here!" Then he ad-libbed for another twenty minutes and everybody had a great time.

NO BUSINESS AND SHOW BUSINESS

Many people approached me right after the show and wondered what had happened to me these past few years. They were happy to see me sparkle again—better than ever, they said.

Roger Smith was one of the well-wishers. "God, Sammy," he said, "I've never seen you better, even with Elvis. I haven't seen you around Vegas for a while, where you been? Your act is dynamite."

"Thanks, Roger—well, I've been mostly working out of town." Which was bullshit. "You know, working on my act."

Then Roger got the name of my agent and wanted to know whether I was working on November 10.

"As of now, Roger, I know I'm not." I tried not to sound terribly excited. I was going bananas with anticipation. Then he told me that if I was available, he'd like to bring me back to Vegas to open November 10 for Ann-Margret in a two-week engagement at the Hilton. "That room should be familiar to you, Sammy," he said. It would be Ann-Margret's last year at the Hilton, because she was going to start next year with Caesars Palace.

I acted like it was no big deal, like I belonged. Sometimes you have to put on a false front just to show you have confidence.

I couldn't wait to tell Anna. I could have stayed backstage at the Friars until after midnight sopping up all the love I needed as a performer, but getting home was more important.

I got into my car and headed east on Wilshire till I hit Clark Drive, made a left on Clifton Way, and parked in the street. I got my stuff and as I headed up the back stairs I saw the apartment was dark. It was eleven-thirty. I knew Anna should have been home by now, since the meeting she'd been to was a women's stag that let out at ten, and even if she'd gone out to have coffee with the girls, she'd still be home. As I came up to the door I thought, Hey, what am I worried about, maybe she's sleeping—and wait till she hears this news!

I came in, turned on the lights—no Anna. I started to feel an emptiness and anxiety; it was one of those times when a drink would have killed those feelings. But no way tonight. I had a year on the program, I had Anna and what looked like a whole new career.

She'll be home soon, I thought, so I started making myself some coffee. I began pacing. I didn't understand. Here it was twelve-fifteen, and she'd never stayed out that late. Where the fuck was she? I started to burn. I wanted to tell her the news and all the excitement was turning into anger, the joy was gone. It was panic time.

The Warm-up

I heard a car stopping. I looked out and saw her parking her green '68 Caddy and turning out the lights. I tried to act like I was busy reading something on the couch as she came into the apartment. Whatever my feelings had been, I was just happy she was here.

But she looked pensive and uptight as she walked right by me on her way to the bathroom, with a passing, "Hi." I tried to cover up my concern. I gave her the big surprise as she emerged from the bathroom still buttoning her jeans.

"I got fantastic news," I said as she walked into the kitchen to put on water for her usual Sleepytime tea. She acted like she might not have heard me. I got up off the couch and followed her into the kitchen.

"Anna, I've got some great news to tell you."

She turned toward me, half-smiling. "Good news," she said. "I could stand to hear some good news." She seemed remote.

"You know, I did the show at the Friars tonight."

"Oh yeah, I forgot." She was pouring her tea. "How'd it go?"

"That's what I want to tell you. I was an unbelievable smash. It was my night!"

"That's swell," she said with little conviction. She passed by me to sit down at the kitchen table.

My anxiety mounted. Something was up. "Hey, Milton Berle hugged me and congratulated me in front of five hundred people! I got a standing ovation—I just wish you'd been there."

"I'm glad for you," she said. "You really deserve a big break—"

I interrupted. "That's not all. Roger Smith, Ann-Margret's husband, was there, and—are you ready for this?—"

I was like a little boy dying to tell his mommy the good deed he'd done.

I told her all about the great Vegas offer, and tears started to come into my eyes when I told her it was the same room I'd worked with Elvis, except this time would be so much better because she'd be there.

"I want you with me in Vegas, you'll get some new clothes, and opening night you'll be in the same booth Colonel Parker had—I'll be doing that show for you."

There was silence. She'd hardly been looking at me, except for an occasional glance.

Then she said, "Sammy, look, I'm so happy for you. Yet I'm sad—"

My heart stopped. The moment I'd been dreading was here. "What is it?" I said.

"I really don't know how to say this to you. You've saved my life, you nursed me back to sanity. You've loved me, watched over me, smothered me with too much—your kindness, love, whatever you call it. I just can't take this anymore. I feel choked off from growing. I feel so guilty telling you this, but—I have to go. I can't be with you anymore. I have to be a bird and fly, I can't stay here."

I started to sink in tears again. She went right to the closet and started taking out her things.

I pleaded with her to stay. I asked her to wait until at least I'd opened in Vegas, which didn't make a lot of sense, but I was saying anything that might work for the moment. "How can you do this to me?" I said. I started losing control.

"I wish you well in Vegas," she said. "I know you'll be a smash. Take care of yourself, Sammy—and thanks for everything you did for me. I'll never forget it."

She walked out and down the stairs. I followed. I even opened her car door, all the time trying to change her mind. No good. She said she was sorry, then drove away.

I had done it again. Once again I was a shell. Or, to be more honest, I was always a shell looking for something to fill me up, and now it was gone, just as everyone had predicted. I had to call several of the prophets that night, just to have someone to cry to and help keep me from drinking.

I had an act to put together with just a few weeks to go, but I felt like a walking bomb crater. Connie Stevens invited me to stay with her and her children in Malibu. I worked out of her house, calling my writers, taping jokes off the phone, making arrangements, and now and then running alone on the beach and screaming, "Please, God, take this pain away."

I walked out onstage in the Hilton's main room on November 10, 1977 and got a nice round of applause. I felt good as long as it lasted and I grabbed the mike.

"Good evening, ladies and gentlemen, it's nice being back in my favorite town—"

"We missed you, Sammy!" a voice said in the back of the room. "You're the greatest!"

"My agent," I said, and people started to laugh.

But my stomach was in knots. I had not been able to make it back from Anna. When I got into my act, it wasn't happening. I'd had nothing this time to quiet the anxiety, no more J&B to get me through the rough ones. I was cold-cocking it.

I had been in this position before—floundering in my act—but never as bad as this. I was losing my composure entirely, and I was thinking more about my pain than the job I had to do.

The audience became very uneasy. They couldn't figure out what was happening to me, and the more I realized this, the more frightened I became and the faster and more mechanically I talked, until I just wanted to run off the stage.

But I managed to get to the last part of my act, my trademark, Brother Sam.

"Gimme an amen!" I shouted.

A few amens were heard.

"Are you ready to be healed?" No response.

"Are you ready to be saved?" Nothing. But by now I was just reciting.

"Will you give me your money?" Absolute silence.

"Good night, folks," I said as the orchestra played "Bringing in the Sheaves." Some people applauded in their embarrassment. I headed down the back elevator in tears. I had never done so badly in all my years in show business.

I fell on my hands and knees as I entered my dressing room. I looked at the bar and all the bottles of booze and I prayed for the strength not to drink.

There was a knock at the door.

"Just a minute, I'm in the bathroom!" I shouted. I took a towel and washed my face and tried to get back my composure.

I opened the door.

Shecky Greene.

I was thunderstruck.

I shouted his name, we embraced.

We'd seen each other a couple of times since that little brawl in the Riviera casino and were back on speaking terms, but he was about the last person I expected to find at my door.

"I didn't know you were out there," I said.

"I just stood in the back. I wanted to watch you."

"I was terrible, Shecky, I really bombed. I feel just awful."

"What happened out there, Sammy? You seemed lost. I know it's not the greatest room in the world for comedy, but you've always done great here.''

I told him about Anna, and it turned out he had known her when she'd been with Mickey Black. And he told me the same thing had happened to him when his wife walked out on him.

"You can't let someone have that much power over you," he said. "You've got to save something for yourself, you can't give all of you away.

"You know," he continued, "we comedians are a special breed. We work with inner heart and soul, the comedy comes from within. And if your will is broken, you just become unnatural.''

He told me not to worry, I had twenty-seven more shows that would be a hell of a lot better.

Then Dick Lane, Hilton's head of entertainment, came down and wanted to know what was wrong. I told him I was sorry, that I didn't want to let him down. I also said I didn't want to talk about it and I'd get it together for the next show. And in the next couple of days I did start to put it together and the shows improved.

When the reviews of that first show came out, they were devastating. One reviewer said, "I can't believe Ann-Margret picked Sammy Shore to open for her. It must be politics." Another said, "I've seen better acts on *The Gong Show*."

Even though I'd been sober for over a year, I was finding out that it didn't mean all my character problems would just vanish. In fact, they were now more prevalent than ever because I couldn't drink them away. All the fear, insecurity, and neediness had surfaced, and with Anna out of my life, they were magnified many times.

I was finally beginning to realize, after all the pain I'd been through in my life, that with all these women the problem was mine, not theirs. I chose disturbed ladies to fix things for me. It wasn't their fault that I needed them so badly.

Ann-Margret understood what was going on with me, and talking with her gave me the strength to come back during the engagement. There were good nights, some brilliant nights, and by the close of the fourth day, I was my old self. The last night of the engagement Roger came back to congratulate me—and asked me to open for Ann-Margret the following March at the Sahara Tahoe, and then, best of all, at Caesars Palace in May. I was ecstatic.

I had done it on the natch.

The Warm-up

I was back in LA the next day, at an AA meeting in Brentwood. As the meeting ended and I headed through the crowd to the back door, I heard that voice.

"Sammy!"

I turned. Anna. My heart started to jump. I tried to stay cool. "Oh, hi."

"Hey, I heard you did fantastic in Vegas."

"Yes—thanks."

"I tried to call. Did you get the message?"

"Well yes, I did. But I really had nothing to say."

"Oh look, Barbara's waiting for me. I've got to run—I'll see you." And she ran off to another woman's Cadillac Seville. I had found out the lover Anna left me for was a lesbian. I still had very strong feelings for her, though, and I knew I had a way to go before I could forget her.

As Shecky told me that night at the Hilton, comedians are indeed a special breed. Most people think we're the brave, brassy few. But underneath all that moxie we know that the audience is a beast who can tear us apart. No matter what level of comedian you are—novice, veteran, warm-up, or star—the same thing is at stake: "Will they like me?"

I never really understood this until recently. I always thought stars of great stature would never be insecure. After all, why should they be?

My revelation came one night in Atlantic City, at the Resorts International. I was then appearing at Caesars Boardwalk Regency with Tony Orlando and was becoming an Atlantic City favorite, having done well in front of Bobby Vinton a few weeks before. I went over at dinner to meet Masholem Riklas, owner of the Riviera in Las Vegas, and his beautiful wife, Pia Zadora, who was appearing there at the Resorts International with Buddy Hackett. I knew both Rik and Pia very well from my appearances at the Riviera, so it was like old home week as I sat down at the table.

Just then Buddy Hackett came wandering by. Buddy has always been my idol, a comedic genius. "Hi Pia, Rik, Sam—did ya catch the show?" Buddy said right away.

"You know," Buddy said, "I did a completely different act for the second show, totally different than the first."

We all mumbled our approval.

"You know," he said, "I haven't done the same show twice since I've been here."

Business hadn't been very good for Buddy, and as I sat there I felt his insecurity coming through. And, believe me, I'm an expert on insecurity. It was hard for me to believe that Buddy had to persuade us he was a genius as a comedian.

"Look at all the weight I've lost," he said, not giving us a chance to notice on our own. He started in on his salad. "I'm in Overeaters Anonymous, lost over twenty pounds," he said.

I felt he wanted all of us to tell him he was the funniest man alive. But we couldn't do that, if only because he was pushing so hard for it. And for the first time in my life I felt relaxed and on a par with Buddy Hackett. I started to get funny and was joined by Stewie Stone, a young comedian doing the warm-up for Englebert Humperdinck. We all sat around as equals. I realized we're all the same. At any given moment we can become afraid—even in a restaurant with friends, when things aren't going our way.

Don Rickles is another comedian whose talent is phenomenal but who can be just as insecure as he is brilliant. Sometimes I think the two qualities go hand in hand. As much as Rickles can be an animal onstage, putting people down in that special way, offstage he can be the lost little boy looking for approval.

I was in the audience the night that he and Steve Lawrence first tried working together at Harrah's in Lake Tahoe. I was with Tony Orlando, who had just closed the night before. The show wasn't received that well by the audience; it seemed too long, and Don was straining a bit to make it work. He was just a bit off his stride. Steve was marvelous; you could put him in the middle of a field and his voice would carry through the skies.

The protocol in show business is that if an entertainer comes to see your performance, near the end of the show you introduce the celebrity and have him take a bow. Tony was introduced, but I wasn't. I didn't know why Don had snubbed me, but I didn't feel comfortable about going down with Tony afterward to Don's dressing room. I waited a while, talking to friends, and when I went down, Don shouted: "Sammy! Where the hell have you been?"

He embraced me and, in my ear he said, "I'm really sorry I didn't introduce you—we go back a lot of years—Detroit, Washington—" Then, to the people there, he said, too insistently, "You all know

Sammy Shore, everyone, one of the funniest comedians around." In fact everyone did know me. They waved.

"How long you gonna be in Tahoe, Sammy?" Don went on. "Let's have lunch."

He was embarrassed about not introducing me, but what was really bothering him was his feeling that the show had not gone well. I left with the realization that we all walk around with the same clay feet.

People seem to forget that comedians are not always comedians. We are human beings first. We do something out on that stage that is just not a natural way of life. We can't be that way all the time. Yet many people think that at any given moment they can turn us on for an instant laugh.

"C'mon, say something funny!"

I'll admit that the desire to be loved can be overpowering, and at times we do succumb.

"C'mon, say something funny!"

But just once I would love to say, when given that command, "FUCK OFF!" I don't know how other comedians feel, but I abhor the idiot with a martini in his hand and the breath of old sneakers who stops you dead in your tracks and says, "Hey, I know I can't tell 'em the way you do, but I got this joke I heard, maybe you can use it in your act." Turns out to be about these two sailors who are walking down the street and this woman pulls up in a new Mercedes.

" 'C'mon over,' she says. 'I'll give you something you've never had in your life.'

"One of the sailors shouts, 'Run like hell, she's got leprosy!' "

You have to stand there like a nice person and listen to this jerk screw up what might have been a good joke. Then as an afterthought he goes into his tirade about how he's always so funny at the office. And they tell him he ought to go to The Comedy Store and try to become a comedian.

Let him try it!

When you're standing out there and it's not happening for you—I truly don't think I can explain the feeling. It's the pits. The emptiness and pain of failure on the stage at times can be excruciating. "We don't love you anymore," the audience says. "Get out of our lives. We don't have time for you. Get us somebody new who can make us laugh. You're not it!"

172

Yet when it's happening, the feel of the audience, the exhilaration, the warmth and laughter create an incredible high that I think only a comedian can feel. It takes over your entire body, like scoring a winning touchdown. When they want you back for more, it's like you're on your way to the Super Bowl. And how wonderful it feels when you go offstage and the crew hands say, "Hot audience tonight, ya really killed 'em." The crew isn't out there, they only hear the laughter or the silence.

I believe that it starts within yourself and radiates throughout the room. The audience senses it: "I know this guy's gonna be funny."

For a well-known comedy star, the audience is there especially for him. They know him; they've seen him on television. When a Steve Martin walks out, the audience knows his act better than he does. For those fans he's God. Not that stars like Martin did not have to come up from the pits—they've all paid the price.

But if you're unknown—the warm-up—you'll never get a second chance to make that first impression. You've got to hit them fast and make them like you in the beginning, so that by the time you get to your strong material you're really rolling. If by chance you're out there struggling, for whatever reason, by the time you've rushed to get to your strong material, you're in deep, deep trouble. The flop sweat, the gut full of anxiety, the rubbery legs all contribute to making your strong stuff sound like you're reciting instead of performing it. Your speech pattern becomes too rapid as the fear sets in, and you just want to hurry and get off and go into some corner and die.

The gift of comedy is given to a very few. Our agony pays for the joy we have of standing among the many and, on any given night, being able in a few minutes to relax every muscle in their bodies—to make them forget the past, the future, the pain.

Sometimes I think we're divine healers, put on earth to spread the word of joy and laughter. That it's a healing gift was well demonstrated by Norman Cousins in his book *Anatomy of an Illness*. Comedy films were an essential ingredient in his self-cure. Cousins found that getting deep belly-laughs from his favorite Marx Brothers flicks jogged his internal organs and relieved his pain so that he could sleep.

Who knows, maybe in the future doctors and psychiatrists will give way to clowns and comedians with their own offices.

"Hello, Comedian Shore? I have these terrible stomach cramps and I feel just lousy. What do you suggest?"

"I'll send over a fifteen-minute Laurel and Hardy and a Three

173

The Warm-up

Stooges. If they don't help you, I'll come over myself and do twenty minutes.''

When Marty Feldman died, critic Charles Champlin said of him, ''He was a kind, warm man who took his friends and the world more seriously than the world, too often, was prepared to take him.''

Indeed, most comedians I know are truly serious-minded people. Sit with us sometimes and you get the feeling that the world is coming to an end. We also like to philosophize without ever getting to the point. We just love to hear ourselves talk.

Milton Berle, whom I love dearly, is usually very serious when you're sitting with him alone late in the afternoon at the Friars Club. But get a few more men around his celebrity booth and—well, he never stops talking when there are more than three. It's not as if he's craving company; in fact it's an honor to get the chance to sit with him. But when the people are there, God forbid you try to break in on him when he's got a roll going! Forget it! And when Uncle Miltie picks up the phone—a red one, yet—and starts to talk very softly, as he usually does on the phone, do *not* carry on a conversation with anyone else at the table. He'll shush you down.

The comedian's ego never dies. We need that constant confirmation: you were funny, honey. That's rough on our spouses and close friends.

I'm speaking here of the nightclub type of comic. Comedy actors, like a Harvey Korman, are out of their element when they sit with us. Korman once told me he could never stand out there alone, he'd die. Give him a Carol Burnett to bounce off of, however, and he's brilliant.

We comedians are really not a handsome lot. Not that we're ugly, but many of us have faces only a mother could love. Now I'm speaking of my own generation of comedians; many of the new crop are very handsome young men. And it just seems that the good-looking ones are the less funny ones. Go shoot me if I'm wrong.

Having been rejected by women most of our lives, we comedians have staked our psychological survival and also our slim chances of getting laid on trying to make a girl laugh. ''Oh, you're so funny and cute,'' she'd say.

Then, when I'd try to run my hand up her leg, she'd get angry. ''Stop that!''

Well, we've always got the same cop-out. "I was only kiddin'. I'll try anything to get a laugh."

"Well, that's not funny!"

Although comedians typically try to act like macho make-out artists, the fact is that both warm-ups and star comedians have problems getting women to take us seriously. Women don't want to believe that we have a serious side—and if we have a *somber* side as well, that's even worse. They just love to laugh at us; they find that wonderful and appealing. But we still can't get laid.

Of course, I'm not saying that all of us are unattractive to women. There have been a couple of giants, as we call them in the trade. And I don't mean tall people. *Cocksman* is the word for these guys. In fact, Milton Berle is known for this very attribute.

Now I didn't go up to Milton and say, "Milton, I hear you're a big star. Can I look?" I happened to be sharing a room with him in Palm Springs when we were down there to do a benefit for his brother, Frank. Milton was in the bathroom.

"Hey, Sam, could you bring me my hairbrush? It's on the dresser," he said.

As I walked in with it, his back was turned to me, but he turned around with the reputed genital in his hand, as he had just finished taking a leak. I was shocked, and I guess my reaction was obvious.

Milton stood there smiling at me. "You didn't think there was one around like this, did you?"

I had heard through the years that Milton was the biggest guy in show business, but . . .

Hey, don't get me wrong. I don't go seeking large genitals to gaze upon. You sit in the steam room with your fellow comedians—and let it all hang out.

Comedians can be very vindictive. Ask Marty Brill, a comedian out of Chicago who more than twenty years ago got his first big break opening for Merv Griffin at the Riviera in Las Vegas.

On that night in the same hotel, Shecky Greene was to open in the lounge, in one of his many engagements at the Riviera. Shecky was by now a very big lounge star. He and Don Rickles were the two hot comedians on the horizon. Neither of them had any reason to worry about other new young comics coming around to take away from their laurels. Although I must say that Shecky always had a fixation on

Don, for whatever reasons. Maybe Shecky heard that Don farted a certain way one night; Shecky would scream "He stole my fart!"

Marty Brill was ecstatic that his friend and fellow Chicagoan Shecky Greene, whom he'd idolized all his life, would be appearing at the same time with him in the same hotel. Marty had invited his family and flew them all in from Chicago—his mother, father, and sister—to be there for his opening night.

Marty did well in front of Merv, then headed with his family to the lounge to see Shecky's show. Shecky's opening, as usual, had an array of celebrities in the audience—Bob Hope, Danny Thomas, Dean Martin. Any stars working in town would drop by sooner or later to catch Shecky's inventive style. Bob Hope had recently said that Shecky Greene was the funniest comedian then working, an opinion then shared by many of the people coming to see him.

Unbeknownst to Marty Brill, a struggling young comedian whom I'll call Joey Vee happened to be in Vegas that day trying to find work. He heard that Shecky was about to open the Riviera and figured maybe Shecky could put in a good word for him there. Shecky was known as an easy touch. When he was sober, he was a pussycat and would give you the moon.

So Joey called Shecky and, as Joey had hoped, Shecky invited him to come over for coffee. As Joey arrived at the hotel, he noticed on the marquee that Merv Griffin was opening the main show room—and underneath Merv's name was Marty Brill's. Now, most comedians on their way up are very envious when they see one of their peers on the same level moving ahead. How did he get that job? they think to themselves—I'm funnier than him! And sometimes they'll do destructive things to hurt the other comic.

As Shecky and Joey were rapping about the foibles of show business that day, Joey happened to ask if Shecky knew Marty Brill, who was opening for Merv.

"Sure I know him, I know him very well. We're both from the same neighborhood in Chicago," Shecky said. "He's a funny kid, I'm glad he got a break."

"Yeah, he sure is funny," Joey said. "He should be—he's doing part of your act."

"He's what!"

"Really, Sheck—I just saw him in Chicago working at the Casino of Tomorrow, on the South Side."

"No wonder that bastard hasn't called me," Shecky said.

Now as kind as Shecky was at heart, all he had to hear was that someone was doing even a line of his act and he'd become so paranoid he'd literally walk up onstage where you were working and try to pull you off. So, having written this, I have to prepare myself for a possible onslaught by that raging Jewish bull somewhere, coming up onstage and pulling me off for saying these things about him. So I'm in training. (But I have to be honest—the closest I ever got to a black belt in karate was a seat belt in a Toyota! That's a joke, but it about sums it up.)

Shecky became furious. He told his manager, Frankie Ray, about it and asked Frankie to catch Marty's opening show.

But Shecky never waited for Frankie's report. When he came out onstage to face the audience that included Marty Brill and family, he was fuming.

"Good evening, ladies and gentlemen," Shecky seethed. "Did you all get a chance to see Merv Griffin tonight?"

Some of the audience started to applaud.

"Well," Shecky said, "opening the show was a young comedian I used to know in Chicago. In fact, folks, he used to follow me all over town—mimicking me. Always had his face up my ass."

Some of the audience started to wonder what he was doing. They all knew Shecky was a wild man and figured he was about to come up with something funny.

"And he's sitting ringside here," Shecky said, "right down here ringside. How about a nice hand, you might have seen him in front of Merv—*Doing My Act! Marty Brill!*"

With that Shecky came off the stage and lunged at Marty. He had become possessed. Marty's sister grabbed Shecky before he could hit Marty.

"How dare you insult Marty, you vicious sonofabitch."

The maître d' also grabbed Shecky and held him.

"Why'd you do this to me, Shecky?" Marty pleaded as tears started to roll down his cheeks. "I'm not doing your act. I don't understand, man. I'm your friend!"

The entire room was in shock. But the people there who were intimate with Shecky already knew he was capable of such things.

Shecky soon learned that he'd been completely out of line, that Marty wasn't doing any of his act. If he had stopped to think, I'm sure it would have occurred to him that if you were a comedian doing another guy's jokes, you'd have to be insane to be doing them in the same hotel at the same time as the person you were copying.

Shecky tried to make amends. But Marty was shattered and bitter. "I'll accept your apologies," he said, "if you bring all those people back into the lounge who were there last night—Bob Hope, Danny Thomas, my family—and tell them openly, 'I made a mistake, I'm sorry.' Then I'll accept it!"

Of course Marty was saying that the damage could never be repaired. "I'll never forget what you did to me," he told Shecky.

And twenty-three years later, Marty Brill apparently still feels the same. Now a successful comedian, actor, and writer, Marty was recently at a meeting with some producers at NBC, where he'd just finished writing a comedy pilot. The producer of the projected show mentioned that Shecky Greene would be a natural for the lead.

Marty looked around the room and said, "Yes, that's a marvelous idea, Shecky would be great for it. But as you probably don't know, Shecky has cancer."

End of discussion. Even though Shecky underwent successful surgery and his career is still going great guns, Marty put the hex on him.

Looking back on my career as a warm-up, I realize that the fact that my marriage wasn't going well had a lot to do with intensifying the turmoil I always went through as an opening act. However, there are always many factors that complicate life for the guy—or woman— who opens. For example, let that warm-up go out and destroy that audience or even get an unexpected standing ovation—especially on an opening night—and you could be in deep trouble and not appreciated at all by the star and his manager. Our job is just to go out there and get them loose, set 'em up.

Only if a star feels very secure within himself will he appreciate the brilliance of an opening act. Tony Orlando is one of those who loves to follow a dynamite opening act.

I'll be honest. Some stars want you around just for the laughs and to get them girls, and they really don't care how funny you are out there. As long as you do a pleasing job in your allotted time, offend no one, and don't make waves with the management—well, you could work with that star for eternity.

NO BUSINESS AND SHOW BUSINESS

But the stars of yesteryear were true stars in every respect. The Nat King Coles, the Berles, the Bennys loved the performers who opened for them. There was respect for the opening act because these men were secure. For one thing, they didn't rely on a chemical for their high.

It's sad how many young performers have taken their lives because of drugs and alcohol, because our business is so pressure-packed and painful. Usually they're just looking for someone to say, "Hey, man, you really killed out there tonight—great set."

I don't want to sound like I'm preaching. After all, I once couldn't even walk out to do a benefit for a B'nai Brith lodge without the aid of several belts of Scotch.

The irony of all this is that we warm-ups are no less petty than some of the stars. We get jealous if another comic gets the job we might be up for, saying, "Him?! I'm funnier in my sleep!"

Another sad thing is the fact that it's a young man's business. The networks and the new concert stars are always looking for the latest breed of warm-up. After all, it feels a little unbalanced when a twenty-four-year-old star has a fifty-five-year-old comedian trying to warm up his young audience. The middle-of-the-road journeyman comic is no longer sought after unless a big star like Frank Sinatra likes him—and even then the work is only occasional.

It's time for us, the comedy vets, to move over and do whatever we can do to help the younger generation. Age is meaningless. We can do it till we die. That's exactly what Joe E. Ross of *Car 54* fame did. He was doing a date in his apartment complex for a crowd of older people; he was down on one knee, doing a bit with arms outstretched, when he fell backward and died. You always hear about an act dying—

But, Joey, that was ridiculous!

Milton Berle recently told me a funny story about the origins of the warm-up comedian. It happened in 1936.

Nineteen thirty-six was a good year for radio. Remember radio? That was also the year that Milton Berle came to California, after he had established himself as a well-known nightclub star.

The Texaco Star Theatre was one of the biggest radio shows and featured stars such as Ed Wynn, Bette Davis, and Paul Muni. One day the Buchanan Agency, which handled the Texaco account, asked

The Warm-up

Bill Grady, Milton's agent, if Berle could come by and warm up the studio audience. This had always been the announcer's job, but now they had the bright idea of using a comedian.

Grady was hot for Milton to try it out, but he ran into a wall of resistance from his client. Milton just wasn't thrilled about the idea of warming up an audience for somebody else. After all, he was a star in his own right and what he really wanted was a show of his own. But Grady persisted. He argued that the exposure would do Berle good and might give him the break he wanted.

So Milton agreed and walked out in front of the studio audience and killed them. The same day Grady was telling Berle just how excited the Buchanan people were about what he had done; they had set up an appointment to see Berle and Grady the very next day. It looked like the agent had been right.

The next day Milton and Grady went to the Buchanan offices, and sure enough, the Buchanan people were excited as hell about Milton's performance.

"You know what the agency guy says to me," Milton recalls. "He says, 'Mr. Berle, we are so impressed, we want to sign you for thirty-nine weeks of warm-ups!' "

Comedy and comedians have become big business in the past few years. Of course, comedians have always been important in show business, but what singers were to the business in previous years, comedians are today. All three TV networks, as well as the hotly competitive new cable companies, are eating up most of their air time with various forms of what they say is comedy. Comedy is the big supplier to the networks, which need people all the time to keep the comedy shows running.

And where do the networks go for their comedy supply? They go to virtually only two people: Mitzi and Budd. That's right—Mitzi Shore, my ex-wife and owner of the four Comedy Stores in California, and Budd Friedman, who operates The Improv in LA. These are the houses or factories that supply most of the young comedy minds and performers to the media. Of course, there are acting workshops and the like, but their contribution is relatively minimal.

You could say that Budd and Mitzi are the Mr. and Mrs. of Comedy. Only they don't live together—thank God! Get them together in the same room and there might be a nuclear explosion.

180

NO BUSINESS AND SHOW BUSINESS

On any given night, and especially on a weekend, you can see, at the main Comedy Store on Sunset and at The Improv on Melrose, more than seventy-five comedians working at twenty-five dollars a pop to fill these establishments with people who pay five and six dollars plus a two-drink minimum. These two clubs are responsible for a wave of carbon-copy establishments around the country and even around the world. In fact, there's a very successful Comedy Store in London. Not only did they steal the idea from Mitzi, they even stole the name.

You would think that with all the business each of these comedy empires is doing—Budd even has a syndicated TV show coming out of The Improv—the two principals involved would be friends and, at least at times, help each other. No way, Dr. J!—no chance. The resentments run deep, especially for Mitzi, who has insinuated that Budd once tried to buy The Comedy Store from underneath her. And of course Budd has no love for Mitzi. So there we are, two people controlling the pipeline of the future of comedy regarding each other as enemies.

What's sad, and incredible, about the entire fracas, is that if you work one place you can't, in most cases, work the other. Only the better-name, more successful comics can work both sides, since Budd and Mitzi need them to bring in business. But when it comes to the lesser names, the new boys and girls, forget it. They'll cut off your comedy balls if you cross that Maginot Line.

Another kind of barrier persisted until a couple of years ago, when all the comedians got together and decided not to work for Mitzi and Budd. A strike! The comedians didn't have any kind of union at the time, but one was formed as the strike went on for weeks and then months. The comedians had finally realized that, yes, these places are great training grounds for us, a place to be seen and discovered, but if Budd and Mitzi are making so much money, why can't they give us something? They'd been working for nothing at all. Now they decided, we have to eat while waiting for Johnny Carson to discover us; we need something, even if it's just fifteen or twenty bucks a set.

But Mitzi became very adamant about "her" comedians, her babies whom she'd nurtured. And she did do that—a lot of them were just kids new to California when they showed up at the Store. Today Mitzi still takes it very personally that they rebelled against her, and she still can't fathom it all.

The Warm-up

I had to look at both sides of the fence, as comedian and cofounder of the club. Rudy DeLuca and I had opened The Comedy Store in 1972 as a place for all of us comedians, young and old, actor and stand-up, to come by, jump up onstage, and have some fun. Every comedy person could experience our stage. That was the joy. No one knew what was going to happen. Rudy and I ran it and made no money—that wasn't the purpose. We left the back bar and refrigerator open to all comedians at any time of the night. "Go back and have, a beer." Of course, as with any good thing, they took advantage and we nearly went broke doing it.

When in my misery I gave Mitzi The Comedy Store as part of the divorce settlement, I hoped that she would keep the tradition of what it was originally intended to be. But I guess Mitzi was still very angry about having always been in the shadow of my Sammyism, my career and my personal problems. She had had it with being the housewife tending to four kids. Now she had a new domain and it was her time to show me and the world that she could be a very successful operator of nightclubs for the funnymen. She had always been business-oriented, and now she made The Comedy Store—and Stores—a financial bonanza.

What upset me most about the strike was the action of a young comedian who decided to take his own life by jumping off the roof of the Continental Hyatt House and splattering himself in front of The Comedy Store, where his fellow comedians had been pacing back and forth with signs that read BUCKS FOR YUKS. He'd left a note and tried to explain in it that Mitzi was not at fault: "I am sacrificing my life so you can all end the strike and get back together again." Of course, we all know that such a note is not the expression of a well person, which he wasn't. But he was a very good friend of Mitzi's.

I love Mitzi, and I love the comedians. But I'm a comedian first. And I feel that what Budd and Mitzi are doing—both in their attitudes toward each other and in the pressure they exert on young comedians—is totally out of keeping with what their establishments should be for. The idea should not be to instill fear in young minds. How can the kids create and be natural if they're frightened? The doors of both places should swing open anytime a comedian passes by.

Then you might hear conversations like this:

"How did it go at Mitzi's tonight?" Budd asks a comic.

"Great, Budd. I think I got the Carson show. One of the talent buyers was in the audience and I didn't even know.''

"I'm happy for you, Ron. How'd you like to do my TV show next Friday? One of the comics fell out.''

"Gee, thanks. Oh by the way, Mitzi says hello.''

Budd smiles. "Yeah, she's quite a lady!''

I know I can't tell a young comedian: "Be patient. You have a gift to use the rest of your life.'' I know I was the same way: I wanted it now, no matter what. My comedy came first and my family was just a deterrent. They were in the way. But in those days everybody seemed to get married, that was the thing to do. Today the young comedians either live with a girl or just use them for the moment. Few get married. They want so badly to make it that they allow no one to get in their way.

Another thing that I find kind of sad among the young guys is the lack of camaraderie. Jealousy and resentment run deep. They really don't care about each other, only about themselves and how they can get on the Carson show. They're waiting for that big break.

There's a warmth and love that radiates when you sit down with a Milton Berle, Red Buttons, or Dick Shawn. They have respect for each other. The things they say at Friars roasts—the hugging and kissing, the "thanks for coming,'' the tributes—these are not just pretty words or empty gestures. They all feel part of a wonderful gift, the gift of comedy. We know how precious that is, especially in these grim times.

Why are they all so loving? I really can't answer that. Maybe it's because most of them have attained a special place in the annals of show business—they're legends. But the difficult time in their lives is now, when they're no longer sought after, despite their fame. The exceptions would be George Burns and Bob Hope. George Burns is having the most successful period of his entire career. And Bob Hope is Bob Hope—the Kate Smith of comedy—Mr. America!

But ask *any* of these guys to do a benefit and they're always there, free, to help. Try asking a plumber to come unplug a drain for free for some elderly people who can't pay—forget it! The same with doctors and lawyers. Yes, there are some kind professionals who'll devote their time to the needy—but very few.

It's funny but I've never heard of any comedian, unless he had a job that night, refuse to help out, to fill in, to raise money for a fund.

The Warm-up

Yet all musicians are paid, no matter what the occasion.

The people who ask us to do these things often assume it's easy for us. "Oh, come on over and just do a few minutes. We don't expect you to do your *act*." Well, we aren't singers—we just can't sing a couple of songs and run. It ain't that easy. It takes time to walk out there, say hello, it's nice to be able to come by, and then work up to something funny. Now this crowd of maybe a thousand people has paid a hundred dollars a plate to raise money. Even though they know you're doing it for free, they've come to be entertained. And for a hundred dollars a plate, you'd better get funny. It may be a free and easy situation in theory, but in fact there's nothing worse than going out there and bombing in that situation. Even on the Friars roasts, it hurts your career if you don't do well—and that's a free one too!

But the risk is just the other side of the payoff that makes us so special. We have the power to turn people on—to make you laugh, cry, forget, remember. We can get into the deepest part of your soul and ignite the frustration, the sadness, the anger that lies there waiting to erupt. We're magicians who can then turn around and evoke the laughter and joy that will dissipate the frustrations of the day— that'll flush you out like an enema.

Isn't it great to be able to walk away feeling so good, so relaxed, not taking things so seriously? For that night we comedians are the gladiators, the knights in armor with swords of merriment, allowing you back into your childhood, when you were able to laugh at the silliest of things. Look at how *E.T.* brought us all back to those days. People need and want that kind of pure entertainment today. And we comedians are the E.T.'s of the nightclubs.

What a sad state of affairs we are in when our future comedy stars, the bright young creative minds, have to resort to bad-taste material for their laughs.

The only way they, the young comedians claim, can survive in the Comedy Stores or Improv's is to use off-color or drug-related jokes to get their laughs. I totally disagree with their concepts.

The blame lies with the nightclub operators. If Budd and Mitzi did not allow their comedians to use profanity in their establishments, they would not use that type of material—just as I requested the young comics when I operated The Comedy Store that no vulgarity should be used on my stage. And it wasn't, and they all did well.

NO BUSINESS AND SHOW BUSINESS

Doug Bushousen, talent buyer for all the Harrah's hotels, will not go into a Comedy Store or Improv to find comedians. He says, "I can't use hardly any of them because of the bad taste and blue material they use."

As I got to know Ann-Margret, talking with her practically every night in her dressing room before the show, I started to realize how shy she was. Here was this brazenly sexy woman throwing herself all over the stage in production number after production number, dancing, singing, and sliding her body every which way next to her male dancers, yet in her dressing room she was quiet and always in the shadow of her husband, Roger, who is a very strong guy. Roger ran the show—he practically pointed her to the stage—she did not do anything important without his approval. She adored him and was very much in love with him. I could really identify with Ann because she felt about Roger much the way I always felt about women.

Roger did everything, including putting up the sets, and for that spring engagement at Caesars Palace in Vegas he had a monumental job. We had just finished two weeks at the Sahara Tahoe, where Ann had broken in an entirely new act that cost two hundred fifty thousand dollars, and we were all set to go into Caesars for the first engagement of Ann's long-term contract.

Paul Anka closed at Caesars the previous night, and he has dozens of platforms that he works on to make him look much taller than he actually is. So after Paul's show it took the backstage crew just about all night to dismantle his sets. Ann-Margret's trucks were outside the stage entrance waiting for the last of Anka's equipment to be loaded. It was already seven-fifteen in the morning and Roger and the crew were waiting patiently, knowing they would have to do the impossible. Not only was Ann-Margret bringing in her largest ensemble ever of singers, dancers, and musicians, but she was using perhaps the most elaborate sets ever constructed in Vegas. It all had to be ready by the evening, right down to the laser lighting, and they'd be starting late.

Just to add to the tension, Roger had seen to it that every important columnist in the country had been flown in by Caesars to witness what he hoped would be Ann-Margret's greatest show. Caesars had also just installed, for the first time in Vegas history, Ticketron. No more dinner shows. Now you had to go to a box office and pick out where you wanted to sit, like for a ball game. The waiters and captains were furious because you'd no longer have to tip them to get a good table.

185

The Warm-up

Caesars wanted that era to end. No longer could the poor customer from Iowa be shoved into the back of the room. Now he could say, "I've got a ringside seat for Sinatra," and show you his ticket stub.

So the day was filling up with hostility from all the show-room help. And no wonder. I remember some nights with Elvis when Emilio, the maître d', made more in one night than I did in a week. Word around town was that Emilio was making somewhere between ten and fifteen thousand a week. So all the maître d's and captains around town were shitting in their pants at the idea that all the hotels might follow the new Caesars policy.

The hotel was a fiasco that day: people lining up in the casino for the box office, the workmen pounding the sets together backstage and rushing to get it all together before showtime, the orchestra rehearsing music, the captains and waiters milling around trying to figure out a new way to screw up the seating so the hotel would go back to its old policy. It felt like *Mutiny on the Bounty*. I was sitting in the show room waiting for the orchestra leader to call me for rehearsal, while the waiters and waitresses set up the room with clean tablecloths, knowing that food would no longer be served on them and looking at me like it was my fault.

Then it was eight o'clock and in thirty minutes I would once again have to go out there and fight the beasts. Pat, the stage manager, came back to my dressing room and said, "Sammy, ya got thirty, but the way it looks it ain't gonna start on time, no way. The opening set is only half up, so just hang in there."

I wandered around backstage and there was Roger with a hammer, pounding, pushing, and shoving sets and moving lights.

"Stay close, Sammy," he said. "We're not going at eight-thirty."

Then it was nearly nine and you could hear the restless people out front starting to clap, waiting for the main event, which of course wasn't me. There was no familiar sound of the clearing of dishes, because there were none, just drinks and ashtrays.

In all the years I had worked Vegas this was the first time that a show—and an opening show at that—had not gone off on time. The casino bosses are adamant about starting on time—and finishing on time—so they can get a shot at the people. Whenever the show starts to run over schedule, for whatever reason—the star doing extra time, the comedian getting a few extra laughs—word is sent backstage by the casino, actually telling you to cut two minutes out of your act.

186

And if by the next show you're still taking extra time, literally one of your balls is removed.

It was getting close to nine-thirty, and both the casino and the people were shouting, "Get the show on the road!" But the pounding of the sets was still going on.

Roger came to me. "Sammy, you're going to have to go out there and get them quiet, and you can't use the band, just go out and talk to them." He was really angry and frustrated and was not in a position to give a shit about me; all he wanted was someone to tame the crowd.

"I'll introduce you and just go out there." He started to grab a backstage mike. "You're going to have to work in front of the curtain," he said.

"Roger," I said. "There's hardly any room to move out there!"

"Then just stand still and talk!"

Terrific. It takes me all this time to get back to Vegas from my last opening-night fiasco—after Anna—and now I get another one.

"And now, ladies and gentlemen," Roger shouted into the mike, "here's Sammy Shore!"

No music, no build-up, not even at least a mention that I was a comedian. I came through the center opening of the curtain and looked out at thirteen hundred pissed people, plus pissed-off help. Some people were still wandering around ringside looking at their tickets and trying to find their seats; the maître d's were so disgusted, they were letting the people search on their own.

"Hi," I said. "Welcome to Dodger Stadium."

I ran down into the audience and grabbed a lady's ticket. "These stubs are for the Lakers game," I said. "That's tomorrow night at The Forum!"

You could still hear pounding backstage. "They're putting up a new wing of the hotel back there!"

I felt like one of the boxers from the championship fights that were often held at Caesars, only I had thirteen hundred opponents and it seemed like they were all dying to hit me below the belt.

I kept trying to find things to do. I knew that if I went into my act they would bury me. They didn't want to hear jokes about my divorce and gambling.

"Do another fifteen minutes!" Roger's voice came bellowing through the curtain. I glanced at my watch; it was nearly ten o'clock and I'd already been out there twenty-five minutes. I was sweating, but they all knew I wasn't doing my act and they were starting to come around. They were beginning to laugh at all the tumult concerning tickets and tables.

At about ten-twenty, Roger yelled, "Get off, Sammy, we're ready!" and everyone around ringside could hear him.

"Get off?" I shouted back into the mike. "Now that I've got 'em you want me to leave? No way! These are my people!"

They all started to applaud. In my hand I had a few tickets I had taken from the audience. I looked at them, ripped them up, threw them in the air, and said, "Take these tickets and shove 'em!" and walked off as the drum roll for Ann-Margret's music began. Now the crowd was not only steamed up but ecstatic.

Roger greeted me as I came off. He put out his hand. "Sammy, what can I say?"

It was a great moment for a comedian. I thought of my mom, how much she would have enjoyed tonight. Her Sammy, the talented stomach-shaker, getting all that applause, all that love. Maybe it could have made up, a little, for the applause she never got.

Print dresses, with floral designs weaving in and out, are my mother's favorite kind of attire. Most of her time, while I'm growing up, is spent cooking and cleaning, so she's never had what you would call a wardrobe. But come rain or shine, she always manages to wear a floral-print dress, even if it's in sad condition. Even though her days, from first sunlight to dusk, are spent cooking, scrubbing stairways, cleaning out the rooming-house toilets and urinals, she always manages to maintain her dignity—with her floral-print dresses.

Maybe she's just hoping that someday Hyman will say, "That's a nice dress."

But except for an occasional ride in the truck on a Sunday, she never gets a chance to exhibit herself. And never do I see my mom really decked out—except for this one Sunday, in mid-August.

That morning I've slept late. It's about noon. I open the door of my room and the apartment seems quite still. Unusual for that kind of day, even a Sunday. The dining-room door, leading to where they sleep, is closed. They might still be sleeping. But noon?

I quietly turn the knob and open the door. There in front of her dresser mirror stands my mom.

Fingernail polish is glowing on her hands. Her lipstick is pale red. Earrings are set in her tiny lobes, and a string of pearls fits loosely around her neck. An immense bosom-buster, ass-catcher type of girdle is squeezing red color into her face so she looks like she's about to explode. I stand in amazement as she finally puts on a new—well, somewhat new—flowered dress.

"Ma, what's the matter?" I blurt out. "Are you moving out? Are you all right?"

"I'm fine, Sammy."

"I've never seen you so dressed before!"

"Pa and I are going over to the Levines'," she says. "It's their twenty-fifth anniversary. Look, Sammy,"—she opens a box on the dresser—"I bought Mr. Levine this nice tie, and Mary this handkerchief. I hope Pa doesn't get upset because I bought 'em these."

I nod. "Where is Pa?"

"Downstairs in the store."

"But it's Sunday. Since when does he open on Sunday?"

Ma explains that he thought he might get a customer walking by, while waiting for her to get dressed—that he doesn't really want to go, but she's talked him into it just this morning.

"Well, have a nice time, Ma." I head back to my room to get ready to meet the guys to play ball, and after a few moments I hear the door shut. I've just got to see my mom dressed up again.

I open the apartment door and see the new queen of Wells Street slowly descending three flights of stairs. Perfume fills the hallway. She looks elegant.

"Ma," I shout, "you're beautiful!"

She just looks up and smiles. Today she's going to be Cinderella, no matter what.

A few hours later I come back home to find my mom sitting out in front of the store.

"Did you have a good time?" I ask her. She looks sad.

"We didn't go. Pa got mad because I spent a few dollars on the gifts. He just left me here and went to Newberry Park."

My dad always runs to the park when he gets pissed.

I tell her I'm sorry, and ask her if she wouldn't like to come upstairs. But she insists that she wants to sit in front of the store.

Maybe a neighbor will pass by—and tell her what a beautiful flowered dress she's wearing.

7

BOZO THE BEAUTIFUL

Beverlee Dean, the well-known psychic, has been a good friend of mine since we met a few years ago at a writers' seminar in Lake Arrowhead. I had been invited to talk about nightclub humor before an audience of comedy writers and producers. That night I happened to get very lucky and funny in front of my peers. Beverlee was taken with me, and as we talked she predicted a few things that were to happen to me in the coming year. And what she predicted came true.

One of her predictions was that in the month of May I'd meet a very beautiful lady.

I was waiting around outside the auditorium of the Sheraton Hotel in Honolulu. I had just finished my performance preceding Tony Orlando, who was onstage at the time. We'd been working the Islands for the past ten days and this was to be our last performance on a wonderful tour. We were all to go back to Los Angeles the next day. It was Sunday night, May 31.

All that month I'd been waiting for my lady, but she just didn't show up. So I'd more or less forgotten about what Beverlee said. I was just sitting in one of the chairs, munching on some macadamia nuts and feeling kind of sad that tomorrow I'd have to go home. I'd made some wonderful friends here, and my comedy was well received by the local people. Tony, of course, had torn the Islands apart.

You'd think they'd never seen anyone like him before. Tony is all love, and so are the Islands.

My chair was in a corridor that led to the restrooms, and of course all kinds of people were coming and going. Tony was in the middle of his "Colors of My Mind," from *Barnum*, which is so beautiful and touching. I reached down to put my empty jar of nuts next to my chair.

As I started to get up, a blond girl dashed past me. Her small, curvaceous body and beautiful legs trotted back into the auditorium like a champion filly. My heart started to pound—I just had to see her. Where were these feelings coming from all of a sudden? I see beautiful girls all the time and don't have heart palpitations.

I started my chase . . . and luckily, I had my jogging outfit on. She was standing in the back of the room watching Tony. I guess she was waiting for him to finish his number, as Tony was already among the audience, standing on the tables.

I stood for a moment and just gazed at her. She was beautiful. My insecurities flared up. Maybe she wouldn't even recognize me, especially in my gym clothes. But I had to meet her. I meandered over.

"Hi," I said. "I'm Sammy."

She just looked at me for a moment and said nothing, but smiled.

"Isn't Tony great?" I said.

"He's wonderful," she said.

She stared at me again, and then her eyes lit up. "Aren't you Sammy Shore?"

"Yes," I said, nearly swallowing my tongue.

"You were fantastic . . . I just love comedians. You look a lot younger off the stage."

"Yeah. The lights make you look older." But I really didn't want to talk about *that* subject.

I could really see her now. She was indeed beautiful, but young.

I took her by the hand and rushed her out into the corridor.

"Come on . . . I want to talk to you." And she came along freely and easily. Out in the hall all I could do was basically stand there and lust. We agreed to meet the next morning and spend the day together until I'd have to go.

That night I couldn't sleep. I waited for Barbara in the Sheraton lobby. I saw the willowy pixie sauntering over with her little beach bag, sun outfit, and petite sandals. She put her arms around me.

"Good morning, Sammy, my funny man," as she kissed me on my mouth. It's sure good to see you again."

"Oh hi, Barbara," I floundered like a teenager. "Good morning, and aloha."

"Let me go into the ladies' room and I'll put my suit on. I'll only be a minute."

I just waited like a puppy. Was Beverlee right? Was this the girl? Barbara came out of the ladies' room with a swimsuit that hugged her most unbelievable body.

Of course there were many beautiful women who live in or frequent the Islands. But I never saw more heads turn than when Barbara walked along the beach with me. She literally stopped traffic.

I brought her over to the Hilton, where Tony and the guys were staying. She was not well received by the women around the pool, only by the men. Tony sat with us. When Barbara left for a moment, Tony said, "Holy Christ, Sam, where did you get that?"

I told him. He proceeded to tell me that he felt she was into drugs and that she wasn't all there, that I should forget her.

Tony was my closest friend. He knew what I had been through and he did not want to see me get hurt. But at that moment I was once again blind, fulfilling another one of my fantasies. I simply wanted her.

In the next couple of hours she told me practically her whole life story. I listened to every word, trying to remember what Tony had said.

She started to cry. "Sammy, you're so wonderful. You just listened to me—no one listens to me. No one cares on the Islands. All they want to do is use me."

We went up to my room. Before she could put her bag down, I grabbed her, turned her around, and passionately kissed her. She reciprocated by just about putting her tongue down my throat. I gently unpeeled her swimsuit and lifted her sensuous body into bed.

In a few hours I was to board a plane back to LA. We had dinner in the hotel's Polynesian restaurant, with Hawaiian songs of love in the background. She apparently couldn't keep her hands off me.

"You're such a sensitive man, Sammy. Do you really have to go back tonight? Why can't you stay a few days with me? I have my own three-bedroom condo on Maui. It would be just wonderful. I want to get to know you. You're so special."

My ears were ringing. I hadn't had such accolades from a girl, especially this kind of beauty, since the days with Elvis. I was in sheer ecstasy. "I can't stay, Barbara. I have a show tomorrow night in LA."

"Can't you get out of it? Tell them you have the Hawaiian flu."

I really wanted to. I hadn't felt this good in years. Why not enjoy it? You deserve it, Sam. Make the call.

But something healthy inside said no. "Take me to the airport, Barbara, it's getting close."

She cried all the way. "Can I come to LA to see you this summer? My daughter will be staying with my mom and dad for the summer. I'll have the whole summer to be by myself."

"Great, Barbara. Come over for a week or two."

She put a lei around my neck, and I felt like I was leaving Pearl Harbor on furlough from the navy, leaving my girl behind to go back to the States.

"I'll write to you!" she shouted as tears flowed from her eyes. "You're gold, Sammy."

"Flight two-oh-three just landed from Honolulu, sir."

"Thank you," I said as I rushed to the gate. The weeks of waiting, the phone calls—she was finally here. My friend who owns a limousine service got me his long-stretch job with a driver, as a gift for me to use at my disposal.

"I'll wait here in front of the baggage for you, Mr. Shore," Joe, the driver, said. I was enjoying this whole trip. Champagne waited, chilled, in the limo for her. I felt and acted like a star.

The gate was filled with well-wishers welcoming friends and family to California. Everyone coming down the ramp wearing leis and looking so healthy. Where was Barbara? I hope she didn't miss the plane. Among the many people milling and moving I saw her beautiful face.

"Barbara!" I shouted. "Over here!"

She looked like she had stepped out of *Vogue*. She was bronze and wore a light linen suit with a very short skirt and gold lamé sandals. A white lei of the most exotic Hawaiian flowers I had ever seen circled her neck. Her face was specked with gold dust. She had come prepared.

"Hi, Sammy." She kissed me tenderly. "It's so good to see you."

As we stood at the baggage claim, she handed me the baggage checks. There were five!

193

The Warm-up

"I just brought a few things, I really don't know how they dress here . . ."

Five enormous bags rolled off the belt for Joe to put into the limo as we both entered the car.

"This is beautiful, Sammy."

Joe opened the bottle of champagne. "Can I pour it for you, ma'am?"

My apartment in the Marina was just ten minutes from the airport. We exchanged niceties on the way. She knew we were to spend July 4 weekend in Palm Springs. It would be at my newly purchased hotel, consisting of nineteen villas. I didn't want to tell her about those—kind of a surprise later, I thought.

Joe broke his ass carrying up her luggage. She started to hang her dresses and take out some of her things to bring to Palm Springs.

Her bags were open, and there facing me was a bag that held about fifteen pairs of shoes. As she sorted her things, out came a couple of framed pictures of her daughter, which she promptly placed on the dresser in my bedroom.

"Isn't she gorgeous? You'll just love her, Sammy." She continued to move her things in. "I'll take this, I'll leave this. Is this dress too hot for Palm Springs? I'll take all my cottons."

I mean this girl came to stay the summer. I just went along with it, knowing that at least at this point I was still in control. I had experience—the battle scars of my past encounters.

As we lay on the bed, I got so excited, I wanted to make love to her so badly. I started to move close and slowly touched her breasts.

She seemed distant. "Please Sam, I don't want to now. I have cramps—and I'm tired." She pulled away to go to sleep.

What was this?

As soon as she found out my son and I owned the Palm Springs place, she was putting down the present managers and hinting that this would be a nice place for her and her daughter to live in and run. When she drank she sometimes became vicious, as I discovered that weekend in Palm Springs, where we had a party with two of my sons and the other guests at the hotel.

The barbecue grills were blistering with hot dogs and hamburgers, and the guests kept offering Barbara "Long Islands"—drinks containing nearly every known alcoholic substance poured into fruit juice. The more Barbara drank, the more her tongue became like that of a poisonous snake.

194

BOZO THE BEAUTIFUL

"You know, your manager is the pits. She really doesn't know what she's doing. I've been watching this whole operation, I could really make this place wild." And she had something negative to say about everybody.

She basically was a nice girl, but I guess got caught up in always being taken care of. She revealed to me that she never had to work. In fact she'd never had a job in her entire life. So it really wasn't my gold heart, my comedy, the warm wonderful me, that she wanted to come and live in LA with, and I was to be her springboard. Living on the island of Hawaii for the past five years, she was being taken care of by an older, married Japanese bank president. She probably fantasized that the little Jewish comedian would dance for her, too.

I have to admit she learned her trade well. She had it all. She was funny, charming, emotional, childlike and evasive anytime she wanted to be. I really hadn't experienced anyone like her in years. I was enjoying it. And some of her qualities I really adored—until my old insecurities started seeping through. My gut was filling up with anxieties, because I really started liking her a lot.

I was taking her all over town trying to show her a nice time and show her off, and we were bombarded by the usual assholes, especially the young Lebanese guys. They cared less who she was with; they came right over to her in a bar, at a restaurant table, even waiting in line for a movie. They just couldn't figure out what this old man was doing with this young, beautiful blond creature. And that perception started once again to haunt me—that I was old compared to Barbara. She was twenty-five; I was fifty-five. She would have been perfect for my son Scott. But not for me.

I just knew the time had come—growing-up time. The party had to end. She was already planning to stay longer than I had anticipated. It had been ten days.

Yes, she could have stayed the whole summer. I had nothing else to do, except to continue to take a class at Santa Monica College. I had no work. We could have honeymooned all summer between Palm Springs and the Marina. Many guys would have given their paychecks and jobs just to be with her in that situation.

I came back from class that eleventh morning and knew I had to tell her how I felt. I walked into the apartment and she was sitting in my robe, just out of the shower, her hair still wet. She was doing her nails. I wanted to throw her down and make love to her, but I knew that would just put off the inevitable.

"Hi, Sammy," she said. "How was school?"

"Fine, Barbara. How's your day been so far?"

"Wonderful, it's so beautiful out. Sammy, could you take me to Disneyland? I promised my daughter I'd bring her back a present from Disneyland."

"Barbara, I want to talk to you."

"What about?" she responded very directly.

"I really think it's time for you to go back to Hawaii."

She looked at me, shocked.

"Sammy, I thought we were having so much fun together. I was just getting to know you. And you know I love it here. I just don't understand."

"Yes, we did have fun. The bottom line, Barbara, is that I really could learn to love you. It's really not that hard, you know. But, I'm twice your age. I think down the road it would eventually catch up to me. You're young and vital—I'll be approaching sixty in five years, and you'll be thirty, hot to trot."

"Sammy, age has nothing to do with it. I love your maturity, your experience. It really doesn't matter to me. I've been with a lot older men than you."

"Thank you for those kind words, Barbara. But this is the way it's got to be. I want to thank you for allowing me to feel love again, knowing I can still get excited over someone. It's been a wonderful experience for me. And someday if I get back to the Islands again, I'll call you, you can be sure of that.

"I made reservations for your flight back tomorrow afternoon—two-thirty on American."

She sat on the couch and cried. I wanted to take her in my arms and say, "Barbara, I love you. I want you to stay as long as you like." Eventually it would have been death for me.

She packed her clothes the next day and I drove her to the airport in my car, not a limousine. Reality had set in. It was over. No more fantasies. It was sad. Not a word was said all the way to the airport. Her bags were taken out of my car by a porter.

"Wait here, Barbara," I said. "I'll get your ticket."

I handed it to her. I put her in first-class to Honolulu. She was a special lady to me and deserved a special place.

"Good-bye, Barbara. Have a safe trip. And thank you again."

She threw her arms around me and kissed me. "Thank you, Sammy.

Say good-bye to Peter and your other kids for me. Give me a call once in awhile.''

I smiled, nodded, and said I would. I got into my car and headed back to the Marina. I was sad, but content with myself. This was the first time in my entire life that I had told a girl she would have to leave, that this was truly how I felt. That I had my home to come back to. That my key fits my lock to my apartment. That this is my home. And this is my life.

I've seen a star turn down an engagement because another performer was going to get more billing on the marquee and in the ads. I've always paid attention to billing, too, but recently the issue took a new and different turn for me.

What's happening now, especially in Nevada, is that a hotel will want to have two major stars on the same show to ensure business. There are just a few stars who can fill a show room on their own. So the warm-up act is starting to become extinct.

And if two stars have equal billing on the marquee, there isn't room for anyone else. This was the case recently, when Neil Sedaka and Pia Zadora were coheading at the Riviera Hotel in Vegas. Neil insisted he wouldn't follow another musical act, that it just wouldn't work. He asked his agent if he could get a comedian to fill in between him and Pia and just do ten minutes. His agent was my agent, Freddie Moch.

Freddie asked me if I wanted to try to do the ten minutes.

Freddie also said I'd get no billing.

"You mean to tell me, Freddie, they not only want me to do ten minutes, they won't even give me billing?"

It was an outrageous idea, because usually you need time to get used to an audience and get them on your side. You need time to adjust. Is the audience coming in hostile or angry? Have they lost money? Have they won? Are they pissed because their luggage is still on a plane somewhere?

I decided to give it a shot anyway. After all, I'd been through so many ordeals in my life, how could it possibly hurt me?

It was a great challenge to walk out after Pia Zadora finished her act and all the people were expecting Neil Sedaka. Out popped Sammy Shore—no music, no announcement, no name, nothing.

"Surprise!" I shouted.

The Warm-up

My name is Sammy Shore, and I'm the Unbilled Comedian. You notice you didn't see my name on the marquee. You see, folks, if you don't see my name on the marquee, I'm working. I got a big following.

In fact, I got a big following all over the country. One woman in Dayton, Ohio, passed by a local club, looked up at the marquee, and my name wasn't on it. Got so excited and said, "Sammy's in town!" Brought in a party of twelve of her friends, but to her dismay Frank Sinatra was appearing. Got pissed and they all left.

When people ask me for my autograph—they hand me an eraser! They had a celebrity party for Neil Sedaka. I didn't get an invitation, so I automatically knew I was invited.

I used the time problem. I told the people I only had ten minutes, and I kept looking at my watch and counting off the minutes while doing my lines. Got to the end and looked at my watch and said, "That's it!" and walked off. The response was tremendous.

I was held over doing the same thing between Bobby Vinton and Donna Fargo. Columnist Joe Delaney wrote a column the next day that almost erased memories of the Eden Roc blank space and my Vegas *Gong Show* review. "Sammy Shore came out as the Unbilled Comedian," Delaney said, "and did the most hilarious ten minutes this reviewer has ever seen. In fact, to be honest he actually stole the show. . . . The people kept yelling for more."

I stayed on another two months, doing my thing for other twin bills such as Kenny Rogers and Debby Boone, and soon all the stars and hotels were seeking the services of the Unbilled Comedian.

So who cares about billing?

Growing up is tough—even when you're old! We all want to be like "him" or "her." I know that I'm a lot like both my parents, although of course I wasn't trying to be. My idol, growing up, was Harry James, with his shiny new trumpet. Studying trumpet at the age of ten, I tried to emulate him. Bought all his songbooks. Still couldn't play. Then I went to the best trumpet teacher in the city of Chicago. His name was Nicole, and he had taught all the great trumpet players around Chicago, including quite a few who'd gone on to bands like Woody Herman's and Stan Kenton's. Every week, religiously, I got on the bus downtown for my lesson with Nicole.

When I first started trumpet lessons, at the Wurlitzer School of

BOZO THE BEAUTIFUL

Music, my lessons cost two dollars. But Nicole was famous—I had to pay him three. And getting that extra dollar out of my dad was murder.

"What's the matter with the teacher you got now?"

"Nicole is famous, Pa," I would say.

"Famous, shamous, I never heard of him. Harry James yes, him no!"

"Taking lessons from him, Pa, I could learn how to play a lot faster, and then I won't have to take any more lessons."

That he could relate to. Nor more lessons, no more three dollars. He was a financial genius.

No computers, no adding machines—his fingers did the counting. He knew exactly where to go in his furniture store if he needed money to pay a bill. He knew what he had where—what mattress, tool box, dresser. He usually kept the singles and twos in an old mattress he knew would never sell. And he never liked to go to that particular site for money if he could help it, because then the bedbugs would come charging out. He didn't want to disturb them, as they might move on to a newer, more salable mattress.

The fives and tens were usually kept in his tool box underneath the basement stairs. We all knew that every time he opened the basement he was heading for his tool box. He'd say nonchalantly, "I got to check the furnace—it's cold in the store." To this day I can't say for sure why he kept going to that tool box. Because he never went anywhere, did anything, or spent anything unless it was to pay a few bills. Meanwhile, the big stuff like the twenties he usually hid in brown paper bags in a couple of the old stoves.

I honestly think that he went to these sacred money tombs just to count it and see that it was still there. And I'm afraid I have to admit that I can truly understand it. I find myself hiding money in a drawer underneath a pile of papers. Inside a telephone book. Even sometimes hiding a few hundred in a shoe, then messing up all my shoes so that no one would think to look there. But who's going to look? I live alone! I even find myself at times hiding money underneath the mat in my car—and never really knowing why I'm doing it.

In the news this morning I see someone is getting a mechanical heart. You plug it into a power source. If it was my dad, he'd want to know first how much the monthly electric bill would be. He was crazy in many ways, but at least he was honest with his feelings.

The Warm-up

In the early days of my involvement in the Alcoholics Anonymous program, I was reaching out to anyone to show me the way, to help me. I was very vulnerable. Everyone tries to help you on the program, but what I was looking for, I guess, was something like a father image—a strong male figure. All my relationships with women had faltered. I knew only that I could no longer go on looking for a mama.

Then I met him. He spoke at a meeting. His words flowed like poetry. He was incredibly articulate. I thought I was listening to a guru. He was handsome and confident, a writer with more than a dozen books published, mostly on Freud and psychology. We met and his charm, his quiet profile, his way with words, completely intrigued me.

I asked him to become my guiding force on the program, my sponsor, as it's called. He obliged, and we became friends.

I became obsessed with his superior knowledge and his philosophy and I hung on to his every word. I would call him and ask his advice on every little thing—on everything, literally. And no matter what, anytime of day or night, Norman was always available for my calls. There were many times when he would stop his writing and meet me for coffee, or we'd go to a meeting together.

As I finally started to become more independent and my calls to him grew less frequent, I sometimes felt a need on his part to continue as my sponsor and protector. I guess he saw my growth, and at times it seemed to make him uncomfortable.

I felt I didn't need crutches anymore, and what he had become in my life was a wheelchair. So I now saw *his* humanness, his vulnerability, his need to be needed. For a while things between us were very difficult and painful.

I ended up cherishing the entire experience. I learned that I had become dependent on someone who was just as human and vulnerable as me—that I can't put my survival into another human's hands and that my role model will have to be a person just like me. Best of all, I was eventually able to help the man when he really needed it, and today we're dear, dear friends. He's ecstatic about my newfound interests and the new closeness in my family.

And I'm delighted with him rather than dependent on him—the way it should be.

***

BOZO THE BEAUTIFUL

I never realized until my middle years that girls can be as needy as guys. I swear I always thought we were the needy ones. They rejected us. I never thought that women had the same feelings we do—that when they're rejected by a man, they too go through that experience with the empty hole in the stomach big enough to drive a tractor-trailer through.

The funny part of it all is that women think that *men* don't go through that pain—or any pain, for that matter. They think the men are strong, that they don't feel like we women feel, that women are more sensitive to feelings and emotions.

I agree with this last point, *but* women can get over a traumatic breakup much faster than a man. They can bounce right back and get on with their lives.

Men just seem to wander around aimlessly, looking to get laid. They'd put their dick in a light socket—just to make that hole in the pit of their stomach go away. If only they could pick up that phone and talk to her, to make it go away for just a moment.

Pretty soon you're not even there—you're just one big hole. You walk into a place and you just know that everyone is looking at you, thinking, "There's Mr. Empty."

It's an endless search, trying to close that gap. I can just see me at eighty-five, on my deathbed, still worried about being rejected. Should I call her back? The hell with her! I just don't want to get involved. I'll go out just the way I came in—alone and empty.

Doctor finally comes over. "What did he die from?"

"We don't know, doctor—never saw anything like it. He's got this big hole in the pit of his stomach—no heart—nothing, just this hole . . ."

Her name was Zel Leifkowitz. I knew that with a name like that, she wasn't going to be a Jessica Lange. But listen—when you're horny and lonely and at this stage in your life, anything'll do.

She lived in the San Fernando Valley, which might as well be the other end of the world as far as I'm concerned. It was about an hour-and-a-half drive from where I live in the Marina—about forty deadly miles on the freeway, in rather heavy traffic.

You start fantasizing: well, maybe she's got a nice body. I just want her, whoever she is. I can't fathom a relationship with her. Maybe if I was a truck driver. I'm a comedian!

201

The Warm-up

Hey listen, I say to myself, it's Thursday night—be grateful to have a warm body to talk to.

As I arrived at her abode, I calculated that I was already out a half a tankful of gas—that was about twelve bucks invested already. Plus wear and tear on my middle-aged Jewish body—boy, that could be quite a toll!

I looked at her address: 175671 El Caballero Drive. It was one of those huge apartment complexes put up with spit and a lot of spray-gun adobe. It was the kind with a very impressive front and a name like the El Toro-Cliente Mananas Apartments. And underneath it: VA-CANCY. CALL MANAGER IN APARTMENT 5.

I looked at the enormous directory case on the entryway wall. It looked like the World War II casualty list of the Second Infantry Division, U.S. Army. Smith, Johnson, Jones, Clark—and there it was—Leifkowitz, Apt. 2F.

I rang the bell and a voice blared through the tiny speaker, *"Hello, who is it?"*

"This is Sammy."

"Oh—hi—Sammy, did you get lost?"

"No, why—was I supposed to?"

"You said you were coming at eight-thirty—it's already nine-oh-five."

Holy fuck, I thought, one of those.

The front-door buzzer started its gnawing sound, releasing the palatial door that looked like the front of a Taco Bell stand that had gone out of business. The complex was posted as "security guarded," which amused me. I was pretty sure my remote TV-channel changer could have opened the door.

These complexes are usually owned by syndicates of doctors and lawyers who desperately need tax write-offs. And they usually hire, as managers, people who have themselves been written off as human beings. These angry, old, bigoted, redneck types are usually a man and wife who hate each other and feel the same way about the people living in the apartments. And don't ever try to ask them, if you happen to be lost, where one of the tenants lives. They are there to rent and only to rent—not to give you the blueprint of the building.

But a blueprint was what I needed. You'd think that apartment 2F would be on the second floor. No, 2F was in the second phase of the development, which wasn't quite finished. Each phase had a special number—2F meant that her apartment was on the sixth floor, since the letter *F* is the sixth in the alphabet.

I found it. Apartment 2F. On her door was a gold mezuzah, the small parchment that tells visitors you're a Jew. I seemed to recall that since I was Jewish I was supposed to kiss it, but it was kind of high. I kissed the doorknob.

I quietly rapped on the door. Again I heard that rapturous voice come shrilling through the door.

"Who is it?"

Who the hell did she think it was, Richard Pryor?

"It's me, Sammy."

"Okay. Just a minute."

I heard bolts unlocking, chains sliding, latches being pulled open. What was she hiding in there, family heirlooms?

That's one thing about a Jewish princess. A noise outside her door— anything that can be heard to move—and she becomes totally panicked. Surely someone is about to break down her iron door and rape her.

The door was finally unsealed. There she was, standing in a long evening kimono that looked like it was designed in Hawaii during a devastating typhoon, with the lava from a volcanic eruption still on it.

"Hi, you must be Sammy?"

"Yes, as you must be Zel."

"Please come in and make yourself comfortable."

As I followed her toward the couch, I was trying to get some idea of what she actually looked like. I knew I was in trouble. When they wear that kind of clothing, they're usually covering up "el gourdo." Shiksas, on the other hand, wear tight jeans that show their ass. The only problem with them is peeling them off when you both get hot on a couch.

The game started. I really didn't know what to expect, but I knew there was going to be a problem. Everything in the apartment was covered with something. The couch had plastic slipcovers, just like her mother's had, I guess. It seems all Jewish mothers have slipcovers on their sofas so their husbands won't get them dirty. My brother Morris was married for over twenty-five years and his first wife, Dorothy, hated him so much she skipped the slipcover but simply wouldn t let him sit on the couch!

"Would you like some wine—red or white? *I have them both.* Or if you'd like, I have a bottle of Dom Perignon."

"No thanks," I said. "I'd like some Perrier. Or a diet drink."

"You're kidding. Let me open the Dom Perignon."

"I really don't drink," I said.

"How about some J&B Scotch. Or Jack Daniel's."

"Soda water's just fine."

"Let me make you one of my mixed drinks I learned while I was in Hawaii. It's got a little bit of everything in it."

"A glass of water would be fine."

"What kind of music do you like?"

"Middle of the road. Barry Manilow," I said.

"I've got some great jazz records. Ella Fitzgerald's first album."

"Fine."

"Let me put on Dizzy Gillespie. I love him."

"That's okay."

"Is it too loud? I'll play it softer."

"No, really, it's not too loud."

"How's the temperature in the room? If it's too cold—"

"No, that's all right. . . . Why don't you come over here on the couch, next to me. I'd like to get to know you," I said.

"No, not just yet. I'm listening to the music and enjoying the wine."

Her dog kept jumping up on my lap and licking my face.

"You like my dog? If you don't like him, I'll ask him to leave."

"No, he's a nice dog."

I just love it when a dog starts to sniff your crotch. He knows you're in heat just like he is.

"Here's a picture of my mom and dad. Aren't they just so handsome? You like them?"

"Yeah, they're a very handsome couple."

"You like the picture of me over the fireplace?"

"Yes, it's really a nice picture of you. You look a lot younger than your picture."

"I could have taken a better picture. It was a bad time in my life. I was going through a divorce at the time."

"I see."

I figured now was the time. I wasn't there to listen to her résumé or to study her family tree. So I said to her, "I find you very sensual."

She sprang up off her chair. "I don't do that! Would you kindly leave now?"

Now that I'm in my middle years I'm realizing that there's more to life than comedy. I'm smelling the roses—I mean really smelling the roses. And you want to know something? They really smell like roses.

The pressure is finally off. I have choices now. If I want to do a stand-up, I can, and really not worry what that particular audience thinks about it. I'm doing it for me. I have the freedom and clarity to believe that, and that's truly the gift.

I don't know what you call these feelings. Maturity? Part of it is knowing that the ultimate ahead is death—seeing some of your friends pass on. Even young, vibrant men felled by massive heart attacks at thirty-five.

I know that if I can combine spirituality and fitness in my life, I have a good chance of going the full span. However, it seems the level of one's success today is measured by the quality of his heart-bypass operation. When I'm in the steam room at the Friars Club I see the elderly gentlemen with the scars that run from the neck to the navel.

"Who did your bypass?"

"I had the best, Dr. Matloff."

He must be the best, I'm thinking, because they're all here still talking about it. And it's amazing—all of Matloff's scars look the same.

Maybe his father was a *moil*—a rabbi that does circumcisions. All the kid's parents knew if it was a certain rabbi because all the penises looked alike. In many cases this meant not much was left. Much to my regret, I had one of those rabbis.

Knowing my father, he probably made a deal. "What does he need such a big one for?"

Thanks, Pa.

Three thousand people were standing and cheering as I left the stage. I came back out to take another bow and the ovation was thunderous. "MORE!" they shouted, three thousand members of Alcoholics Anonymous cheering their fellow alcoholic at their annual convention in Palm Springs.

The Warm-up

I was drying myself off in my dressing room, and Mike and Perry, the show's producers, were standing around marveling at what had just occurred.

"We remember you," Mike said, "when you first came into the program. You were a battered and beaten man, and look at you now. Your growth is phenomenal. And on top of that, you're a brilliant comedian."

As I thanked Mike for the kind words, there was a knock on the door. I asked Mike to get it.

He opened the door. "Sammy," he said, "there's someone here to see you."

I turned and there was former President Gerald Ford and his wife, Betty, surrounded by their security guards.

"Can we come in?" the President asked.

I was speechless. He and Betty came over and he put his arms around me and hugged me. "Sammy," he said, "I don't know if I've ever been so taken as I was by what happened out there tonight. Betty and I were ecstatic, you were hilarious. We were just gasping for breath, we were laughing so hard. You made our evening, and we want to thank you."

Mrs. Ford hugged me and thanked me in that warm way of hers.

I was in shock and groping for words. "Gerald," I said, as if I knew them, "I didn't even know you and Betty were in the audience." I was so excited. We talked a little more and then they left.

I just stood there, hardly able to believe that a President had taken time to acknowledge me.

When I watch Robin Williams and Richard Pryor on the stage at the same time, I want to put my head in the sand and never have it come out again. That's how awful I feel as a fellow comedian.

I saw them recently at the taping of a Home Box Office special at The Comedy Store. For the audience on that particular night, the event was the ultimate in exhilaration and euphoria. People sat there mesmerized for more than three hours of the most insane impromptu off-the-wall humor I've ever witnessed in my thirty years as a professional comedian.

The power, the laughter, the release of that evening might be the equivalent of a weekend of intense psychotherapy—Doctors Richard and Robin at our service, there to flush out our innermost innards.

BOZO THE BEAUTIFUL

The emotional state that night was the closest thing I could imagine to the Resurrection or the Second Coming. The audience, more than seven hundred people, turned soul and mind over completely to the masters. "Here—take me—do what you want with me—you are my gods!" The hysteria, the adulation for these two men of genius, was unforgettable.

As Robin exited through the audience, he walked through like Jesus (an impression strengthened by his current beard). People were standing and screaming for more. Women were touching him, wanting him. It seemed he could have had any woman of any color or persuasion in that room, that's how devastating he was.

And most of what he did was not an act in the usual sense. He doesn't have an act; everything he does is improvised.

For a comedian to watch all of this—and especially someone like me, who has been around for thirty years and has always done an act per se . . . well, I walked away feeling empty. I never wanted to grace a nightclub stage again. And I knew there were plenty of other comics in that room who were feeling much the same way. Among them was Henny Youngman, the oldest of all.

As Henny left his table and was heading out of the room, he spotted me. He wore a look of disdain. "Hello, Sammy," he said, half-smiling.

I shook his hand.

He grabbed at his sleeve and rolled it up. "You wanna buy a watch?" He had three watches strapped to his arm.

I laughed. "What did you think of Robin?" I said.

"He's cute."

It seemed he really didn't want to discuss Robin's performance.

"Sam, did you hear about the guy that walked into an antique shop. Walked over to the owner and said, 'What's new?' . . . Well, gotta go, got a club date tomorrow in Cleveland. See you around, Brother Sam."

"Hey, Henny!" someone hollered. "Take my wife—please!"

If you're a young comedian watching a Robin Williams, you can come away with a dream of your own—that someday you'll be like him. But if you've been around the horn as I have and you see these new monsters of the midway, you know in your heart that you can never, ever become them—in any way, shape, or form. And if you're in that transitional period between fifty and sixty years of age, as I am, at the beginning of the autumn season of life, and you haven't achieved your goals as a comedian, the empty feeling in the pit of your stomach starts to enlarge.

That empty feeling is familiar to every comedian; it comes anytime the laughter, the applause, the audience appreciation isn't there. For us older funnymen, that pit will just keep growing into a gulf, unless we come to terms with it. Nights like the HBO special with Pryor and Williams are nights of reckoning.

I know that I can never be a Robin or a Richard. God did not have that in mind for me. He had it in mind for *them*. And even they will eventually have to come to terms with age and changing taste. How will they do it? We already have some idea, especially from Richard's well-publicized life, of the demons such performers face. Sooner or later, God willing, they'll face the fiercest beast—time.

Many years ago, when I was a fledgling young comedian, I was in awe of such stalwarts of the nightclub genre as Jan Murray. But Jan sobered me one night with a confession. What he told me may look on paper like a show-business cliché, but it was plenty real.

"Sam," he said, "it's fun on the way up. The praise, the laughter you hear night after night—there's nothing like it. Then one day you wake up and look in the mirror and say, 'I'm old.' You just stand there and stare at yourself. What happened?"

That realization can be devastating for a comic: will I be funny, being older? You know you still feel good inside. You're healthy. But you look down at your naked body. The skin around your stomach and knees is starting to sag. You just never noticed it before. But there it is. The elasticity is gone. You reach down and grab your thigh to stretch the skin upward, you let go—old again!

We're all so vain. What does sagging skin have to do with being funny? All your faculties are intact. But it's undeniable—a slowing-down process is unfolding. No longer are you "the fledgling young comic," "the bright young talent," or "the up and coming star." Now you're "the veteran." "The guy has paid his dues," they say. "He's a real pro."

It's wonderful to become a star when you're young and then be able to sustain the mystique of never really growing old, like George Burns. But *he's the only one*!

So what's the answer? For me, reeling from that HBO taping, I realize that for several years I have eased away from the constant push to be funny, to be a hit. Rather than always straining upward, I've begun to appreciate my roots and real interests, not all of which are going out onstage. I've learned that I have other needs and a contemplative, often sad part of my nature that also needs to be resolved and fulfilled. And in this way I'm no different than Richard Pryor or Robin Williams or anyone else.

The sensational nights will come and go. They're meant to be savored—by performer and spectator alike. But life not only goes on, it goes deeper and branches out. The comedians who retain their great gift and who still understand this—Milton Berle, Jan Murray, the incomparable Red Buttons—are the ones who show us the way. They're the ones who can give and who can gracefully and eagerly acknowledge phenomenal young talents.

So, Robin, Richard: you're the best.

And I truly love the September of my life now—because I'm booked!

Venice, California is known to many as the chic ghetto of southern California. Although the property values have skyrocketed and there are elegant restaurants and what they used to call "trendy" shops, the area is ridden with derelicts, drugs, and crime. The small Jewish temple survives near the recovery houses for drug and alcohol addicts.

On any weekend you can pedal down the ocean bike path and hear the conga drums beating at fever pitch, with the groups of mostly black people gathered around shouting and singing. Scattered among the punks and freaks and the incredibly shaped girls on roller skates are always people of all ages and colors who are looking for loose change.

Just a few blocks away, in the old synagogue that sits facing the ocean, in the back hall of the temple, on any given Sunday at least a hundred older Jews gather to be fed bagels and cream cheese by people from the Beverly Hills chapter of the B'nai Brith. These volunteers are usually elderly themselves, but fortunate enough not to have to be the ones served. Many of the local Jews act ungratefully, grabbing extra bagels and danishes and stuffing them into purses. They're bitter and angry that their children have left them here to die, in Venice, among the addicts. Many others in the group, however, sit in joy, able to appreciate their long lives. Modern medicine has in some cases allowed them to live well beyond three score and seven. And

209

yet within a block, the younger generation lies on the beach, stoned out of its mind.

A stone's throw away, off Washington Place, there sits an old American Legion hall that on any given night becomes the meeting place for AA members of all ages and backgrounds. Former drug addicts and whiskey heads sit together and share their experiences, strength, and hope.

It was in that hall, in December 1978, that a couple of guys came up to me and suggested we put together a show for Christmas Eve And December 24 saw the first Venice AA show and Christmas party. The tiny hall was jam-packed with people; some had even brought their children. They were sitting on folding chairs, on the floor, and three-deep around the walls. The stage, improvised from boxes and wood scraps, had just enough room for two people.

The love was in that room that night. And when I came on, to that group I was a *star*! They all laughed, and it was a huge success.

So every year thereafter I was called again to participate. The third year it had to be moved to a larger hall because of the reputation and following it had earned. Last year, I was working in Atlantic City at Christmastime, but I knew I had to be there in Venice. It was part of my gift to the program.

I took a couple of days off from the show I was appearing in and flew back that night and did the show with no sleep. It was wonderful to see hundreds more hanging from the rafters. All new scenes had been written, there was a cast of more than fifty, with two spotlights, stage crew, props, everything. Jerry, who was also the emcee, had helped make it all very professional and thought out. And when he grabbed the mike and introduced me as "the star of our show, who just flew in from Atlantic City," the applause was tumultuous. They laughed again, and I was happy.

This year I was not away. Things were slow and I was not working, so I was around at various AA meetings. A week before Christmas Eve people were coming over to me: "Hey, Sammy, ya gonna do the show again? . . . Looking forward to seeing you." I didn't know what to say; I was uneasy and a bit confused. No phone call from Jerry. Why?

Five days before the show and still no call. I was with my friend Shery, and I had a gut feeling that I should go to Zucky's, a Jewish deli in Santa Monica. I very seldom go there, but for one thing, with Shery not being Jewish, I wanted her to experience matzoh ball soup.

As we were being shown to a booth, there was Jerry, sitting with two girls.

"Hi, Jerry," I said. "How's it going?"

"Fine, Sammy." He was uncomfortable.

"How's the show?"

His face seemed to drop. "Great," he said. "You know—a lot of hours, a lot of work."

I sat in our booth, feeling rejected. Not a word. It just wasn't like Jerry to act like that.

I told Shery what I was feeling, and she understood. "Forget about it," she said. "It's really not that important."

But it was important; it meant a lot to me. I wanted to walk over to his table and ask him why. But as I started to get up, he was leaving.

In the next couple of days I tried to call him, but he was never in. I was really becoming frustrated. Then finally, two days before the show, I reached him at his office.

He was a bit defensive when he came on the line. I guess he knew why I was calling. I could feel the tension. I told him I felt hurt and left out—that we'd been part of something wonderful together in past years, and now, not even a call. Why?

There was silence, and then he spoke. "Sammy, I'm sorry. You're absolutely right. I got so caught up in the show, doing it a new way, and I didn't even think about it that much. I just took it for granted that we'd skip you this year and you'd come back the next. We just wanted to do some new things and use some new people. I'm really sorry. I should have called."

I told him I understood, that it was fine, and all I wanted was for him to call and tell me. We cleared the air, and Jerry asked me to please try to make it to see the show.

I hung up the phone and still felt a little unwanted, although I understood. I was sitting answering phones, as I did every Thursday at the Westwood AA office. I was about to leave when the phone rang. It was Jerry.

"I was thinking about what just happened," he said, "and I feel terrible. I want to make amends and to thank you for making me aware of my obsessiveness about planning the show. And you showed me how much self-esteem you have by calling and telling me how you feel. I really love you, Sammy."

I told him that *that* was the phone call I wanted from him, and I tried to tell him how much I appreciated his feelings. I wished him Merry Christmas and felt glad that I really meant it.

When Christmas Eve came, I wanted to experience what it would be like to attend without being in the show. I sneaked around through the back door. Again, the hall was crammed—I'd never seen so many people per square foot in all my life.

In front of me was Al Syns, one of the guys who had originally approached me about the first show. Al grabbed and hugged and kissed me, and then so did his girl, Pat. "Watch the end of this sketch," they said. "It's hysterical." And it was.

I looked at the audience. They were laughing and applauding, and in their smiling faces was the look of elation. And they were all sober.

The comedian-magician who had replaced me in the show then came out. He was wonderful, and the people loved him, as they had loved me in the past. A glow grew within me as I stood and applauded him. I knew that it was truly all right to simply be standing there as one of the members, enjoying myself.

I left a few minutes later. I knew in my heart that everything was taken care of and the show would be great without me. Once again I realized, as I was driving home, that it was time to move on to other things. And they'll all still love Sammy . . . even if he doesn't do his show.

Around this time I paid a long overdue visit to Shecky Greene. Before I could tell him what I had come to say, he told me that when I was good, I was the greatest opening act he'd seen.

"Well," I said, "Shecky, that's part of what I wanted to talk about. You see, I really owe you an apology. I've resented you for years. I was always in awe of your talent and how far you went with it, the fact that you could earn a hundred twenty-five thousand dollars a week. It made me dislike you. I envied you.

"I don't feel that way anymore because I've accepted myself, the real Sammy Shore. I know I'll never go hungry. I have a talent that will support me. I'll always have people laughing at me and appreciating my talent."

Shecky gave me a big hug. A bear hug from someone I'd mistaken for a gorilla.

Then the day after Christmas, I was lying around at my home in Marina del Rey when I got a call from Jim Martin, an entertainment consultant for the Caesars Boardwalk Regency in Atlantic City.

"Hey, Sammy, guess what?"

I told him I couldn't.

"You've been voted by the Atlantic City press as the top opening act of the year. Diana Ross was the top female entertainer, Tony Orlando the top male, and Shecky Greene the number-one comedy star."

So Shecky and I were teamed up for honors. It felt right.

"Aren't you Sammy Shore, the comedian?"

"Yes," I said, a smirk on my face.

He signed the register, and I immediately recognized the name. He was president of one of the biggest film studios.

". . . I own this place," I said.

"*You* own La Siesta Villas?"

"Yeah, I just bought it. And aren't you president of Colossal Pictures?"

He nodded. "I always stay here when I want to get away from people in the industry." He cleared his throat and gave me what I thought was a wary look.

"Oh, don't worry about me, I'm not in pictures. . . . But if you want me to come to your villa, I'll do a fast ten minutes!"

"No thanks, Sam, I've seen your act!"

Wow! President of Colossal (not the real name, of course) staying at my place in Palm Springs. Instead of a Gideon Bible in the dresser, I'll put in my picture and a résumé.

"Hey, Sammy," bellows a voice from the poolside. "Ya got any extra towels?"

"Sorry, man, Oscar nominations do *not* entitle guests to extra towels. Not even for Best Director."

I've got the studio president checking in; the hot new director needs towels; Tony Orlando wants me to jump into the pool; the recording star is blasting his new album from his villa; and the managers of La Siesta Villas are on a three-day vacation. So I've got to watch the store. It's like I'm back in the hills of Wisconsin. Here I am thirty years later broiling in the desert sun, pumping up plastic rafts, pouring lemonade, checking people in, carrying bags. Am I a comedian or a bellboy?

I've got a captive audience here—the same people I'm used to seeing on those big opening nights in Vegas—only now I don't have to perform, I'm just opening for the villas and they do all the work.

What am I doing owning a hotel in the middle of the desert at a time when nobody's working, much less taking vacations? I blame it all on my hotshot son Scott, the real-estate investor, who lives in San Diego and is slowly coming to own it.

"Dad," he said, "now's the time to buy real estate. We can steal the place—the owner's just about to go bankrupt! I know; I've been staying there the past five years, and I went to school with the owner's son—he says his dad is ready to sell. You've got to take your savings and buy some real estate, Dad. It's a hedge against inflation."

My father's voice kept echoing: "Sam, don't buy! Save the money. Scotty will take your money like Phillip took mine. Don't invest. Keep the money in cash and hide it in paper bags! Like I did. Wasn't I right? Look at all the money you had when I died." And my dad never paid taxes, either.

I took my "blood and sweat" money, the savings I'd put away for retirement, and gave it to my son Scott. I had broken my father's bond of never trusting anyone. I finally did it—I trusted Scott. It wasn't easy for me. So much of my father was still inside me—the part I hated. Scott also had many of those same qualities—Hyman was in him too. It wasn't his fault. All he ever heard growing up in our house was me telling his mother, "What do you need it for? Get the other one, it's cheaper!" So now, when it comes to picking up a tab, for example, Scotty often finds he has an impediment in his reach. Just as I once had. I've broken that part of me; to do it, I had to start reaching for the tab every single time, even when it wasn't really necessary, just to experience that awful feeling—the feeling that I might go broke.

I've learned that it's useless to try to understand and control everything. Like money. When it seems like I'm not going to have enough, something happens and there unfolds a gift from God.

"Dad, this is Ted Pelton, owner of La Siesta Villas."

"Nice meeting you," I said.

We all stood poolside with the sun beating down on us. Ted was smiling, undoubtedly because he knew Scott really wanted this place, no matter what it took. I wasn't so enthusiastic, although the thought did creep into my brain that it would be nice to bring a girl up here once in a while. But that thought zoomed right back out when Ted told us how much he wanted.

Ted was a very impatient and frenetic man of about fifty-five. As he talked, he kept twitching and scratching and rubbing his face.

"Damn mosquitoes, they kind of come around in the summer," he said as he also stepped on a waterbug and half-smiled.

I said, "Yeah, I know. The snakes eat 'em up."

He didn't think that was too funny. He didn't think anything was too funny, because the man had no sense of humor—none whatsoever. All he was interested in was telling us about the stars who had stayed there, like Tyrone Power, who of course was dead—just like the place!

It was less than thirty days later. It had been the fastest closing of escrow in the history of that particular escrow company. Scott and I were sitting in the Jacuzzi the night of the closing of the deal, and with the air temperature hovering at 110, I felt like the natives were boiling us in oil. To our left, hanging in a tree, was one of those bug-catchers that looks like a neon sign. The way the bugs were hitting it, that lamp must have felt like the U.S. *Arizona* at Pearl Harbor. It was really exciting to know that I now owned twenty-five percent of the bug catcher.

"Gee, Dad, isn't this great?" said my balding son as we wilted away in the boiling water. "You know, Dad, what I really wanted this place for was this Jacuzzi. This is the best I've ever been in. I just love it!"

I just knew that the heat must have inflicted some sort of brain damage on my poor son. This was just not like him. He had always been so practical—so conservative. So cheap!

I could just imagine my dad screaming at me: "You needed this? With all these goddamn bugs? At least in my rooming house we had rats—you could at least see them! And where's the people?"

"Pa, it's the summer. No one goes to Palm Springs in the summer. It's a winter resort."

"Winter, my ass!" he would say. "I'll send you some of my black roomers—they like the heat! At least the place would be filled."

I could just imagine him owning this place. He'd shut off all the air conditioning, even in his own villa. The lights would be off, the pool would have no water, and my mom would be cleaning the villas every day. And he'd be sitting in the office, complaining, *"Where's the customers!"*

Is my dad right? Time will tell. The one great thing is that he's wrong about not trusting my son.

So if you ever plan to come to Palm Springs, look me up. I should be running around La Siesta Villas yelling something appropriate, like, "Everybody out of the pool!" And, for a limited time only, if you bring this book with you and show it to the manager, you'll get one free night.

By the way, my father told me to tell you that!

Palm Springs is just before death. The cavalcade of wheelchairs starts to arrive around Christmas and stays till Easter. The ones who leave are the ones who survive. The very wealthy have their nurses wheel them into their winter abodes to hibernate and to complain, "It's too cold. Where's the goddamn sun? I coulda stayed in Philadelphia, it was warmer than this. Turn up the heat! Have my kids called yet? Ungrateful bastards—they sent me to the desert to die."

The sounds of the paramedics swirl through the streets at all hours of the night. Palm Canyon Drive: Heart-Attack Row.

Bob Hope, Gerald Ford, Frank Sinatra—they all live here. Who cares? Dinah Shore has her tennis classic every winter with a bunch of aging ladies chasing a ball.

The only real movement in this town is at Cecil's and Zelda's, the two remaining discos catering to the young and hip. They're so hip none of them are working. But go by these places any night and you'll find them packed with beautiful tanned bodies. The young girls are looking for an old cocker to take care of them, while the young Richard Geres are trying to latch on to Mrs. Stretch Face.

One of the most exciting attractions in this town is the Aerial Tramway, which for $8.50 will take you to the top of Mount San Jacinto, a height of 8,516 feet. From here you can gaze down on all the beautiful homes that are up for sale. With a good set of binoculars, on a clear day you can make out some of the newer attractions, such as the Bob's Big Boy Restaurant.

The cultural offerings of Palm Springs include the Desert Museum, which I have to admit is very nice, and the new art wing of a place called Denny Western. This offers, so far, three paintings and two baskets by the ancient local Indian tribe, the Agua Caliente. Two of the paintings are of the Agua Caliente standing alone in the desert, hands outstretched, looking up to the sky. They're probably pleading to their God, "Okay, let the white man take our land, but please, no more condominiums!"

An innovation at some of the newer hotels is to offer guests a "concierge," a person experienced in the hotel industry and prominently positioned in the lobby to make life easier for guests. They used to call these people bell captains, and they were the ones who could get you a hooker. Of course these concierges do the same thing, except with the hooker you now also get her résumé.

The truly young people arrive only twice during the year, at the Christmas holidays and the Easter or spring break. Then it's like locusts taking over, swarming over everything, screaming from their caravan of high-assed pickup trucks. The college kids and the crewcuts from the local marine base seem to be in competition for who can be the first to repave the city with beer bottles.

Saturday night in Palm Springs is Häagen-Dazs and a walk. The conversation is all about "the season"—the winter. And from Christmas to Easter it is indeed fairly exciting, with such happenings as the Bob Hope Desert Classic. Then comes summer. Sweat time. Dante's inferno.

"I love the heat," a Palm Desertite would say. And why shouldn't he, he's working for the chamber of commerce. In summer the town will go to any length to get people; the hotels advertising STAY ONE NIGHT, GET THE REST OF THE WEEK FREE. You can't even manage to walk around the pool, the cement is hotter than the sands of Africa. The pools aren't heated—they're supposed to be cooled. But it feels like every kid in Palm Springs has done his thing in the water, that's how cool it is.

The few shop owners who try to stay open will say to each other, "Really cooled off today." Sure it did. His sign melted and fell off and as it hit the ground there was a draft. Palm Springs will never make it in summer. And now with the recession, I don't think the winter looks too good either.

But my son and I are proud motel owners, with leaking roofs and some of the tree roots inching their way underneath the villas and making them rise. The villas all have to be painted, the air conditioners have to be replaced, there's a crack in Scotty's favorite Jacuzzi, the main water line is jammed. The old owner knew just when to get

The Warm-up

out. It seems all old owners know when to leave. But I love Palm Springs. Both winter and summer. Because we're open.

"Sam, that looks terrible. Are you trying to grow a beard? It makes you look old! You've got a cute funny face, you're going to hide it!"

That was John Francis, entertainment honcho of the Friars Club. I thought the remark was uncalled-for—but par for the course for John, because he loves to kid comedians.

I think my decision to "mask one" was just something I always wanted to experience but never had the guts to go for. I was always worrying what people would think. But I thought, if my insides are changing, why not go for the outsides? It's something that grows, it's natural . . .

I just wish it would grow on my head.

Almost all my adult life—and I mean including my early adult life—I've been bald. Yet in my teens I'd been called Bushman by all my friends, for my beautiful full head of curly brown hair.

I was devastated when, slowly but steadily, the hair follicles decided to abandon my cranium. Here I was, starting a career in show business, with nothing on top! What was worse—it would make me just like my dad, Hyman.

Panic! Here I was at twenty-two with an unadorned head, standing up in front of people trying to make them laugh. I wasn't making it. Did I look too old, or was I just not funny? What was I to do?

GET A TOUPEE—LOOK 10 YEARS YOUNGER! the ad in the paper said.

"Ten years younger? That'll make me look twelve!"

I finally got the toupee, as it was then called—"hair replacement," as we know it today—and was I hot shit when it was all fitted and trimmed. Curly brown, just like the sides of my real hair, and made of real human hair.

I felt just like a teenager again. Bushman was back!

On my first date after I got the new hair I felt really confident; I wouldn't be tormented by any more "baldy" remarks. I'd always felt intimidated, naked, with no hair. And in those days being bald wasn't really the in thing, unless maybe you worked in a factory.

Her name was Audrey and she was twenty-one and beautiful. But after we left the movie and drove to my usual parking spot on Lake Michigan, I began to feel a little apprehensive.

As we started to neck, she said, "I love your hair, Sammy, it's so curly and natural—" and she ran her hand up through the back of it.

218

Holy shit, I thought—how was I going to stop her? She was in the height of passion, and I was about ready to come in my pants.

In those days the toupee was put on with spirit gum, and when your head perspired, the piece would begin to come loose.

I made a move to pull her hand away, but it was too late. She screamed as the toupee started to come off in her hand. "What's *this!*"

I didn't know what to say; I was stunned.

"Is that not your real hair, Sammy? That beautiful, curly hair is— is a—" she started to sputter, "a *toupee?*"

"Well, not really. I have lots of hair all around my head, it's just a little in the back where I don't have any, because of when I had diphtheria as a kid and almost died and was lying in the hospital for two weeks practically in a coma and some of the hair fell out while I was lying back in that bed. And being a comedian, I couldn't go around explaining that to people all the time, so I just had a little put back there. You know, Bing Crosby has no hair at all. Completely bald. And he's a big star. So I thought—hey, if he can wear one, it's okay for me!"

I went on to tell her that Gene Kelly, Fred Astaire, Ray Milland, and Fred MacMurray all wore one, and she felt a little better about the situation. But for me the ship had sailed; there was no going back to our intimacies as Audrey inquired, "How old are you?"

From that day on I had to be careful how much spirit gum I used, and was *very* careful not to let a girl's hand get too high on the back of my head, even in the height of passion.

I find that most women just love to grab your hair, especially just before they come to orgasm. I just have to say, as blandly as possible, "Please don't touch my hair—that annoys me. It's a turn-off!"

Eventually I had to face the uncomfortable situation of having a girl stay overnight. This was going to be a calamity. The don't-touch-my-hair routine always seemed to work, but sleeping all night with that thing would be quite unpleasant. I'd always taken it off when I went to sleep.

After my first guest and I said good night, we turned out the lights, and there I was staring at the ceiling trying to figure out a way to get this hair-ball off.

I'd think: It's dark, she can't see. I'll take it off and put it next to the bed. In the morning before she gets up I'll go to the bathroom and put it on, then crawl back into bed like I've never left. But what if she wants to go to the bathroom in the middle of the night and a

The Warm-up

little light is seeping through—and there lying in bed is a bald person. Then it's gonna be get-dressed-and-go-home time.

Well, I tried it a few times and wound up getting no rest at all. Every time she'd turn over, I'd reach down and put on the piece. When I thought she was sleeping again, off it would come. I wound up feeling completely exhausted. And if she liked me a lot and wanted to stay over another night—I was in deep trouble.

I once dated a girl for a year and a half, saw her at least four times a week—she would come stay with me when I'd spend a week on the road—and she never knew I wore a piece. *That* was total insanity, trying to figure out ways to get it off and on. I had to end the relationship, for any stupid reason I could think of, just so I could finally take the damn thing off!

How could I keep this up? I had to find some way to break the horrendous curse I had put on myself. I had to expose myself, once and for all—to let someone (besides my wives, from whom I was now divorced) see me "without." It took me *twenty-five years.*

One day I found the gimmick, the way. How many times as a kid had I seen the Barnum and Bailey Circus and loved the clowns—the ones who had no hair and who'd jump up and down with their bald fright wigs.

My night arrived. The girl was someone I'd taken out a few times, and she liked me. This was the third time she'd stayed over with me, and it was tonight or never. I'd just plain chickened out the last two times.

"Shery," I said, "I want you to sit up in bed. It's show time!"

She looked at me kind of strangely, but she knew I was a little off-the-wall, so my announcement wasn't very disturbing.

"Get ready for the greatest show in town," I said. "I'll be right back."

I walked into the other room and put on a record I'd just bought—circus music, the real stuff from the Barnum & Bailey shows, was blaring through my apartment.

I put on a clown's nose and some makeup, took off that sacred hairpiece, and—totally nude—entered the bedroom jumping up and down and shouting, "It's Bozo the clown, everybody!" As I continued to jump up and down on and off the bed, my heart was pounding—and she was laughing.

I ran into the other room to shut off the record, then headed slowly back to the bed.

BOZO THE BEAUTIFUL

There she was, smiling at me. "You know, Sam, you're insane. But I loved it." Then she added nonchalantly, "You know, Sam, I didn't know you wore a hairpiece. You're so cute without it."

I was in shock. "Really?"

"It really doesn't make any difference. You just look more natural without it . . . Kind of sexy."

I realized, right then and there, that nobody really cares if you have no hair. And it's also okay to wear a piece.

Maybe what I'd been doing all that time was trying not to look like my father. He couldn't have cared less about the fact that he was bald. There was no time to be vain in those days—there was no time to be a lot of things. Same thing was true of my brother Phillip, the Chicago cop, bald in his early twenties. He was tough and didn't care.

When some men begin to go bald, I see desperation in their eyes. They'll do anything to save or exaggerate that last clump. Some let their hair grow long down the sides, then comb it forward and spray gook on it so it sticks. The last guy to get away with that look was Napoleon. The new thing is hair transplants—the most idiotic thing I've ever seen. Guys think it's cool, but it looks like an asparagus patch.

Some guys get such bad pieces—everyone in the world, even preschoolers, can see he's wearing one. It doesn't even match his hair; it looks like he's wearing a hat that doesn't fit.

My latest and funniest experience on the hair front has involved my twenty-nine-year-old son, Scott, who has been losing hair for the past few years and is nearly bald like his pop. He came to me recently and said he'd like to try wearing a piece. I don't think he's terribly vain about the hair issue; he just wanted to try out the experience of toting a piece.

He asked if I'd set up an appointment for him with Don Jeffery, my guy, whom I've been with for years and who is the best around.

"What do you think he'll charge me, Dad?"

"I really don't know," I said. "I assume, you being my son, maybe the same as me. I've been paying him five hundred fifty dollars for years."

I didn't give it much thought because, after all, Scott is practically a millionaire.

Scott went to see Don, all excited about the prospect of a new crop of hair.

When Scott came back that day, he said, "I don't believe him,

221

Dad. He wanted to charge me twelve hundred fifty dollars. And I'd have to have two made, because he said you have to 'switch them off.' And he said I'd have to come in every six weeks for 'service.' It's like getting your car fixed! And he said that the total, with the service, would run around five thousand dollars a year! How come he only charges you five hundred fifty, Dad?''

I thought for a second. "I guess it's because I was one of his first customers. I was sort of his guinea pig. I mean, I went through a lot in those early stages of his trying to find a new way to make them so they wouldn't look like you had one on. I mean, Scott, I sometimes had those damn things slipping off my head in the middle of a performance, because he was experimenting with some new adhesive.''

And today Don is the premier hair-replacement service in Hollywood.

Scott just stood there listening to me and every once in a while glancing up at my dome. "Dad, how many pieces do you have now?''

"Gee, Scott, I really don't know. I have two right now that Don keeps changing. I know I have about four or five old ones lying around that I don't use anymore. . . . Why?''

"Well, I was thinking, Dad—you know we have the same color and the same curly hair. Maybe Don can take one of your old ones, reshape it—take the gray out of it—and I can have one.''

I sat there amazed, listening to my millionaire son expound on how maybe one of my retreads could be salvaged for his hairless head. It was as if my own dad were still alive, whispering to his grandson, "What do you need a new one for? The old one's good enough, why spend the money?'' Two peas in a pod.

And now here I am starting to front a beard, probably just because of the sensation that this thing is truly mine. It actually *grows*. If it would just move upward, taking over my face and the top of my head. I think I'd go around as the wolfman, one entire clump of thick hair, just to know that feeling again.

This was going to be my first AA meeting in the desert. I knew I'd be spending a lot of time down here, and wanted to make contact with the people—to see if I could be of some service and to stay in touch with the problem I once had.

I saw the converted house in the middle of nowhere. People were driving up in their battered cars and pickup trucks. And here I was, with my new Cadillac convertible, parking alongside the oldies. I knew that it's just a car, that those other battered ones get you to the same places. One thing I've learned in the program is that the people really don't give a shit what you drive, who you are, what you do. All they care about is that you don't take that first drink. Most of the people are truly happy about any success you've achieved—and are ecstatic if you get it while you're on the program. It gives them hope that while they're with the program, they'll finally be able to achieve some of their goals.

Not many people were here yet, since the meeting started at eight-thirty. A long table extended across the entire room. At the other end three guys were talking, another was reading. I walked over to what looked like a converted bar—I guess it was put in just to remind the folks where they came from. On the bar were a coffee pot and cups. I reached for a plastic cup. A young guy grabbed the pot.

"Let me," he said as he poured. "My name is John."

"I'm Sammy."

An elderly lady sat at the end of the long table playing cards with a young man. She looked up.

"Hi, Sammy," she said. "I saw you last night in a movie. I really enjoyed it."

"Thank you," I said. I sat in the middle of the room at another table, watching all the men and women as they casually drifted in and, in many cases, hugged and kissed each other. The meeting, which had been coming to this house for years, was known as the dirty dozen group. They were the type of people who were from "all walks of life." Let's say they weren't from Bel Air. They were the hard-nosed former alcoholics, many of them from the streets. It was a mean-looking group!

The meeting started. An elderly woman who was sitting next to me stood up and introduced herself. "I'm from Hungary," she said. She sounded like one of the Gabor sisters.

In the ensuing moments some pretty horrifying experiences were being told by these people, and there was plenty of strong language to go with it, from both men and women. They were simply sharing their experience, being honest about who they are and who they have been, and telling how they felt.

A petite white toy poodle came over to me under the table. I had seen him going around and being petted by different people. He just sat up at my feet, looking up at me, saying in his eyes, "Pick me up." Which I did. I felt his warmth. The tiny body just wanted to be held, like most of us in that room. He licked my hand and snuggled up and went to sleep in my lap for the rest of the hour. He knew that I felt lonely sitting there, just as he did, and only wanted to be wanted. He made me feel very peaceful.

I was asked to speak and so I shared what had just happened with the puppy. I said that I feel love most of the time—if you want to come over, my doors are open.

After the meeting, some of the people came over and thanked me for sharing that experience with the puppy. I could have gone to Cecil's disco, which a friend of mine owns. Every time I walk in there he introduces me to all the girls and guys, shuckin' and jivin'. But this particular night I wanted to be here. I knew I had come to the right place.

After all these years in the stressful business of comedy, with its wear and tear on the mind and body, I was one of the lucky ones who'd never had to have any kind of surgery. No triple bypasses (knock on wood), no interesting scars to talk about in the steam room. The only time I'd seen action in the operating room had been at age nine, to have my tonsils removed, when the doctor had told me I could have *a whole quart of ice cream* when I woke up. Of course, it took me three days to be able to swallow a glass of water, let alone a spoonful of freezing ice cream.

Here I was, more than forty years later, being driven by my friend Shery to see Dr. Jon Perlman. Jon Perlman, M.D., A Medical Corporation; Plastic, Reconstructive and Aesthetic Surgery, in the great medical beehive of LA's Cedars-Sinai. Perlman's suite encompassed two complete operating rooms, with every modern facility to lower your ass, raise your tits—or, as in my case, to give you a bilateral blepharoplasty. In other words, my poor eyelids were drooping over my squinty eyes, and Dr. Perlman had resolved to rid me of this menace.

I sat in his outer office at eight in the morning, reading *The Los Angeles Times* and waiting for him to show up—for someone, anyone, to come and get me.

The office door opened. It was Susan, whom I knew as the doctor's secretary, clad in operating greens, her shoes covered in plastic bags, as was her hair.

"Good morning, Sammy," she said.

"Why are you dressed like that?"

"Why? Because I'm also a nurse and help Dr. Perlman during surgery."

I was about to ask her, "Do I get ice cream when we finish?" when she added that she also did the doctor's books.

As Susan led me to the changing room, I just couldn't fathom the fact that I was on my way to surgery. It flashed through my mind that maybe Perlman could take the skin from my eyelids and add it to the foreskin that my rabbi had so cleverly removed.

The door was slightly ajar. I could see Susan—bookkeeper, secretary, nurse—preparing the IV drugs and the instruments. Scalpel, sutures—big-time shit!

Now I sat on the edge of the bed, still nervously reading my LA *Times,* while Susan continued her preparations. In walked Dr. Perlman, in his greenies and looking a little bleary-eyed.

Jon Perlman was not from the old school. Young and handsome, graduate of a Boston school, he was a true M.D., which is more than you could say for many practitioners in southern California.

But a bookkeeper-secretary for a nurse? ' was already a little leery.

"Good morning, Sammy," he said.

"Hi, Jon. How ya doing?"

"Oh, I'll be okay. Had a bit of a rough night. One of my buddies I went to school with in Boston came in and surprised me last night, so we all kind of tied one on."

Oh boy. I could definitely smell his breath, or so I thought, as he came close to mark my eyelids with his pen. I remembered that hands shook when too much alcohol passed through the body. I knew, of course, from experience—times when I was drinking heavily and my hands would grab the microphone and shake.

I mean, it's bad enough to sit in a dentist's chair and have him lean over you with bad breath. But this was a surgeon, about to cut out my eyeballs!

It wasn't that I didn't have faith in his ability. I was probably just nervous and paranoid. So I steadied myself by recalling that the doctor had come highly recommended, by Dale Gibrow, a Beverly Hills attorney I'd met one afternoon at the Friars Club.

I'd happened to pass by his table on my way to see Red Buttons, who was at the next table.

"Sammy, come on over!" Dale had said. "I'd like you to meet a friend."

Dale goes to all the show-business functions in Hollywood and is very taken with show people.

"Sammy, I'd like you to meet Dr. Jon Perlman. He's one of the best plastic surgeons in this town. He does everybody."

We exchanged pleasantries, and I took a seat. Perlman kept looking at me as we talked.

Finally, he said, "I saw you at the Friars affair last week. I love your comedy—but not your lids," he added, half-smiling, as if he'd just told a comedian a joke.

Well, I thought it was a clever remark and told him so. But he kept staring at me, and I just had to ask why.

"Sammy, I was just noticing that the lids of your eyes are protruding lower than where the lids would normally be. It's quite a common dilemma as you start to age. That skin above your eyes is some of the most sensitive skin you have. And as the lids lose their elasticity, it slowly starts to fall over your eyes and eventually it hampers your vision—especially when you try to look at something above you."

I knew I had squinty eyes—but drooping eyelids? I took his card, and he invited me to his office for an explanation of the whole procedure.

I got up and turned toward Red's table, but by now it was empty. I felt left out. I stood alone in the room, in the throng of old Jews gnawing at their bits of food like it was the Last Supper.

I sauntered around to various tables saying hello to some of the men, shaking their hands—and looking right in their eyes to see if *they* had drooping eyelids. Their eyes looked fine to me. And these bastards were old! I kept thinking, Where are the drooping eyelids? I honestly couldn't find one pair. I started to panic. Am I the only one who has these eyes? I'm younger than most of these cockers!

I headed for the bathroom to take a look. I shoved my face close to the mirror and looked closely at my Marty Feldman eyes.

I lifted my lids. There it was, the skin that Perlman was talking about. The evidence unfolded right in front of me. Drooping eyelids! He was right!

I never really noticed them before. After all, I could see.

Shit, you hear about women going in and getting their faces done. But me, brought up on the near north side of Chicago, in the toughest

226

of neighborhoods—with black kids, Greeks, Italians, Poles?

I could just see them now, standing on the corner. "Where ya goin', Sammy?"

"Gonna have my eyelids removed—they're protruding! See you guys in a coupla days. Doctor says I won't be able to play stickball for a while . . ."

When you're told you have some kind of defect, it seems to double the problem. The lids suddenly become bigger, and now you think you're going blind.

So I sat there on the edge of the bed as Dr. Perlman marked my soon-to-be-gone lids, lids that had been with me for over fifty years. Lids I never knew I had! Those lids had been in the company of the biggest stars in show business! Elvis, Sinatra, even Jerry Ford had seen them, and not one had ever said, "Sam, your lids are drooping. I think you'd be a lot funnier if you had them removed."

"That should do it, Sam," Dr. Perlman said as he finished chalking me up.

The next thing I knew, I was looking up at the doctor through a haze.

"We'll be finished in a couple of minutes," he said. He seemed to be suturing my eyes.

What had happened was that the wicked bookkeeper had put something in my IV while the doctor was marking me. I knew she was a sneaky lady, not to be trusted.

I didn't take any of her Häagen-Dazs; it was a matter of pride.

And I knew that everyone would notice the difference in me.

My young son Pauly sure did. "Dad," he said. "You look like a guppy!"

The long-stretch limousine pulled up in front of 49 Greenwich Avenue. The driver opened my door, ending the two-and-a-half hour drive from Atlantic City.

I hadn't been in Greenwich Village for more than twenty years. It reminded me of my old Chicago neighborhood. I stood and reflected for a moment on the last time I had been here. My friend and writer Rudy DeLuca was then living here—struggling—living five flights up in a dismal rathole. Literally, with live rats chasing the cockroaches. But that was Rudy's home.

The Warm-up

Some of the people passing by stopped for a second to notice the stretch limo, especially the black kids, who seemed to gaze at it.

The door of 49 Greenwich opened and out came my friend Gary, bearded and quite handsome. Gary was writing and was working on the screenplay for a forthcoming TV movie. He lives in California, but as a native New Yorker, he just felt that he needed to write this movie in his hometown.

We hugged in the street. I hadn't seen Gary in a few months. I had just finished an engagement at The Sands Hotel in Atlantic City, and coming to New York was a delight for me. But the Village? I remembered Rudy's pad—and my own humble beginnings. I wasn't eager to be reminded of them, and in the past, every time I came to New York I usually stayed at a plush midtown hotel. But Gary wanted me near him and had told me that a musician friend of his was out of town and I could use his place.

"Sammy, why don't we go over there and look at it? You might not like it," Gary said.

So we both hopped into the stretch and Gary gave the driver directions. Gary was a little in awe of the limo and enjoyed the fact that I was a star in Atlantic City and that they treated me like one.

"It's really a classic pad, Sammy. The building is a historical landmark."

Already I wasn't too thrilled. Not being a New Yorker, the idea of Greenwich Village, and especially an *old* place in Greenwich Village, really didn't appeal to me. We arrived—just a pigeon's hop away from where Gary was staying.

As we headed out of the limo for the front door I got the feeling that this place would take me back to my father's rooming house. Gary opened the door as if handling treasured keys to a vault, but I was thinking, Why would they bother to lock this place up?

Then the ascent up the stairway. One floor, two, three, then four—and finally, cardiac five.

The frail-looking door was bolted with two King Kong latches. After a couple of minutes of twisting and turning the locks, Gary gave out with the immortal words, "I think I got it open!" But then he had to kick it.

"I think the weather must have warped the door," he said.

He kicked it again, it flew open, and, lo and behold, there it was.

"Rudy's old apartment," I muttered.

228

"What did you say, Sam?"

"Oh nothing, Gary—it just reminded me of a movie I saw."

"Well, Sam, what do you think? I mean, you're only going to be here for a few days, and I know it'll cost you a hundred fifty dollars a day in midtown."

"Yeah, you're right, Gary, I never thought of that."

I stood in amazement at the relics this man possessed. He was a musician, and usually New York musicians are very hip. I mean, they don't have to be rich. But an orange crate for a coffee table? He did have a TV, though. A black-and-white, called a Muntz. Years ago that was the Edsel of the TV sets.

"Come on, Sam, I'll show you the kitchen."

I just had to turn my head and we were in it. And there it stood, against a darkened wall of peeling paint, a Kelvinator—the epitome of old-time refrigerators. It blended into the wall very nicely.

Atop the fridge sat an antique vase or urn—probably containing the remains of the previous tenant. It was a swell kitchen. Bob, the musician, had lived there twenty-two years.

Gary had used this place to do some of his writing, so I guess in a way he was proud of it. He just loved the Village; every rat nest was precious to him.

"You probably won't eat here. But the kitchen's okay if you want to have some coffee in the morning."

"Yeah, Gary. Fine."

"I'll show you the bedroom. Over here."

Again, all I did was turn and there I was. The boudoir: sunken bed—and a raft of debris to give it that funky look.

"Well, Sam, what do you think?"

We had already carried my bags all the way up, and the limo had gone. I really didn't want to embarrass Gary. He had gone out of his way to find a place for me to be nearby.

"It's nice, Gary. Reminds me of where I came from."

—And now that I've been here a couple of days, I kind of like it.

The first night was horrendous; I kept rolling into the center of the sagging mattress. I couldn't help remembering Rudy's rats and thinking they were going to jump in after me. Some gay guys were screaming and fighting across the hall. Paramedics blasted their sirens on the way to St. Vincent's Hospital down the street. Ah, New York.

But after a while I gave up worrying and just lay there, really feel-

The Warm-up

ing good. The whole thing made me smile. I was tired, but I was also aware of how grateful I was to have all the things I do have. And of all the things I had, perhaps the most important was the ability to feel comfortable wherever I was.

I had never felt at all comfortable in New York. The city really intimidated me. It was like the song says—if you made it in New York, you could make it anywhere.

There's the legendary intensity of the people—the harsh words shouted at you in the street if you slow them up. Sometimes it seems they never show any feeling unless it's anger. But as I was lying there, I already knew better—knew that once you break down the barrier to a New Yorker's soul, you have a friend for life.

Bernie Swartz was lying on his back in the sauna at The Sands in Atlantic City. His stomach rose up like a slab of glob. It looked like he didn't have a penis—because you simply couldn't see it for the rolls of flesh. He was bald, in his early fifties. He had a lit cigarette that he had smoked down to the filter, and what was left of it was still hanging from between his lips. I'd never heard of anyone smoking in a sauna, but this was the East, and sometimes people do things here that are really unheard-of.

I was sitting nearby talking with a young black fighter named Tom Hall who was going to fight next day at the hotel's monthly fight event. Tom was twenty-two, sinuously built, with not a scar on his handsome face.

I sat down next to him as perspiration was pouring out of my skin. I kind of secretively glanced down at Tom's genitals. Holy shit! I quickly covered up my own. Between Bernie's and mine, we couldn't match even half of his; it was definitely a sledgehammer.

Tom was a kick boxer. It's becoming quite a popular sport. The fighter is allowed to use both hands and feet—and you have to kick the opponent at least eight times during a round.

"Who you fighting tomorrow, Tom?" I said.

"Joe Louis."

"Isn't he dead?"

"He will be when I finish with him."

At just that moment Bernie the walrus started to move. He slowly began to sit up and take heed of what we were saying. And as he looked at Tom, he quickly grabbed a towel to cover himself.

BOZO THE BEAUTIFUL

I never could figure out why fat men usually have small dicks. God gave them all that extra meat but couldn't spare a few more ounces for something they could get so much use from. Touching, feeling, scratching, masturbating, fucking, pissing—man through the ages has always touched his cock. I really empathize with fat guys.

I asked Tom if he'd like to see my show that night. He said that would be great.

"I'll see if I can get you comped," I said. "Call me at six-thirty and I'll see if I can get a couple of tickets for you and your trainer."

Bernie broke in. "So you're a fighter—and *you're* a comedian." Slight pause, then: "I never heard of either of you!" This was said in sort of a kidding manner—a typical New Yorker remark.

After a few minutes of bantering back and forth—about how Bernie the New Yorker has seen every star and every fighter and knows most of them—he said to Tom, "Look, I'll get you comped for the show. I'll see you tonight, Sammy, and Tom, I'll see you tomorrow in the ring."

Yes, Bernie the tough little Jewish New Yorker got Tom and his trainer in to see my show. And the next day he was sitting right next to Tommy's corner yelling and rooting for him to kill his opponent— which Tom practically did.

Tom told me the next day, after winning the fight, that Bernie was going to put up fifty thousand dollars to bring him to New York to fight. And the next time I work Atlantic City, Bernie will be there cheering me on.

That tough New Yorker was a pussycat!

After my third day in the Village, I started to feel its heartbeat, the uniqueness of it. In fact, I didn't even try to kill a cockroach making its way down the side of the sink.

Somehow people in the Village are real people. George Furth, the famous new playwright, strikes me as an example. Apparently, he never takes a cab. If he goes to the theater, he prefers to take the subway and walk a few blocks if he has to.

I wanted to experience that myself and headed uptown on a train entirely covered by elegant spray-painted graffiti. People sat there staring at each other, fear in some eyes. Women held purses close to their bosom. A couple of Puerto Rican kids who were about to exit shouted, "I don't want no fags sitting next to me, man!—those fuckin' queers!'' and laughed, giving a very embarrassed gay man the finger.

I was astonished at the slogans and profanities written on every square inch of space inside the car. Everyone in that city knows it's just the symbol, the expression, of frustration.

Recognizing, expressing how things really are—that's what New York is all about. People really couldn't care less what you do. If you come on like a person, you're welcome. But try to lay some shit on them—forget it. They've heard it all.

Like, ''Hi, I'm Sammy Shore, the comedian.''

''Oh yeah . . . you want some tomatoes.''

The other night I was at a quaint corner supermarket and saw Rod Steiger picking up a quart of skim milk. Now we all know that Rod Steiger's face is recognizable. They didn't care. Yet give your keys to one of the shop owners and tell him you have a friend coming in from out of town and could you give him the keys—they just love doing favors. That's something tangible and real.

Many people are afraid of New York, because it can break you down. It says, ''You're not really special. You want to be special? Prove it on our level.''

New York is energy. It's good for people who don't need to be reminded who they are. But there's a sense of physical tension that goes along with the city, because it's so dense, inconvenient, and dirty. No matter how rich you are, if there's a strike, no one's collecting your garbage. And unless you have a limo, you've got to wait for that cab. And no matter who or what you are, some waiter's going to tell you, ''Fuck off!''

I have to go to New York often—to get rejuvenated, uplifted, excited, and accepted. LA is a haven for emotional misfits. It just seems that people in LA are isolated and afraid. In their eyes I see tremendous fear.

I was recently on my way to Palm Springs and the Villas when I decided to stop at Smith's, a supermarket just on the outskirts of town. I got my cart and started moseying around looking for my favorite things to eat. I headed for the deli section, since I just love Jarlsberg cheese. Got my cheese and was making for one of the check-out stands.

A voice that sounded strangely familiar bellowed out from one of the aisles. ''Is that you, Brother Sam?''

I turned around and from a distance, I saw him waving and scampering toward me with a wide smile on his face. It was Colonel Tom Parker, Elvis's manager. I hadn't seen the Colonel since that fateful day in the steam room.

He hugged me and told me how good I looked. I introduced him to my friend Shery. And he started rattling on about what fun we'd all had—how great the tour with Elvis had been and how I used to get all the sweet rolls and pies from the hotels and bring them on the plane for us.

Was I hearing right? Was he really coming out with all that stuff? Sweet rolls and pies and the tour?

"My wife is an invalid now. This is José; he takes care of Mrs. Parker," he was saying.

He turned to Shery. "Sammy was a real funny guy. . . . He did a good job for me and Elvis." Somehow he sounded like Elvis was still alive and staying right down the street waiting for the Colonel to bring all the little Cornish hens he had piled in his basket.

"I'm still working for the Hilton, doing some promotion for them. And I'm still over in LA at RCA—why don't you come and see me, Sammy?"

He finally ran out of steam. "How you been doing?" he said.

"Just fine, Colonel. Still working. Doing my comedy standup."

"Nice seeing you, Sammy. Call me when you get back to LA."

It was as though he hated to leave. He seemed lonely—and lost. I thought of all the nasty things that were said about him and how even the Presley estate was suing him. From the power he was—to the sad soul he seemed at Smith's. And I had stuck it to him a couple of times, too.

When the Colonel fired me, I couldn't understand it. I was devastated. But what if he hadn't fired me and I had stayed on with Elvis through those years of his decline? Perhaps I would have continued on my frenetic pace, eventually to lose it all, just as Elvis did.

Elvis died from it. The Colonel stayed the same and is probably still looking for another Elvis. And I'm going to my villa to have some Jarlsberg cheese.

This past August—the Hilton Hotel—Las Vegas. Tony Orlando invited me to spend the weekend with him there while he worked the main show room. We had just finished working Atlantic City together and wanted to continue our friendship.

233

The Warm-up

When I arrived the immense lobby looked as gaudy and pretentious to me as ever. I remembered very well the first day I'd arrived here to work with Elvis, when boothsful of Elvis banners, hats, and all the Elvis paraphernalia the Colonel could think of were for sale. I thought, in another week Elvis will have been dead six years. Our lives are so short, all we have is time.

I came up to Tony's suite on the thirtieth floor—the same one Elvis had had—and was greeted by Robin, Tony's personal secretary. She was young and tall and her hair was in rollers.

"Tony wanted me to greet you," she said. "He's still in the shower. My hair's a mess," she added. "I'm sorry."

I said her hair was adorable and I walked into that enormous suite for the first time in almost ten years. Everything was so different since the changeover from the International to Hilton; the decor, the furnishings were totally bland. It looked like they had simply emptied a couple of other hotel rooms somewhere and put the furniture in the star's suite.

Tony came out wet in his towel and we hugged. He said he'd be back out soon.

Robin went to get us some coffee and I just stood there and contemplated the room and the memories of all the parties Elvis had had—all the karate demonstrations he used to do. We all thought it would never end. How still it was now and how different it was for me to simply stand and feel that silence.

It was getting near show time and Tony came out in his beige suit, cowboy hat, and smile. We talked for a while and then it was time for Tony to get down to the stage. We all headed for the back elevator.

"Is this the way Elvis went down every night?" Tony asked, kind of teasing me.

"Yeah," I said. "The couple of times I went with him, this was the way, down through the back kitchen." As we walked through the long tiled corridors cluttered with dirty dishes and bus trays, I felt like an old padre leading the accused to his execution. We finally arrived backstage. Fred Travalena, Tony's opening act, was just finishing.

As we approached the side curtain to the stage entrance, a voice called out, "Is that you, Sammy?"

"Yeah, who is it?"

"It's me, Terry Little." He came around to where I could see him.

BOZO THE BEAUTIFUL

Terry was stage manager when the hotel first opened.

"Jesus Christ, Sammy, how are you?"

"Fine, Terry, it's good to see you again."

"It's coming up six years since Elvis died," he said.

"I know, Terry—I miss him," I said. Just then the orchestra started playing "Tie a Yellow Ribbon."

I walked over to Tony and stood by him while he bowed his head and crossed himself. I remembered the opening night I came offstage and shook Elvis's hand, when Elvis was standing just where Tony was, and how cold and clammy his hand was. I reached out my hand to Tony. "Have a good one," I said. His hand was warm and firm.

As the music got louder, Tony walked out onstage like the star he is. The audience stood up. He's alive and Elvis is a memory.

I reflected on what a nice feeling it was not to be warming up the star's audience this time, to simply be there for a friend.

The next afternoon I woke up in the suite and came out to the living room, where silence still prevailed. I sat on the couch and looked around. Tony was still asleep. I thought, What if I were the star, sitting in this huge, tasteless suite?

Robin came in with coffee and took some into Tony's room. I followed a few minutes later with a metal coffeepot lid on my head and a cloth napkin over my arm. The room was still half dark and Tony was slowly emerging from the covers.

"Haro, Misser Orando," I said, going into my Japanese houseboy gibberish. "Here's your coffee."

We laughed and started carrying on and then we had a nice, long talk. Mainly we talked about what it means to have a good friend.

"The only truly close friend I have ever had," Tony said, "was Freddie Prinze. His death saved my life. His illness, his drive for stardom, that empty well he couldn't fill with drugs and alcohol, that finally made me realize how precious life is and what my priorities are."

I knew what Tony was talking about. I knew that I too no longer had to look up to the stars or anywhere else for my survival. I had reached a plateau in my life, where I could finally accept myself just the way I am, and simply know that I'm one of the best warm-up comedians in the business.

And that ain't bad.

8

WARMED UP

Hold on, folks, it's not like I graduated and now the struggle's all over. Maybe it never will be. It's just that I'm more comfortable and I learn more easily from experience. Like the time this past summer when I was "lost on the mountain."

I was chauffeured in a Cadillac limousine, compliments of the Caesars Boardwalk Regency in Atlantic City, all the way to the Catskill Mountains for Labor Day weekend. I had once again done a fantastic job for them at the Regency and was becoming the new-old fair-haired boy of Atlantic City. They were happy to give me whatever I wanted, like this long-distance lift in the limo.

I had signed to do a couple of dates out here in the Catskills, because I wanted to relive what I'd been through twenty years before. At least that's what I told myself.

As I pulled up in front of Brown's Hotel, the memory of a Saturday night in the summer of 1959 was still vivid. Then I had just finished driving in from the Poconos, in the Italian Borscht Belt seventy miles away, where I had done my third show of the night. It was two-thirty in the morning and Mitzi and our two kids were half sleeping in the car. I got out, changed my shirt, grabbed my props, and headed into Brown's for my fourth and final show.

WARMED UP

For decades the Catskills have been a training ground for comedians. If you did well in the mountains you had a good chance of working in New York. And most comedians who worked the mountains were actually from New York. Occasionally, someone from the Midwest worked the mountains but most often they were not successful. You had to have a certain rhythm and attitude to work to New York Jewish people. I was one of the lucky ones and did well. I guess because I was so different from most midwestern types.

Certainly my act was different. "And now, ladies and gentlemen," the announcer would say, "here's one of Mexico's favorite flamenco dancers, formerly with José Greco, let's welcome Señor Rodríguez Shore." Music from *The Brave Bulls* would begin and out I would come, parading around with a black-and-red sequined cape over my shoulder. For a few minutes I would have most of the people believing I really was a flamenco dancer, until the music stopped and I twirled around and said, in a Jewish accent, "Tanks a lot."

It always worked for me and got the audience immediately.

I finished my act that Saturday night, gathered up my props, and headed back to the car. Mitzi and the kids were sound asleep. I waited outside the car for a bit, not wanting to wake them.

I sat against the car watching the people walking to their rooms. Mitzi finally stuck her head out the window.

"Hi, how'd it go?" she said.

"Oh, just fine, I really killed 'em. 'Course there weren't that many people, it's so late."

It was about four.

"Let's see if we can get over to Charlie Rapp's motel," I said, "and wait there until someone checks out. We're supposed to get rooms today sometime."

Charlie Rapp was the booker of the Catskills, booked almost every hotel there. If he liked you, you could work all summer. He had a motel that housed all the acts who had deals with him. Part of the deal was that you could stay at his motel free and eat at the hotel where you were appearing.

The motel was in the little town of Liberty. The place looked and felt like the Bates Motel in *Psycho*. Mitzi and the kids were scared to death of the place. But we just couldn't afford a nicer motel.

That was my first experience in the mountains, when it was very important for me to do well there. Now, twenty-four years later, I figured I was just coming back to see what it was like. I certainly didn't need the bread, and I didn't need the engagement for career reasons, either. I had virtually a whole new career and could work pretty much when I wanted.

Ironically, I was booked for the weekend by Howie Rapp, Charlie's nephew. Charlie had passed away a few years before and Howie was the new boy in town.

All the rooms at the nice hotels were booked, so Howie had me stay at a Howard Johnson's—one step up from the Bates in my book. So now I was starting to feel funny. I was pissed about the accommodations and told Howie. But I knew I wasn't going to walk out on an engagement because of a room.

I did start to think, though: What the hell am I doing here? Who needs this?

Apparently, for some reason, I did.

The next night I arrived at Kutscher's Hotel, one of the biggest and nicest in the mountains, where I was to appear. They have stars on special weekends. I was there on Friday; Glen Campbell, Saturday; Robert Goulet, Sunday.

The show room was beautiful à la Vegas and seated about fifteen hundred people. And all fifteen hundred guests were there. That's part of the deal: room, food, and show. The Labor Day weekend was traditionally the biggest of the summer, the last shot before everybody headed back to the jungle.

"Who's Sammy Shore?" was the comment around the hotel. "I never seen him before," another guest said. "Is he on television? Is he a singer—or a comedian—who knows? Sometimes here they give us pot luck!"

"If he's a comedian, I hope at least he's funny. We've had some real turkeys up here lately."

The band was playing the kind of cha-cha music I hadn't heard in twenty years. The dance floor was packed with all the Jewish people struttin' their stuff. It was their chance to show off their clothes and look important.

There is something about my Jewish people. They always have to look good. They're so proud. None of them had it easy, and what they have they earned. Yet they just have to flaunt it. They love each other and will kill for each other. But get them all together at once, away from their homes, at their favorite hotel that they've been coming to for years, and *then* put them all in the same room—well, then they truly are the beast, ready not only to swallow you but also to spit you out.

The band stopped playing and the bandleader took the mike. "Show time," he announced, and everyone went to their seats as in a deluxe summer camp. The house lights dimmed, there was a drum roll.

"And now, ladies and gentlemen, a very funny comedian who just closed a successful engagement at Caesars Boardwalk Regency in Atlantic City—let's welcome—Sammy Shore!"

A few scattered bits of applause and I knew I should have brought back my Mexican dancer.

"Good evening, ladies and gentlemen," I said. "It's nice to be back here at Kutscher's. I haven't worked the mountains in twenty years."

They all looked at me like, so? What else is new?

"I'm originally from Chicago. In fact, a couple months ago I went back there for our high school reunion. I went to an all-Polish high school. Those Polish kids were smarter than you think. They wanted to go school. They just couldn't find it."

Nothing. Polish jokes were not the kind of subject matter they were used to. They also weren't thrilled with my telling them about my childhood in Chicago. However, they did laugh when I started to talk about my Jewish father and his furniture store.

"It's amazing. My father knew what I was going to become when I grew up. He'd look at my report card and say"—Yiddish accent here—" 'What are you, a comedian?' "

I pulled out all the stops. I started sweating like I used to. I wanted to do well. To show them all I had already made it. But they didn't give a shit whether I'd made it or not. They knew I was struggling and they weren't about to help. And they didn't want to be cheated out of laughs another night.

I finally pulled it out after forty-five minutes and walked off. They all appreciated how hard I worked and how I stayed out there and didn't give up until they liked me. I wasn't going to leave that stage until I was satisfied. It was one of the hardest shows I'd had to do in years.

I had two more hotel dates in the Catskills that weekend, and the next night was a little easier as I got back into the tempo of the people. I was very dissatisfied with my performance on all three nights, and knew I'd made a mistake in going back. I was not the same as I'd been twenty-four years before. I had changed. But the people were still the same. I couldn't relate to them anymore.

I realized that I can't change my style of comedy the way I used to just to please an audience, like the older Jewish folks of the Catskills who only wanted to hear what they wanted to hear. I hadn't understood that when I'd set out to conquer them all over again. Today if a comedian does well in the mountains, you actually have to worry whether he'll be commercially viable elsewhere.

Don't get me wrong—I wanted to do well. My mistake was thinking I had to be able to please any audience anywhere. My need for approval was always so great I'd take on every challenge, even the wrong ones. And now that would change.

I drove my rented Toyota back to Kennedy Airport, looking at all the hotel signs: GROSSINGER'S, CONCORD, THE PINES, and underneath the signs it said, "Vote to Bring Gambling to the Mountains."

Jesus Christ, not here too, I thought to myself.

"Give me an *amen!* Give me a *hallelujah!*" I shouted. I was finishing my act at The Horn, getting ready to head back to Atlantic City for yet another engagement. "I have the power to heal!"

"Heal me, Brother Sam!" came a voice from the back of the room. *"You have the power. . . . Please heal me, Brother Sam!"*

In the dim light I saw the emcee coming toward me, leading someone with a leather jacket completely covering his head. The man's hands were outstretched and muffled tones of *"Heal me!"* came ringing through the jacket. I didn't know who it was and just assumed it was one of the kids at The Horn putting me on as usual.

"Yes, I have the power to heal," I said, as I took my hands and placed them over the headless person. "Heal this poor soul!"

His head popped through the jacket and he shouted, "I can see again! Bless you, Brother Sam!" as he turned and we both exited toward the back.

To my delight it was Steve Bluestein, a young comic whom I'd started at The Comedy Store. I hadn't seen him—in fact, I hadn't even heard about him—in years. We exchanged greetings, we hugged— he had always been kind of special to me in those early days. He said he'd wanted to come by and surprise me, and he sure had.

He'd heard I'd found a new "home" in Atlantic City and I said yeah, and that I thought it would be a great place for Steve, too. No, he wasn't ready yet—he was just getting into a really heartbreaking divorce and just getting over problems with drinking and drugs.

"In fact, one night I really wanted to do myself in like Freddie Prinze. I remembered Freddie's Russian roulette. So I got myself a gun and sat there feeling sorry for myself and chickened out. I feel a lot better now, thank God!"

"Well, I'm glad of that, Steve. You know, seeing you here tonight, Steve, is really ironic," I said, "and kind of eerie. I was just going to leave the club tonight to see Mitzi and talk over some of the things I've never resolved with her . . . and here you are, another part of that same life we had."

He wished me luck, we exchanged phone numbers, and I headed out the back door. The dismal alley brought back the memory of the night I was stopped by Franco telling me Mercedes wanted me back. I was grateful to know that the terrors of the past were nearly all rectified and quiet. And now it was on to perhaps the most important of them all: Mitzi.

I was headed east toward The Comedy Store and a new restaurant, The Annex, which Mitzi had just opened directly across the street. It was about twelve-thirty and Wilshire was dead, just a few cars passing by. I passed through Westwood and the amazing new row of luxury high-rise condominiums, many of them offering units for upwards of ten million dollars, most of them sitting half empty, some unfinished with builders going belly-up. I made a left on Beverly Glen toward Holmby Hills, the neighborhood where Elvis once lived—that is, where he hid when he came to LA. Here was the enormous estate where he and his so-called friends played backyard paddle ball to pass the time, locked up like animals. I reflected on some of the cruel and sensational things writers were saying about Elvis in their best-selling books, even in books by his Memphis mafia bodyguards. As far as I was concerned they were all greedy assholes, using him now as they did then. I honestly feel these are the people who destroyed The King, as much as the drugs.

I turned right on Sunset at the neon-lighted WELCOME TO BEL-AIR sign where Rolls-Royces and Mercedeses turned in toward the enclaves of the very rich. Except now it seemed the Arabs were buying every other available mansion, and the Japanese were taking over the rest of Beverly Hills. But now I was at Sunset Strip and the familiar Hollywood landmarks, starting with the Roxy and the Whiskey. Down the curve past Holloway, up around the bend to the place once fa-

241

mous as Ciro's, now equally famous as The Comedy Store. Up in the hills in back of The Comedy Store and her new restaurant was a mansion Mitzi had bought from Ciro's owner, Frank Sennes. Yes, little Mitzi Lee Saidel from Marinette, Wisconsin, the shy, frightened little peanut head, was slowly taking over the Sunset Strip. I knew that no Arab or Japanese investor could ever tempt her to give up her dream-come-true. Who knows, maybe someday TEMPLE MITZI.

I pulled up in the circular driveway of the restaurant that had once been a very successful in-crowd hangout called Roy's, but which had been headed for bankruptcy when Mitzi transformed it into The Annex. As I was giving my keys to the parking attendant I remembered I still needed them for one thing. I opened the trunk and took out a little puppet. It was Brother Sammy, Junior, a replica of me, dressed in a tiny suit and tie, with kinky hair, glasses, and an enormous version of my nose. I put it in a brown paper bag and tucked it under my arm. I knew she'd laugh at the sight of a miniature me—it was already sure-fire in my act. What I was really using it for, of course, was to break the tension. I was using one of the tricks of my trade, to get 'em laughing the moment you walk out. Little Sammy was my warm-up.

As I entered the restaurant a young girl with a menu said, "Hi. One?"

"Is Mitzi here? I'm Sammy Shore."

She told me Mitzi was in the back booth with a couple of her employees. "Should I tell her you're here?"

"No thanks, I'll just walk over myself." She seemed a little perturbed because she knew Mitzi didn't like to be interrupted, especially when having meetings with her help.

I wandered slowly toward the back, feeling a little uneasy but also feeling confident in my knowledge that this was the last and most influential person with some kind of magical power over my life. I just knew that the puppet would be my magic and that the deadlock between us would disappear once and for all.

What charm the restaurant had. I could see that the warmth, the decorating, the lighting was all Mitzi. It was almost like I was back in the living room of one of our houses. The antique bar stood in front of an enormous bay window overlooking the city. Was I entering her domain to be judged like one of her comics? I really didn't know.

We hadn't spoken in months, and the last time we'd talked it wasn't very pleasant. I knew I had to talk to her on a one-to-one basis. Every time before it was always basic information about the kids or The Comedy Store and not about our past life together, the twenty-one years. Now was the time, and there she was. She wasn't expecting me. She was deep in conversation.

"Hi, Mitzi."

"Oh hi, Sammy," she said quite warmly and surprised.

Before she could say another word I shoved Sammy Jr. in her face and in a high squeaky voice said, "Would you give me some loose change for my little ministry at the Church of the Open Wallet?"

She was hysterical, her eyes lit up. "Sammy! I don't believe what I'm seeing. It looks just like you! It's adorable," she continued. "What do you do with him?"

I explained how I used him in my act. Here he had broken down the walls in a flash. Mitzi invited me to her table and introduced me to her chef and maître d'.

"Please excuse me, Sammy, I'll be done with them in a minute and then we can have some coffee."

I sat there and listened to this petite lady explaining the changes she wanted and why she had just fired the other chef. These two enormous men, one black and the other Italian, were hanging on her every word and giving her a yes after every sentence.

She got up from the table. "Sammy, let's go sit in the lounge. Did you get a chance to see the kitchen? How do you like the place? It reminds me of a resort—remember where you first started?"

"Yeah, it does seem a little like one."

"It just gives me a place where I can get away from The Comedy Store," she said as we sat down.

Before I could open my mouth again she said, "Sammy, you've got to try our miniature bagels and cream cheese." She motioned to a waitress to get some. "How about some lox? I've got twenty-five pounds of lox that's going to rot if we don't eat it. That last chef ordered thirty-five pounds and we weren't even opened yet."

"No thanks, Mitzi, the bagels will be fine."

The bagels and cream cheese arrived with some jelly and Mitzi smeared cream cheese on a bagel and handed it to me. "Aren't they cute?"

"Yeah," I said, "if you're a midget."

I leaned closer. "Mitzi, I just want you to know that the kids and I are very proud of you. Of what you've accomplished in your life.

243

The goals you've attained for yourself. Your determination and pride. You came through it all. You could have failed many times but you didn't, you just got bigger Now you've got this place. You're really something, Mitzi.''

Her eyes started to tear, and a calmness came over her face. "Thank you, Sammy."

"I heard that over the Jewish holidays you went back to Green Bay. The kids told me you went back by yourself."

"Yes. . . . It was a wonderful experience. I wanted to go back to the beginning. I was feeling so empty, nothing was working anymore for me. The Comedy Store, the mansion, the investments, money, it meant nothing. I was just becoming very sad. Me, housing thirty-five comedians and I couldn't laugh anymore. And I just knew there were no answers in this city.

"So I went to Green Bay and I went to the graves of my parents. I threw myself on my father's grave and I was crying, 'Please, Pa, help me!' I prayed for him and God to help me. I really don't know what happened, Sammy, but I felt very dizzy and my body became very warm and tranquil. I got up and left there and I just knew that everything was going to be all right. In my heart I really felt that God touched me.

"I went back to Marinette where I was born, I visited the grammar school where I was in plays and sewed the costumes and read all the fairy tales. And I used to love it, because my home was so sad. You know the story, Sammy. I always thought comedians were happy. I guess that's why I married you. But you were sad, too. I tried to live my life through you. But we know that doesn't work." She spoke softly and tears were streaming down her face. I held her hand.

"It's going to be all right, Mitzi. I'm really happy for you. Your sadness is also of joy. I want you to know, Mitzi, that I really want to be your friend. And anytime you need me for anything, I'm available for you."

"Sammy, thank you. I know you mean that."

It was getting late, both of us wanted to go home. We decided that I'd follow her up the hill. When we pulled our cars into the driveway of the mansion, I got out and just looked at the place. It had been eight years since she'd asked me to leave.

Standing in the hallway I was amazed at how she'd redecorated. "How do you like it, Sammy?"

WARMED UP

"It's beautiful, Mitzi. It's you."

For a moment I wanted her to say, "Would you like to stay over?" That wasn't my purpose, even though I knew she was no longer involved with anyone. I was happy to be her friend once again—to know that her house was once again open to me.

I just stood at the door looking at her, as she smiled warmly at me. I walked over, put my arms around her, and kissed her. "Goodnight, Mitzi."

As I opened the door I turned back to her. "Mitzi, you'll always be my wife."

A little sunlight was starting to seep through the mist as I got in my car and headed back up Sunset toward the freeway and my little apartment in the Marina—knowing in my heart that I was finally back home.

When I was growing up in Chicago I would never have dreamed of walking around the rooming-house apartment without some kind of clothing on. The idea of my mom or dad seeing my genitals was just out of the question, taboo. Of course I never saw them undressed, either—it was all very secretive.

I don't know, it just seems that in those days you could never picture your Jewish mother and father in bed. The only excitement I saw was when a roomer was late with the rent. Or when Dad was pissed at my mom.

I guess all of us felt the same about our parents in those days. It would have been great for my dad to have said to me on the way to school one day, "Got laid yet?"

That's about how far things have gotten with my own two younger boys, thanks to their openness and their frankness about their sexual experience. I was sitting with my youngest son, Pauly, fourteen, in the Jacuzzi at the Friars Club. As we'd come out of the shower to enter the tub, Pauly had nonchalantly whacked my penis with his towel.

"Where is it, Dad?" Then, "Dad, I got to tell you what happened the other night." He proceeded to tell me the story, in detail, of how he had almost made it with a girl for the first time but had left the room in disgust when he discovered his girl was asleep.

Pauly has always been very open with me—but that was a bit much for me to handle.

***

The Warm-up

It was my son Peter's seventeenth birthday. I had taken him to a camera store in Hollywood because there was a certain lens he wanted. He loves photography and was becoming quite good at it. In fact, he and his friend were starting a little business; Peter gave me his card as we were driving into Hollywood.

The clerk handed him the box with the lens. Peter took it out, started adjusting it, and asked the clerk all kinds of technical questions which I knew nothing about.

Peter had everything. He wanted a high-ass Chevy truck; his mother bought it for him. He got rid of that and wanted a Rabbit convertible for school. His mom spent ten thousand dollars. There was nothing Peter wanted that he did not get. Pauly, too, but Pauly really didn't care about all that stuff. Give him a surfboard and he was in heaven. A Jewish kid with a surfboard, I could never figure that one out—that part of him was not Jewish. Mitzi spoiled them to death, she even admitted it to me. I guess it was her way of compensating for not being able to spend the time with them that she wanted to when they were growing up. Judging from the way they are now, whatever time she did spend with them must have been special.

"How much is the lens?" Peter asked the clerk.

"A hundred sixty dollars."

Peter seemed a little uncomfortable. He knew I'd buy it for him, but he also knew I wasn't in the same league with his mother. When he wanted something from her, it was automatic. He knew that $160 is a lot of money, at least to me. Anytime I'd bought him a birthday gift or something for Chanukah, he'd really shown appreciation.

"If it's what you want, Peter, get the lens."

"Okay, I'll take it," he told the clerk.

We headed out of the store and he threw his arms around me and kissed me. "Thanks, Dad!"

"Happy birthday, Pete."

As we drove away he kept turning the lens in his hand and feeling it. "Dad, this is the most special gift I got for my birthday. I really appreciate it."

"I know you do, Pete. . . . I just want you to know, Peter, that whatever you decide to become—photographer, actor, director, all the things you've talked about—it really doesn't make any difference to me what you choose. You don't have to prove anything to me.

"For so many years I tried to make my dad proud of me. All I

246

wanted him to do was tell me it's okay—he just didn't know how to say anything, really. But he gave me money every week for my trumpet lessons, as hard as it was for him to give any money. And that was his way, the only way he knew to tell me he was proud of me. 'Here's another two dollars, take another lesson until you get it right.'

"So what I'm trying to say to you, Pete, is it's okay. Just go for it. As long as you're happy and you don't hurt anybody doing it. I'm proud of you, Pete."

As we pulled into Greenblatt's deli, he said, "You know, Dad, I'm going to look for a job next week. I think I could get a busboy's job over at this new club that just opened. . . . I just don't want to take any more money from Mom. I want to start doing it on my own."

I smiled warmly at him and put my arm around him as we headed down the stairs.

"You want to split a roast beef sandwich with me, Dad?"

My son Scott is the oldest. As I've said, he's very successful in real estate in San Diego, and is now partners with me in Palm Springs. It's kind of bizarre. Here I'm his father and he's getting me involved in his real estate. Shouldn't it be the other way around? The father takes the son into *his* business. I know I can't take him into mine, he's just not funny. He is, around his friends, but not professionally, thank God.

It's actually been very difficult for him to have me become involved in his projects. He's never had a partner and doesn't want one. It was just as much a breakthrough for him to invite me to help him as it was for me to begin loosening up about money. But I'm at the point in my life now where I don't want to be involved with anyone in a business venture, and especially my son. I can see that now. At the time it was my own anxiety and confusion, and nothing Scotty did, that got me into the project. I thought that my son the real estate developer could take some of my savings and make me rich with a few investments. It just doesn't work that way.

Now I realize that I don't care to be really rich. I just want to be able to pay my bills and come and go as I please. I don't want to have to deal with my son telling me that the Villas are empty! Once I confessed this to Scott, we both felt a great sense of relief.

I love my son and want to be available for him twenty-four hours a day—but only as a father. I don't want our relationship to be tarnished by anxiety because we're not making money. I'm at peace with myself doing my writing and my stand-up, Scotty's happy making lots of money in the business world, and we've both learned a lot in the process of discovering our respective places.

My daughter Sandy was recently divorced after six months of marriage, which was not surprising if you considered what kind of care she had from me, her father, in her early years. I know now that I wasn't truly what a father should be. I was "The Comedian." I was away a great deal. When I was home, I slept late, having been out at work almost all night. About the only times Sandy saw her daddy in those first years was when I'd come home late at night from a club I was working in Detroit. There she would be, standing at the top of the stairs, two fingers in her mouth and her blanket held up under her tiny nose. Her big brown beautiful eyes and her smile a mile long looked down the stairway at her daddy. It was like a puppy dog waiting for its master to return. I'd scurry up the stairs, pick her up in my arms, and give her a kiss.

It was New Year's Eve 1979 at Charlie Brown's restaurant in Marina del Rey. I had asked Sandy to dinner. We were sitting there, not saying much to each other. I was just asking how she was doing, trying to make light conversation. She leaned across the table and said "Daddy, I hate you."

I was speechless—literally unable to say a single word in my shock. I knew Sandy resented me, that there were good reasons why she felt as she did, and that there was nothing I could say or do at that moment.

I also knew that Mitzi had a big influence on her at the time; Sandy was living in one of Mitzi's houses. Mitzi's resentments for me ran deep, and many times she'd let Sandy know how she felt about me, how much she hated me. And all the while Mitzi was the talk of the town with her Comedy Stores, her name in all the papers. I was merely trying to find my way back.

I knew I couldn't deny Sandy's feelings, regardless of whether they stemmed from her mother's vendetta or my not having been around. Part of it was simply human nature: when you're down for the count, as I had been, people tend to want to leave you there. When you're riding the crest, everyone wants to be part of it. Your kids tend to be that way, too. And if there was not enough love in their childhoods, chances are they won't be around when you're old. Not that there wasn't love in our house, but it was stymied by scraping and running around the country to various dives, trying to make a living and to get a career going.

When I was rebuilding my life, I couldn't run to my kids and say,"Look at me, I'm really working at being wonderful." When I saw my kids, I made it their time. Their lives became the issue, not my career and not my jokes. I had no career and my jokes were old. I knew that I was a good person and had a good heart like my mom. It had just gotten cluttered up with trying to be famous.

So I stopped trying to make my kids, and especially Sandy, love me. The more I liked myself and started to become the person I'd always thought I could be, the more the kids wanted to be part of me. Kids are much like animals. They sense you. They know if you're honest, if your love is real. But it takes time—God's time. It's amazing how you can be sitting in a room by yourself, not saying a word, and eventually someone, like a child, will come and sit with you. Not that they think you're lonely, but they feel a calmness about you. This happens, by the way, only with people who also feel pretty calm with themselves.

After I started to see the light at the end of the tunnel and not the same old train coming toward me, my kids and especially my sons kept telling their mother how I was changing. Mitzi didn't care to hear about that. She was preoccupied with her new life and success and didn't want to be reminded of the past. And when she was questioned about the history of The Comedy Store, she spoke only in terms of "A.D."—After the Divorce. She really believed that I would never change, and for a while she didn't care. She actually became what I used to be.

Living in San Diego and running The Comedy Store for her mother, Sandy became something of a Mitzi clone. Every time I went to San Diego to visit with Scott, I'd stop by the Store to say hello to Sandy, but she'd be evasive. She'd try to be nice, but it was busy-nice. "Excuse me, Dad. I've got to let these people in." She never wanted to go to dinner with Scott and me, and just didn't care to see me. I was sorry to see it happen, and to see her becoming rigid and business-like, in the pattern fashioned by Mitzi. There was nothing I could say to her.

Then, slowly, as they say it always does in the end, love won out.

The Warm-up

I still called, but only occasionally. I stopped trying to make Sandy like me. I had to let her work out whatever resentment she had for me on her own.

When her male relationships and especially her marriage had failed, Sandy began to realize that the men in her life were not the answer to her survival. She realized that you don't have to marry to be happy. When it came to the men in her life she was very immature—still looking for her daddy. Daddies are humans who fail. Once she realized this, she was able to live alone and become truly independent and assertive about her well-being. And she was able to see and appreciate me for who and what I am, and our relationship finally relaxed.

Now Sandy knows—really knows—that there are millions of single women out there doing very well without a so-called man in their lives. They come home, listen to music, read, travel, date when they want, and pick and choose their own friends without worrying what a husband thinks. And all the while there's the happy prospect that the right person will come along. Being successful running a "man's business"—a night club—gives Sandy tremendous confidence. She also has both a mother and father to call now if she needs them. And if they're not home, she can relax holding her dog, Chester—the kind of animal once known as a man's best friend.

"Gee, Dad, it sure is good to have you down here." That was Sandy speaking, as I got ready to go onstage at The Comedy Store in La Jolla. It was a far cry from the "Daddy, I hate you," of just a few years before.

"I've got your Christmas present, Dad. It's in the office—I want to give it to you."

"Wait till I get off the stage, Sandy."

She couldn't have been nicer—showing me off to everybody.

I felt somewhat nervous as the other comedian was finishing. He was young and went over quite well with the younger audience, the audience which would be mine in a few minutes. Sandy and Scott would soon be watching me on the stage of their mother's club, and I knew this was not the kind of audience I was used to working for.

I had to spend twenty minutes just toying with them, like a fighter who's not too familiar with his opponent. He needs time to find the right combinations and then to pursue the other guy's weakness. I was already into my thirteenth round and sweating profusely. Then I wore them down and cracked them and won them over.

Why did I allow myself to go through it? To prove myself—to my kids? So that perhaps Sandy would tell Mitzi that Dad did a terrific job for us? Still looking for Mitzi's approval? I had that already. Our family was finally in harmony. There was no need to prove anything to Mitzi or the kids anymore.

But I'm a comedian. When I walk out onstage, before any kind of audience, whether I'm getting paid or not, my heart and soul are on the line. It's just me and them. No kids or former wives mean anything once they introduce you. Oh, perhaps they add some pressure, but if you happen to fail out there, they aren't to blame. You should be honored that your kids would want to sit through another performance and listen to the same old shit.

Approval! Approval! Approval! We're all looking for it. The kids are looking for their parents to validate them; the parents are hoping the kids will think they're wonderful. If you all just get through it alive—with the kids grown up and the parents still living to see it—that in itself should be cause for euphoria.

I can't undo the damage I did to my kids in their early years. I can only let them see that I'm human, that I have defects, just as my mom and dad did—and that I no longer have to be that old kind of father. I can let them see that I have honest feelings for my fellowman, that I have nothing to prove, and they're welcome, with no strings attached. Scott said to me the other day, "Dad, I'd like to be like you." Today, that means more to me than being voted Comedy Star of the Year.

If you happen to be one of those parents who gave a lot of love and caring to your kids, you'll always be remembered. Thank God I was able to see my shortcomings before it was too late—to take a good look at my priorities, once and for all. Now when I work, I work at my comedy one hour a night. The remainder of my time is for resting and simply being a person.

It's so sad to be successful and not have someone to share it with. Only the lucky few have the tremendous gift of being able to share something freely with mankind. Many die hoarding it, afraid that it will be taken away. And God usually does take it away if you don't give it away freely.

They say the world is coming to an end. I can't worry about that day, if and when it comes. My days are to be fulfilled today. So if it comes I can say I tried to live it to the fullest. The last third of my life, I can say, has been fantastic. I'm going out blowing my bugle.

On Thanksgiving I drove down to La Jolla with Pauly. Sandy made dinner for all of us—Mitzi, Peter, Scott, Pauly and me, plus a few young comedians. I carved the turkey while Scott taped the festivities with his video camera.

We were all sitting around the table when Scott raised his glass. "Here's to Mom and Dad. We're all finally together for the first time in eight years. May the coming years keep our family together."

I took my glass and tapped Mitzi's.

L'chayim!

AFTERWORD

When I was growing up, every Tuesday night I ran to my friend Rudy's house to watch Milton Berle on television.

On January 11, 1984, at the Friars Club of California, Milton Berle and many of the top-name comedians honored me with a roast.

I sat there in awe of all these comedy geniuses whom I had admired for years. I kept looking around to see if it was someone else they were talking about. No, it was me. They all sounded like my father, using many of the words that once bellowed out of his mouth at my mother.

My feelings sitting there were at times embarrassing; the other moments left me in a state of euphoria.

This was my night. I finally got a dinner. My three sons, Scott, Peter, and Pauly, were there and laughing the loudest. Milton Berle ended the roast by saying, "Gentlemen, this has been a wonderful evening for all of us. Many four-letter words were used tonight, but the four-letter word that filled this room was *l-o-v-e*."

I got into my car with my beautifully engraved plaque and enlarged self-portrait autographed by all the guys.

As I entered my apartment it was still. The roar of laughter was gone. I turned on my answering machine to hear my youngest son's squeaky voice say, "Hi, Dad. It's Pauly. It's after twelve and I know it's late and I guess you're not home but I didn't get a chance to talk to you because all the guys were around you.

"Dad, it really was something, all those things they said about you. I just wanted you to know how proud I am of you—and, Dad, no matter what they said, you're still the greatest comedian of them all. I love you and I'll talk to you tomorrow."